The Formation

The Journal of Philosophy of Education Book Series

The *Journal of Philosophy of Education Book Series* publishes titles that represent a wide variety of philosophical traditions. They vary from examination of fundamental philosophical issues in their connection with education, to detailed critical engagement with current educational practice or policy from a philosophical point of view. Books in this series promote rigorous thinking on educational matters and identify and criticise the ideological forces shaping education.

Titles in the series include:

The Formation of Reason
By David Bakhurst

What Do Philosophers of Education Do? (And How Do They Do It?)
Edited by Claudia Ruitenberg

Evidence-Based Education Policy: What Evidence? What Basis? Whose Policy?
Edited by David Bridges, Paul Smeyers and Richard Smith

New Philosophies of Learning
Edited by Ruth Cigman and Andrew Davis

The Common School and the Comprehensive Ideal: A Defence by Richard Pring with Complementary Essays
Edited by Mark Halstead and Graham Haydon

Philosophy, Methodology and Educational Research
Edited by David Bridges and Richard D. Smith

Philosophy of the Teacher
By Nigel Tubbs

Conformism and Critique in Liberal Society
Edited by Frieda Heyting and Christopher Winch

Retrieving Nature: Education for a Post-Humanist Age
By Michael Bonnett

Education and Practice: Upholding the Integrity of Teaching and Learning
Edited by Joseph Dunne and Pádraig Hogan

Educating Humanity: Bildung *in Postmodernity*
Edited by Lars Løvlie, Klaus Peter Mortensen and Sven Erik Nordenbo

The Ethics of Educational Research
Edited by Michael Mcnamee and David Bridges

In Defence of High Culture
Edited by John Gingell and Ed Brandon

Enquiries at the Interface: Philosophical Problems of On-Line Education
Edited by Paul Standish and Nigel Blake

The Limits of Educational Assessment
Edited by Andrew Davis

Illusory Freedoms: Liberalism, Education and the Market
Edited by Ruth Jonathan

Quality and Education
Edited by Christopher Winch

The Formation of Reason

David Bakhurst

WILEY-BLACKWELL

A John Wiley & Sons, Ltd., Publication

This edition first published 2011
© 2011 David Bakhurst

Blackwell Publishing was acquired by John Wiley & Sons in February 2007. Blackwell's publishing program has been merged with Wiley's global Scientific, Technical, and Medical business to form Wiley-Blackwell.

Registered Office
John Wiley & Sons Ltd, The Atrium, Southern Gate, Chichester, West Sussex, PO19 8SQ, United Kingdom

Editorial Offices
350 Main Street, Malden, MA 02148-5020, USA
9600 Garsington Road, Oxford, OX4 2DQ, UK
The Atrium, Southern Gate, Chichester, West Sussex, PO19 8SQ, UK

For details of our global editorial offices, for customer services, and for information about how to apply for permission to reuse the copyright material in this book please see our website at www.wiley.com/wiley-blackwell.

The right of David Bakhurst to be identified as the author of this work has been asserted in accordance with the UK Copyright, Designs and Patents Act 1988.

All rights reserved. No part of this publication may be reproduced, stored in a retrieval system, or transmitted, in any form or by any means, electronic, mechanical, photocopying, recording or otherwise, except as permitted by the UK Copyright, Designs and Patents Act 1988, without the prior permission of the publisher.

Wiley also publishes its books in a variety of electronic formats. Some content that appears in print may not be available in electronic books.

Designations used by companies to distinguish their products are often claimed as trademarks. All brand names and product names used in this book are trade names, service marks, trademarks or registered trademarks of their respective owners. The publisher is not associated with any product or vendor mentioned in this book. This publication is designed to provide accurate and authoritative information in regard to the subject matter covered. It is sold on the understanding that the publisher is not engaged in rendering professional services. If professional advice or other expert assistance is required, the services of a competent professional should be sought.

Library of Congress Cataloging-in-Publication Data

Bakhurst, David.
   The formation of reason / David Bakhurst.
     p. cm. – (Journal of philosophy of education ; 12)
   Includes bibliographical references and index.
   ISBN 978-1-4443-3909-3 (pbk.)
1. Philosophy of mind.   2. Knowledge, Theory of.   3. Reason.   4. McDowell, John Henry.   I. Title.
   BD418.3.B355 2011
   128'.33–dc22

                                        2010044175

A catalogue record for this book is available from the British Library.

This book is published in the following electronic formats: ePDFs 9781444395327; Wiley Online Library 9781444395600; ePub 9781444395594

Set in 9.5/11.5 Times by SPi Publisher Services, Pondicherry, India

For Christine

Contents

Acknowledgements		ix
Foreword		x
Author's Preface		xiii
1	**What Can Philosophy Tell Us About How History Made the Mind?**	**1**
	What Role for Philosophy?	2
	Wittgenstein and Davidson	3
	Wittgenstein and Davidson Contrasted	5
	McDowell	7
	The Idea of *Bildung*	8
	Understanding the *Bildungsprozess*	10
	The Conceptual and the Practical	14
	Conclusion	16
2	**Social Constructionism**	**24**
	Social Constructionism Introduced	24
	The Social Construction of Reality	26
	Why Bother About Global Constructionism?	28
	Against Global Constructionism	29
	Matters Political	32
	The Social Construction of Mental States	33
	Why Mental States Are Not Socially Constructed	37
	The Social Construction of Psychological Categories	42
	Conclusion	45
3	**Self and Other**	**52**
	Problems of Self and Other	52
	The Problem of Self and Other in One's Own Person	54
	Strawson on Persons	55
	Wiggins on Persons and Human Nature	59
	The Significance of Second Nature	61
	Further Positives	64
	Conclusion: Two Cautionary Notes	66
4	**Freedom, Reflection and the Sources of Normativity**	**74**
	McDowell on Judgement	75
	Owens's Critique	77
	Defending Intellectual Freedom	78
	Freedom and the Sources of Normativity	82
	Sources of Normativity I: Practical Reasoning	85
	Sources of Normativity II: Theoretical Reasoning	86
	A McDowellian Response	87
	Conclusion	90

5	Exploring the Space of Reasons	99
	McDowell on the Space of Reasons	99
	Brandom's Inferentialism	105
	Ilyenkov on the Ideal	109
	Conclusion	115
6	Reason and Its Limits: Music, Mood and Education	123
	An Initial Response	125
	The Challenge Reconfigured	127
	Passivity Within Spontaneity	129
	Mood	131
	Mood, Salience and Shape	133
	Music	134
	Education	136
	Conclusion	141
7	Education Makes Us What We Are	149
	A Residual Individualism	150
	Vygotsky's Legacy	152
	Reconciling Vygotsky and McDowell	154
	Personalism	157
	Final Thoughts on Education	158
References		166
Index		177

Acknowledgements

The vast majority of this work has not appeared in print before, though in preparing the text I have occasionally made use of a few of my published writings. The discussion of David Wiggins's work in chapter 3 is adapted from my 'Wiggins on Persons and Human Nature', *Philosophy and Phenomenological Research*, LXXI.2, 2005, pp. 462–69, Wiley-Blackwell Publications, and my treatment of David Owens's *Freedom Without Reason* in chapter 4 is based on my review of his book published in *Philosophical Books*, 43.2, 2002, pp. 157–59, Wiley-Blackwell Publications. In addition, my presentation of Voloshinov's work in chapter 2 is indebted to my 'Social Memory in Soviet Thought', in D. Middleton and D. Edwards (eds), *Collective Remembering*, Sage Publications, 2000, pp. 203–26, and my exposition of Ilyenkov's views in chapter 5 deploys a few paragraphs from my 'Meaning, Normativity, and the Life of the Mind', *Language and Communication*, 17.1, 1997, pp. 33–51, Elsevier Publications. I am grateful to the respective publishers for permission to draw on this material.

Foreword

There can be few questions more pressing for education than those that appear at the interface between philosophy and psychology, for these are critical to how we learn and how we teach, and inseparable from what it is to be a human being: they are inseparable from what it is to be minded and what it is that makes the mind. But, strangely perhaps, when philosophers and psychologists discuss these things, they are apt to pass one another by. When educationalists turn to such writings, they commonly find that their real concerns are not being addressed, or that they are being broached in a manner that disappears into abstraction, cut off from the realities that confront teachers in their daily lives. These barriers to understanding are symptomatic of deep divisions in scholarly self-conception—not just legitimate disciplinary differences but divergent notions of what a discipline can and should do. Academic specialisation, accentuated by competitive research assessment regimes, amplifies these problems, deepening the division, while the imperative to demonstrate impact, in a culture of supposedly evidence-based policy, is an enticement to some—perhaps for the psychology of education especially—to superficiality or formulaic quick fixes. What then can philosophy do? When one turns to the philosophy of education, one finds, currently, that these questions receive less direct attention that one might expect; or perhaps that their treatment tends to be partial and partisan. All this is regrettable, it goes without saying, and these theoretical and practical deficits cry out for a more creative response.

The Formation of Reason answers to these needs. Drawing upon a rich and varied range of sources, David Bakhurst transcends these limitations with an account of the acquisition of reason—of how, as human beings, we come into the 'space of reasons', in Wilfrid Sellars's memorable phrase—that is remarkable for its breadth of vision. In a text that reflects the influence of Ludwig Wittgenstein and Jerome Bruner, Bakhurst brings Lev Vygotsky and Evald Ilyenkov together with Robert Brandom and John McDowell, forging connections that are sometimes surprising but always refreshing, drawing distinctions that are nicely nuanced and often revelatory: the reader is thus cautioned against too easy an acceptance of received views of any of these thinkers and any acquiescence in formulaic responses. Bakhurst moves adroitly between the detail and the big picture, always maintaining a sense of the practical responsibilities of his task, in a manner professional philosophy has schooled itself to eschew—so, at least, it would sometimes seem. To enquire into the nature and origins of human psychological powers, and the extent of their dependence upon history and culture, is to address questions central to the philosophy of mind, but it can also be to venture into borderlands with psychology that a more scrupulously anxious philosophy would avoid.

The book is an overt tribute to McDowell, and he is plainly the strongest presence in these pages. But it breaks new ground in demonstrating his significance for education, and this is achieved partly by a qualified but highly original reconciliation of his thought with that of Vygotsky. Prominent place is given to other Russian thinkers too, most notably, as we saw, the philosopher Ilyenkov, but this also extends to some acknowledgement of the insights into the semiotic nature of the human psyche of V. N. Voloshinov (that is, Mikhail Bakhtin?). This movement between disciplinary traditions and philosophical cultures gives a critical edge to Bakhurst's discussion such that the expository elements in the text are never merely exegesis but always challenge the reader in new ways.

So too McDowell's turn to *Bildung* in his account of 'second nature' is expanded here in such a way as to acknowledge something of the extraordinary richness of association the term carries. Thus, Bakhurst shows an appreciation of the idea's embeddedness in the facts of human life—of human finitude and sensibility, of human beings as subject to emotion and mood. Hence, his later discussion of music and the arts becomes all the more apposite, and this is just one of the ways in which the significance of engaging intelligently with concrete subject-matter is realised. Rooted in Renaissance humanism and ultimately Ancient Greek thought, and with strong connotations of character formation, *Bildung* is then explicated as a process of self-making. It becomes thus incumbent upon educators to ensure that this process is informed by plausible conceptions of the good, Bakhurst's account of which is resolutely affirmative and pluralistic. This is a vision of education, then, that conjoins freedom and reason.

When Bakhurst foregrounds the idea of autonomy as central to educational aims, he finds connections not only with *Bildung* but also, perhaps more obviously, with that restatement of the idea of a liberal education, in the 1960s and 1970s, that is associated with R. S. Peters, Paul Hirst and Robert Dearden. The interweaving of questions of ethics and epistemology in their enquiry, which, with its strongly Kantian inspiration, contributes to the robustness of that restatement, finds resonance in the present text also with Christine Korsgaard's examination of the sources of normativity. But this proves to be one of the several points where apparently like-minded philosophers are shown to differ, sometimes in ways that would escape the less critical reader of their work. A similar point can be made about the various forms of social constructionism that are evaluated, some of which are clearly congenial to Bakhurst, but many of which are shown to be vacuous—notwithstanding the seemingly religious enthusiasm for them that is sometimes found in educational and social science research. With these differences clearly exposed, the account we are offered of the socio-historical character of mind, and of the salience of this for education, is all the more convincing.

What these brief preparatory remarks should have indicated is that *The Formation of Reason* offers something other than a mainstream approach to these mainstream questions. Yet this is not the work of a maverick. The originality arises from the seeing of connections and the ability to draw these out in ways that are often surprising and always cogent. In doing this, David Bakhurst has succeeded in writing not only a work of philosophy that can speak to that mainstream in philosophy of mind but also a book that should be read by psychologists and educators and, in fact, anyone who has the kind of interest we should all have in what it is that makes the mind.

Paul Standish
Series Editor

Author's Preface

This book begins by posing the question of whether and in what sense our distinctively human psychological powers are essentially social in nature and origin. It responds by developing a socio-historical account of mind according to which we owe our status as rational animals to our initiation into culture. Such issues are the focus of some of my earlier writings, especially my work on Russian philosophy and psychology, and my papers on Wittgenstein and Bruner. This book affords me the opportunity to revisit ideas from those works, expounding them in greater detail and exploring their consequences, especially their relevance to our understanding of education. But there is much here that is new, in part because some of my views have evolved, and in part because my primary inspiration in this book is the philosophy of John McDowell, whose work I have long admired, but have never before given a sustained treatment. I hope the result complements my previous efforts, and offers a fruitful exploration of what we might call the conceptual foundations of the philosophy of education.

I have long been interested in questions of education, a topic dear to the hearts of many thinkers on whom I have written in the past. Nevertheless, I did not set out to write a book in philosophy of education. That came about because a number of friends and colleagues encouraged me to develop my ideas in that direction. I am especially grateful to Jan Derry for her interest in my work, her critical insight, and her marvellous generosity and enthusiasm. Through Jan, I have met many others who have influenced me, such as Paul Standish, Harry Daniels, Anne Edwards, Michael Young, David Guile, John Hardcastle and Andrew Davis (whom I first knew many years ago when he was a graduate student at Keele and I an undergraduate). I associate the writing of this book with good times spent among friends, discussing matters philosophical in seminars, and afterwards over food and wine. Very little of this philosophical camaraderie would have come to pass had Jan not made it happen.

In 2001–2, I was privileged to hold a visiting fellowship at All Souls College, Oxford, where I was able to conduct preliminary research for the book in a setting supremely conducive to scholarly reflection. I thank the Warden and Fellows of the College for their kindness and hospitality. I am especially indebted to Myles Burnyeat and Hanna Pickard for making my stay at All Souls so pleasurable and productive. I am also extremely grateful to London's Institute of Education, where I am now fortunate to have an association as a Visiting Professor. I have given numerous talks at the Institute in recent years to audiences that never fail to be perceptive in criticism and generous in spirit. I only wish I could spend more time there. I am also indebted to Queen's University at Kingston for granting me academic leave to pursue this project, and to the Social Sciences and Humanities Research Council of Canada for funding the research at its embryonic stages.

xiv   *Preface*

I have had the opportunity to present material from the manuscript to colloquia at All Souls College, Bath University, Birmingham University, Durham University, Griffith University, Hertfordshire University, The Institute of Education, London, Queen's University at Kingston, and York University (Toronto), at meetings of the Humanities and Social Sciences Federation of Canada (in Winnipeg), the Philosophy of Education Society of Great Britain (at New College, Oxford), the Philosophy of Education Society of the United States (in Montreal), the International Society for Cultural and Activity Research (in Amsterdam, Seville and San Diego), at the Gregynog Philosophy of Education Conference, and at workshops at Queen's University at Kingston and Laurentian University. I thank the audiences on these occasions for their questions, comments and criticisms.

I would like to thank John McDowell for his help and encouragement over the years. His influence on the text is conspicuous; I hope he likes the result. Many other people deserve my heartfelt thanks. Paul Standish, Andrew Davis and Willem deVries read the whole manuscript with great care and provided countless astute criticisms and suggestions that made the book much better than it otherwise would have been. I am also indebted to two anonymous referees for their comments on the project, and to many friends who discussed parts of the text with me, including David Wiggins, Andrew Chitty, Michael Luntley, Adrian Moore and Hanjo Glock. Jonathan and Sarah Dancy merit special thanks—Jonathan for philosophical inspiration, Sarah for expertly copy-editing the manuscript and managing the book's production. Other friends had a less direct but nevertheless important influence on the work, including Adam Swift, Cheryl Misak, David Dyzenhaus, Peter Jones, George Lovell, Maureen Garvie, Vladislav Lektorsky and my colleagues at Queen's, especially Sergio Sismondo, Henry Laycock, Steve Leighton, Rahul Kumar, Deborah Knight and one other, mentioned below. Queen's is blessed with outstanding students, and I have been fortunate to work with many. I would particularly like to thank Tom Brannen, Anthony Bruno, Octavian Busuioc, Rachel Fern, Jane Forsey, Katie Howe, Ryan McInerney, Rachel Sheffrin and John Symons. I am also very grateful to the staff of the Queen's Philosophy Department, Marilyn Lavoie and Judy Vanhooser, for the superb job they do, and for the tremendous help and support they have given me during my time as Head of Department. On a sad note, since I began this book I have lost several people dear to me who inspired me greatly: Genia Lampert, Felix Mikhailov, Jerry Cohen, and my mother, Peggy Bakhurst. I miss them very much.

The book is dedicated to Christine Sypnowich, my wife and colleague at Queen's. Christine and our two children, Rosemary and Hugh, are the greatest. Not a day goes by without my giving thanks for my good fortune in being part of such a family. Christine is the perfect friend to me, a wonderful mother to our children, and a constant source of inspiration, intellectual, moral and aesthetic. She's also great fun. Many years ago when we were doctoral students in Oxford, I was writing to our friend Hanjo Glock. I asked Christine if she had a message for Hanjo. She answered self-mockingly, 'Just tell him Christine is as lovely as ever and never ceases to delight.' Joking she may have been, but what she said was true then, is true now, and has been true at all points in between. Thanks for everything, Christine.

1
What Can Philosophy Tell Us About How History Made the Mind?

This chapter is concerned primarily with two questions. First: to what degree do we owe our distinctively human psychological powers to history, society and culture? Second: if our relatedness to others is a precondition of our mindedness, to what extent can this be demonstrated or illuminated by *philosophical* reflection?[1]

My interest in these issues goes back to the early 1980s, when I began research on Russian philosophy. I spent the 1982–3 academic year in Moscow, trying to get inside the philosophical culture of the USSR. I was convinced that there had to be more to that culture than the tired doctrines of dialectical and historical materialism that were the official creed of the Soviet state. And I was right. I was fortunate to fall in with a group of talented philosophers, who took me under their wing. These thinkers were not dissidents; they were Marxists, but they were representatives of a very different form of Marxism from the kind peddled by the Soviet establishment. These were so-called 'men of the 'sixties', who had done their most creative work during the brief 'thaw' that succeeded the Stalin period. They were creative, critical and scholarly. They were steeped in German classical philosophy, especially Hegel. Their cast of mind was sceptical, playful and, as you might expect, dialectical. They were typically excellent orators.[2]

One prominent theme in their work was that the human mind is an essentially 'socio-cultural' or 'socio-historical' phenomenon. Now, I had been brought up to think that the idea that human beings are 'socially constituted beings' was a leitmotif of the incorrigibly feeble-minded: the sort of claim that no self-respecting philosopher would advance. So I was intrigued to find the idea flourishing among thinkers whose intelligence and ingenuity were hard to question. I therefore set about trying to establish what exactly these Russians were arguing and to explore similar ideas advanced by other thinkers. As it happens, since the early 1980s, the idea that the human mind cannot be understood without essential reference to culture has come to prominence in certain areas of Western philosophy and

The Formation of Reason, First Edition. David Bakhurst.
© 2011 David Bakhurst. Published 2011 by Blackwell Publishing Ltd.

psychology: for example, communitarian political philosophy, feminist theory, certain readings of Wittgenstein, some forms of poststructuralism, and the various species of social-constructionist, discursive and cultural psychology.[3] Even in cognitive science it is now common to hear reference to the importance of culture. Yet there remains little consensus about how exactly to understand the relation of mind to culture, or society, or history.

WHAT ROLE FOR PHILOSOPHY?

My Russians were convinced that the socio-historical character of mind is something that philosophy can illuminate. But there are grounds for scepticism here, for the influence of culture, or social interaction, or history, on the nature and development of mind must be an empirical matter, and as such one that lies outside the province of philosophy. If you muse about how great the influence of culture is on your own development, you might find yourself asking questions like: *What would I have been like had I been born the child of a Roman centurion?* And you might think that headway can be made by treating this as a thought experiment. But in so far as we can make sense of the question at all, surely the only interesting reading is this: *How would someone with your genetic make-up have turned out had he or she been brought up as the child of a centurion?* That looks like an empirical question about the respective contributions of nature and nurture, not a philosophical one. Questions about the manifestation of genetic traits in contrasting environments are the stuff of twin studies, not thought experiments.

It is interesting that my Russians strongly resisted the idea that they were making a speculative intervention in the nature–nurture debate. In fact, they explicitly argued that psychological development should not be seen in nature–nurture terms (see Mikhailov, 1995, pp. 76–7). First, they maintained that it is a mistake to suppose we can neatly distinguish two discrete causal factors, natural/biological, on the one hand, and cultural/environmental, on the other, and then sort influences on development into one kind or the other. Second, they complained that the nature–nurture debate portrays development exclusively in causal terms. It represents individual development as a product of either natural or environmental influences, or (more plausibly) of some combination of the two. But the position these philosophers were advancing was not one about the causal conditions of human development. Their argument was more transcendental in character: that initiation into culture, social interaction, having a history, and so on are not so much causes of psychological development as preconditions of the possibility of rational agency, and hence of mind, at least in its human form, since these Russian thinkers identified our mindedness with our status as rational agents. We can ask of a rational agent, say, whether she is naturally good at mathematics or prone to fits of anger, but we cannot portray rational agency as determined by nature, nurture, or anything else, for we represent an agent as rational in so far as we see her as autonomous and *self-determining*. The question for my Russians was the relation of history, culture and society to the possibility of self-determination, an issue that, they complained, was rendered invisible by the nature–nurture debate.

But even if we take a nuanced view of nature and nurture, human development is surely in the realm of the empirical, so what exactly is there for the philosopher to contribute? Well, the Lockean job of underlabourer for the sciences is available. But we can probably find more challenging employment even if we concede that the relation between culture and mind is to be explored by empirical investigation. One role might be to integrate material from different disciplines. Understanding the mind is an interdisciplinary project: we need insights not just from psychology, biology, neuroscience, linguistics, anthropology, etc., but from a number of historical disciplines, such as archaeology, ancient history, and so on. There are many reasons why practitioners in one field may be unable to see the significance of work in another, even if they are aware of its existence. So one task the philosopher can assume is to weave insights from different fields into a single synoptic vision. This is no easy job, not just because it is hard to establish a common universe of discourse, but because one has to reckon with all the entrenched reasons for thinking the project unnecessary or impossible.

I want, however, to consider whether there might not be a yet more ambitious role for the philosopher—that is, to argue that the human mind is essentially a socio-historical phenomenon. Might there not be distinctively philosophical arguments that would show what my Russians wanted to show—namely, that there is a more than merely empirical connection between possession of a mind and membership in society, culture or community?

Such a position seems to have been held by two of the greats of twentieth-century analytic philosophy: Ludwig Wittgenstein and Donald Davidson. I shall briefly sketch their respective positions.

WITTGENSTEIN AND DAVIDSON

In the passages in the *Philosophical Investigations* known as the 'private language argument' and the 'rule-following considerations', Wittgenstein argues—or appears to argue—that there could not be a language that is essentially private in character, from which it seems to follow that language is necessarily a public, or communal, phenomenon.

The argument is this: a language in which the meaning of the words was given by entities accessible only by the speaker (such as the speaker's ideas or sensations) would lack standards of correctness. There would be no way to distinguish correct usage of the words of the language from usage that merely struck the speaker as correct. But a language with no standards of correctness is no language at all; therefore, a private language is impossible.

The 'rule-following considerations', which precede the private language argument in the *Philosophical Investigations*, seem to show that we can make sense of standards of correctness in a practice only by appeal to such notions as agreement and custom. There is no philosophical vantage point from which we can declare that one way of extending a mathematical series, or deploying a concept, is correct and another incorrect. Correctness and incorrectness are disclosed from within our practices—activities that cannot be underwritten by philosophy but must be accepted for what they are: namely, aspects of our natural history or 'form of life'. Norman Malcolm concludes:

> When Wittgenstein says that following a rule is a *practice*, I think he means that a person's actions cannot be in accord with a rule unless they are in conformity with a common way of acting that is displayed in the behaviour of nearly everyone who has had the same training. This means the concept of following a rule implies the concept of a *community* of rule-followers. (1986, p. 156)

Given the intimate connection between language and thought, and between rule-following and rationality, it appears we have an argument that represents membership in a community as a precondition of mind and rational agency.[4]

What of Davidson? In several of his later essays, Davidson argues that interpersonal communication is a precondition of the possibility of thought. This is so in two respects. First, communication is 'the source of the concept of objective truth' (Davidson, 1991/2001, p. 209). Invoking Wittgenstein, Davidson argues that a person can be supposed to be engaged in a norm-governed practice—such as thinking, reasoning or speaking a language—only if a distinction can be drawn between her acting correctly or incorrectly; that is, we must be able to distinguish between what the thinker or speaker takes to be the case and what is the case. Davidson maintains that for a mind in isolation nothing can ground this distinction. He writes: '[W]e would not have the concept of getting things wrong or right if it were not for our interactions with other people.' This is not because agreement determines truth, as relativists or social constructionists might argue; rather, consensus 'creates the space' in which the concept of truth has application (Davidson, 1997/2001, p. 129). Only a shared public language can have genuine standards of correctness.

Second, Davidson contends that the very possibility of what philosophers have come to call 'mental content' depends upon social interaction. He argues that our mental states owe their contents to their causes. My perceptual belief that there is a desk in front of me has the content it does in virtue of the causes that engender it. But the causal process in which the belief originates is complex and the number of contributing causal factors enormous. Why should we pick out the *desk* as the cause of the belief—and hence as the object the belief is about—rather than some other part of the causal chain, such as images on my retina or events in the visual centres of my brain? Davidson's answer is that only when we introduce another person into the picture do we have reason to identify the causes of our mental states with the public objects about which we take ourselves to talk and think. Content is determined by a process of 'triangulation', in which two people's responses to stimuli are traced back to a common object. Davidson concludes: 'Without this sharing of reactions to common stimuli, thought and speech would have no particular content—that is, no content at all' (1991/2001, p. 212).

Davidson (1991/2001) maintains that these insights resolve many of the traditional problems of epistemology. Knowledge of our own minds and knowledge of other minds are shown to be 'mutually dependent': triangulation presupposes that I cannot know what I think unless I can have knowledge of the minds of others, and that I cannot know what others think unless I am able to know my own mind. Both these varieties of knowledge rest in turn upon beliefs about the environment with which my interlocutor(s) and I interact. Davidson famously argues that these beliefs about the environment must be largely correct. For interpretation to be possible, interpreter and interpreted must share a significant number of true beliefs about the world. This is not just because the assumption that one's interlocutor has largely true beliefs is a precondition of understanding her; triangulation ensures that speakers cannot be significantly in error about what they take their beliefs to be about. If knowledge of the external world, knowledge of other minds, and self-knowledge are all interdependent, and if many of our ordinary beliefs must be true, then the appearance that there is a gulf between mind and world, or between mind and mind, must be illusory. The traditional problems of philosophy are problems no more.

For present purposes, what is crucial is Davidson's conclusion that 'interaction among similar creatures is a necessary condition for speaking a language' (1992/2001, p. 120) and for possessing thoughts:

> Belief, intention, and the other propositional attitudes are all social in that they are states a creature cannot be in without having a concept of intersubjective truth, and this is a concept one cannot have without sharing, and knowing that one shares, a world, and a way of thinking about the world, with someone else. (1992/2001, p. 121)

If Davidson is right, minded beings are essentially social.

WITTGENSTEIN AND DAVIDSON CONTRASTED

I shall not undertake a detailed examination of the pros and cons of these much-discussed arguments, but restrict myself to a couple of observations.

It might appear as if Davidson's and Wittgenstein's positions are complementary—and hence that the weight of their considerable combined authority presses us to acknowledge the social character of mind.[5] But things are not so simple. Even sympathetic interpreters of Wittgenstein are profoundly divided about just what his arguments show. Among the most persuasive interpretations is the one propounded by Gordon Baker and Peter Hacker, and it is far less bold than Malcolm's quoted above.

Baker and Hacker take Wittgenstein to have shown that a language must have public standards of correctness only in the sense that its rules must be such that another agent *could* understand and adhere to them. It does not follow that there must be other agents who actually do understand and adhere to them. What is crucial is that language practices exhibit regularity, but there is no reason why a contingently solitary person should not establish such practices so long as the practices *could* in principle be learnt by someone else. Wittgenstein treats language as a system of conventions, but a convention could be set up by a solitary individual if the convention were such that someone else—if there were someone else—could adhere to it. This shows that anything that is a language must be learnable by more than one person. It does not show that speakers must be members of communities if language is to be possible (see, for example, Baker and Hacker, 1984, pp. 71–80; 1990).[6]

On this reading, the significance of Wittgenstein's remarks is primarily negative: they explode Cartesian and classical empiricist conceptions of mind and language. They fall short, however, of establishing a substantive doctrine of the socio-historical self. And this, one might think, is to be expected, since Wittgenstein was clear that the aspirations of his philosophy were to criticise and dissolve philosophical misconceptions rather than to advance positive philosophical theories. Moreover, if we look at what Wittgenstein says about persons and selves in his notorious argument that the first-person pronoun is not a referring expression, we see that advancing a vision of the person as socially constituted is pretty far from his mind.[7]

Davidson, in contrast, is committed to the stronger view that more than one subject must actually exist if language and thought are to be possible: 'it takes two to triangulate', as he puts it (1991/2001, p. 213). At the same time, Davidson is profoundly opposed to the idea that language is a system of conventions or that we can understand a language as a kind of social entity or institution over and above the interpretative activities of individual speakers trying to make sense of each other. To understand others, each speaker deploys Tarski-style theories of interpretation, short-term and long-term ('passing' and 'prior', in Davidson's terminology), speaker-specific and more general in character, but none of these describes what philosophers and linguists are inclined to call a language. In fact, for Davidson, there is 'no such thing as a language, not if a language is anything like what philosophers and linguists have supposed' (1986/2005, p. 107; see also Davidson, 1994/2005). What there is is the coincidence of idiolects.[8]

So Wittgenstein gives credence to the notion of language as a set of shareable conventions, but does not require that a community exist to share them, while Davidson insists that more than one speaker must actually exist for thought and language to be possible, but he has no time for the notion of language as a social institution. There are deep differences here.[9]

It is also notable that neither view really has a developmental dimension. Although Wittgenstein's writings are peppered with examples about teaching and learning, he tells us relatively little about how he conceives the child's initiation into a form of life save for a few remarks about 'training'. Davidson recognises that we are owed an account of the emergence of thought and language in the child, but despairs of giving one. He writes:

> We have many vocabularies for describing nature when we regard it as mindless, and we have a mentalistic vocabulary for describing thought and intentional action; what we lack is a way of describing what is in between. ...
>
> It is not that we have a clear idea what sort of language we could use to describe half-formed minds; there may be a very deep conceptual difficulty or impossibility involved. That means there is a perhaps insuperable problem in giving a full description of the emergence of thought. (Davidson, 1997/2001, p. 128)

Davidson wryly concludes this passage by giving thanks that he is not in the field of developmental psychology.

McDOWELL

I want to turn now to the views of a thinker much influenced by Wittgenstein and Davidson: John McDowell.[10] In *Mind and World* (1994), McDowell sketches a view of the emergence of mind that does have a developmental perspective, or at least it has room for one.

McDowell maintains that the distinctive feature of the kinds of minds that human beings have is that we are responsive to reasons. Human beings are not merely pushed about by blind causal forces: our thoughts and actions are guided, and in some cases determined—that is, rationally determined—by our appreciation of what there is reason to think or do. Human mindedness resides in this ability to commune with reasons. We are inhabitants of 'the space of reasons', as he picturesquely puts it, adopting a phrase of Wilfrid Sellars.[11]

McDowell advances a distinctive view of experience. He argues that experience should be understood as exercising a rational rather than merely causal influence over us. In perception, what we take in is not raw data that the mind has to work up and conceptualise before it can form the basis of judgement. The content of our experience is *that things are thus and so*.[12] The deliverances of perception are already conceptual in character and hence fit to yield judgement and to serve as grounds for belief. If we construe experience in this way, we can think of it not as a mediator that comes between us and things as they are, but as openness to reality. Experience discloses the world to us.

If experience is both essentially conceptual in character and is able to reveal reality to us, then reality itself must be conceptual in character or at least not alien to the conceptual (see McDowell, 1994, pp. 25–9). This requires us to think of the world as 'all that is the case' rather than as brutely physical in character. To achieve this, McDowell argues, we must overcome the scientism that insists on representing nature as 'disenchanted', as bereft of significance.[13]

In the present context, the crucial aspect of McDowell's position is that human beings are not born into the space of reasons but are initiated into it by education, or *Bildung*, as he puts it, adopting the evocative German term. The child is born a mere animal, as it were, but acquires a 'second nature' as she develops conceptual capacities that put her in touch with reality in experience. She thereby becomes a conscious rational being—a person. McDowell writes: '[I]t is not even clearly intelligible to suppose that a creature might be born at home in the space of reasons. Human beings are not: they are born mere animals, and they are transformed into thinkers and intentional agents in the course of coming to maturity' (p. 125). McDowell gives 'pride of place' to the acquisition of language in this process of transformation. Initiation into language is our entrance into the conceptual realm. In this, McDowell thinks of language not just as a sophisticated symbolic system, but as a living repository of evolving forms of thought. This is a vision of language in marked contrast to Davidson's: the language that makes 'our orientation towards reality' possible is, McDowell writes, 'essentially the possession of a *we*' (McDowell, 2007a/2009b, p. 149). In acquiring language, the child enters an intellectual culture or cultures, comprising conceptions of the world, styles of thinking and reasoning, values that are epistemic, moral, aesthetic, and so on. She inherits a tradition of thought, 'a store of historically accumulated wisdom about what is a reason for what' (McDowell, 1994, p. 126), and in so doing becomes a minded being. With this, it seems, McDowell arrives at the view that history makes the mind.

THE IDEA OF *BILDUNG*

It is interesting to note that there are significant parallels between the kind of socio-historical vision of mind that emerges in *Mind and World* and the views of my Russians. The latter also portray the child's mind as emerging only through her initiation into culture. They too argue against scientism and the disenchantment of objective reality, urging us to think of the world as embodying meaning and value. And, as McDowell does, they draw a sharp division between the modes of thought and experience available to rational agents at home in the space of reasons and the non-conceptual forms of awareness of 'mere animals'. There are, of course, important differences of emphasis, but the commonalities are plain. This is perhaps not so surprising: the Russians were much inspired by Hegel and 'German classical philosophy', a tradition that has increasingly influenced McDowell since his move from Oxford to Pittsburgh in the mid-1980s.

What, then, are we to make of McDowell's idea of *Bildung*? His immediate source is the philosophy of Hans-Georg Gadamer, whose *Truth and Method* has a conspicuous influence on the concluding pages of *Mind and World* (see also McDowell, 2007a/2009b). Gadamer in turn describes the idea of *Bildung* as one of the guiding concepts of humanism (1975, p. 9), and his use of it puts him in conversation with a tradition of German philosophical and educational thinking whose participants include Herder, von Helmholtz, Schiller, Moses Mendelssohn, and Hegel among many others. The term is related to the verb *bilden* (to form) and the noun *Bild* (image), and is variously translated into English as formation, education, cultivation and culture (though the later translation, once predominant,[14] can mislead). The notion came to prominence in German educational thought in the second half of the eighteenth century to characterise an idea with roots in Renaissance Humanism and ultimately Ancient Greek thought: education as character formation in accord with an ideal image of human development (see Nordenbo, 2003). This became the idea of a process of 'formative self-development' (Wood, 1998, p. 301), in which the individual transcends the particularity of her natural existence through the development of the intellectual, rational side of her being, thereby enabling her to commune with the universal and to enter, in von Humboldt's phrase, 'the most general, most animated and most unrestrained interplay' with the world (von Humboldt, quoted by Løvlie and Standish, 2003, p. 2). Critical in this is the individual's relation to culture and tradition, which are seen as actively appropriated and transformed to become part of the individual's inner life.[15]

These rich themes all find expression in McDowell's philosophy, albeit sometimes parenthetically and in a philosophical idiom rather different from the German thinkers in whose work the idea of *Bildung* is at home. Most prominent is the link to Greek thought, for McDowell takes a modified version of Aristotle's view of the development of virtue of character as his model of the *Bildungsprozess*. Yet apart from this appeal to Aristotle, McDowell tells us little about how he intends *Bildung* to be understood. We can, however, note two important features of his use of the concept. The first is that his conception of the *telos* that *Bildung* aspires to realise is thin. The end of the *Bildungsprozess* is the emergence of an autonomous, critical rational agent 'at home in the world'. To this extent, his work might be thought allied to educational philosophies that stress rational autonomy, such as the so-called London School of R. S. Peters, Paul Hirst and Robert Dearden.[16] But McDowell offers no account of *which* of the many ways in which a life can manifest rational autonomy are worthy of cultivation, let alone a story about their developmental or educational preconditions, assigning questions of what kind of people we should be to first-order ethical and political deliberation and debate.[17]

Second, notwithstanding this thin teleology, McDowell takes a very strong view of what *Bildung* accomplishes. He casts *Bildung* not as the development of an already-existing self, but as the process in which minded beings come to be. He explicitly describes the transformation *Bildung* effects as 'acquiring a mind'; that is, 'the capacity to think and act intentionally' (McDowell, 1994, p. 126). Cultural formation, then, is relevant not just to how rational agents manifest their rationality: it is a precondition of a human being's having rationality to manifest. McDowell's view of *Bildung* incorporates *both* senses contained in the ambiguous term *self-creation*. It is the process of the coming into being of a self able to engage in practices of self-making.

Just how distinctive McDowell's position is in its relevance for philosophy of education depends in large measure on how we are to understand these claims about the transformative powers of *Bildung*. McDowell admits that his position 'risks looking mysterious' (1994, p. 125). He cannot be suggesting that the human infant is literally 'mindless' in the sense of lacking psychological capacity altogether. Nor will it do to lean too heavily on the distinction, favoured by his Pittsburgh colleague Robert Brandom, between *sentience* and *sapience*. For though the child may not yet be sapient, in the sense of being genuinely responsive to reasons, she is far more than merely sentient—that is, capable of being '*aware* in the sense of being *awake*' (see Brandom, 1994, p. 5). There is no question that the pre-linguistic child can 'think and act intentionally' in a perfectly uncontentious sense of those terms. What the infant lacks are psychological capacities that enable her, as McDowell would put it, to hold the world in view. The transformation effected by *Bildung* makes the child not just something *in* the world, interacting with her immediate local environment, but a subject with a view *on* the world that can think and act in light of that conception.

It might be thought that the natural next step would be for McDowell to offer us an account of just how the transformation occurs. It is interesting, then, that he does not venture even a sketch of how such an account might go, or refer us to relevant empirical work. Rather, in his treatment of *Bildung*, he writes as if he is drawing attention to facts of human development that are there in plain view, just so long as they are not rendered invisible by scientism or philosophical prejudice.

How, then, can his account be taken further?

UNDERSTANDING THE *BILDUNGSPROZESS*

Perhaps McDowell is reticent to say much about *Bildung* because he does not think this the appropriate province of philosophy. However, although McDowell would certainly acknowledge that philosophy cannot pretend to discover facts about human development by a priori means, I do not think he believes that, having made room to acknowledge the importance of *Bildung*, the philosopher must simply step aside and leave it for the psychologist, linguist and cognitive scientist to make good on the notion.[18] We can look to philosophy not just to observe the importance of *Bildung*, but to elucidate the concepts that will enable us to *think* its importance: person, rationality, the space of reasons, mindedness, thought, meaning, normativity, agency, second nature, and so on. Moreover, speculative reflection on aspects of human development that are in plain view can be genuinely illuminating. We should not think of such reflection simply as a place holder for a genuine theoretical account, any more than we should see Aristotle's reflections on moral character as merely provisional, awaiting a proper empirical moral psychology.

With these considerations in mind, let us attempt to describe one way in which we might elucidate the *Bildungsprozess*. In this, it will be important to avoid an easy misunderstanding. Reading McDowell, or my Russians, one might think they suppose children to undergo a kind of 'cognitive baptism'. The infant is immersed in culture by her elders and 'acquires a mind', emerging a conscious rational being. McDowell's appeal to first language acquisition serves to mitigate such an impression. Yet it is still tempting to think that we must be able to identify discrete, critical moments of transition that enable the child to cross a line that divides the minded from the unminded, the pre-rational from the rational, 'first nature' from second nature, the merely animal from the personal. But of course there is no moment at which the child becomes rational, any more than there is a moment at which she first qualifies as a speaker of her native language. There are no lines that are crossed, just complex, many and varied developmental processes in which black and white end points are joined by numerous overlapping links in shades of grey. Moreover, the child's location at any point in her development is influenced, causally and perhaps constitutively, by how others relate to her. In our engagement with children, we attribute to them capacities that they do not yet possess, or possess only embryonically, and this 'lending of capacity' is a precondition for the child's coming to acquire the self-standing capacity itself.[19] Any attempt to elucidate *Bildung* must be alive to these complexities.

McDowell identifies the space of reasons with the realm of the conceptual: the child enters the space of reasons in so far as she acquires conceptual powers. It is therefore natural to propose that we enrich our conception of *Bildung* by exploring the development of the child's concepts, and how society, culture and history are implicated in their acquisition and their exercise.

There are, of course, many contrasting accounts of concepts in the philosophical literature.[20] David Wiggins, following Frege, treats a substance concept, e.g., *horse*, as something general or universal (Wiggins, 2001, pp. 8–11). The concept is 'the general thing horse' (p. 79, n. 2). The sortal predicate 'horse' refers to the concept. A concept is said to have 'marks': a property that is a mark of the concept *horse* is a property that anything that is a horse has. On this view, concepts are objective in the sense that they are possible objects of analysis, the nature of which is open to discovery.

It is much more common, however, to treat concepts as purely psychological phenomena, and there are contrasting ways of thinking about concepts as psychological. One is to construe concepts as mental representations. On one version of this view, to have the concept *horse* is to possess a mental representation (a) which has a certain characteristic (i.e. horsey) content, (b) the occurrence of which is correlated causally with the appearance of horses, and (c) which can be deployed to form thoughts about horses.

A second view holds that to possess a concept is to have a certain range of abilities. Opinions differ about the nature of the abilities in question. On the most minimal view, they are recognitional and discriminatory abilities: to possess the concept *horse* is to be able to identify, individuate and keep track of horses—or, more demandingly, to be able to identify, individuate and keep track of horses *as horses*. A stronger view holds that the abilities are linguistic in kind. Brandom, for example, advances a 'linguistic pragmatism' that maintains, following Sellars, that '*grasping a concept is mastering the use of a word*' (Brandom, 2000, p. 6). McDowell focuses on the ability to form thoughts: 'the concept of water is an ability that is exercised in thinking about water' (McDowell, 1992/1998b, p. 289).

Advocates of the second, ability-centred view might say that mental representations underlie the abilities in question, just as proponents of the first view might hold that, although concepts are mental representations, what is important about them is what they enable us to do. But there is nonetheless a marked difference of emphasis in the two approaches. Some advocates of the first view are atomists about concept possession: to have the concept of an *x* simply requires that you have the right kind of mental representation (see, for example, Fodor, 1998). At least when it comes to concepts of the substances we encounter in perception, each concept is a discrete entity, possession of which does not demand the possession of other concepts—a being could in principle have it and it alone. Advocates of the ability-centred view, in contrast, tend to be conceptual holists. Even on a minimalist account of the abilities in question, their exercise requires a whole range of concepts, not just the concept *horse*. These certainly include more fundamental concepts of the kind Kant thought of as 'categories', but they will also include lots of cognate empirical concepts. To be able to identify and re-identify something as a horse, it helps if you can make certain kinds of inferences ('If it's a horse, then …') and if you have a handle on what kind of thing a horse *isn't* ('That can't be a horse because it barks like a dog.').

One attraction of the ability-centred approach is that it represents conceptual competence as a matter of degree: someone's ability to identify, individuate and keep track of something can be more or less sophisticated, just as there can be different standards to which we can hold someone when we ask: 'Does he know what an x is?' Where competence comes in degrees, we can meaningfully ask how it develops.

Let us consider the development of children's understanding of a straightforward substance concept. For this purpose, the concept *horse* will do fine. I shall suggest that we can identify four stages in the child's developing understanding of a substance concept. However, I do not want to make much of this stage talk. It is useful simply because it enables us to illustrate the different ways in which socio-historical influences may be operative.[21] Perhaps the course of conceptual development is not best seen as divided into stages, or, if we can define stages, we should delineate more than four. I want to leave these questions open.

Stage One: At the foundation of the child's understanding of a substance concept is the ability to identify and re-identify the substance in question. So the first stage of the development of the infant's understanding of the concept *horse* is simply her pre-linguistic ability to pick out and keep track of horses. The signs of this ability are pretty obvious: she responds to horses. Of course, early on there may be no clear distinction between the child's responding to the appearance and reappearance of a *particular* horse and her responding to continuants of a type (or a subclass of that type). But equally, there may be: the child may be characteristically delighted at the appearance of the family pet while generally, if differently, excited when any horse is on the scene.

It might be thought that there is nothing socio-historical about this ability: it is primitive, innate, pre-linguistic and individual. In a sense, this must be true: if the child cannot 'lock on' to horses, there is nothing for *Bildung* to work with. At the same time, we should not overlook the role played by the adults and other children who surround the child. From the outset, the activities of others, including of course their speech, play a significant organising role. Many appearances of horses are accompanied by utterances of the word 'horse' by parents and caregivers (and not just utterances, of course; adults respond to, and interact with, horses in characteristic ways): the word starts to anticipate, register and acknowledge experience. Moreover, adults present the boundaries of the concept to the child. The child learns what does and does not count as a horse from the reactions of adults to her responses to the appearance of candidates, which might be real animals, or toys, pictures in books, photographs, and so on. Even the most primitive of conceptual abilities is exercised in a complex social context.

Stage Two: At the beginning of the child's linguistic awareness, she starts to master simple words. She grasps that utterances of 'horse' refer to *this* continuant and to similar others, and she begins to deploy the sound herself, whether to express excitement, make a request, express fear or just for the fun of it. At first the child may overextend the term, calling all four-legged medium-sized animals 'horses', or underextend it, reserving the term only for Dobbin, but the influence of adults and other children brings her usage into line with their own (other things being equal, which they often are not).

At this stage, the child's use of the concept is 'in the space of reasons' in the sense that her usage of the word 'horse' is held accountable to standards of correctness, standards that are upheld by other members of the community of speakers. (Note that even at stage one, the child's non-linguistic responses, while at first seen by others as merely causal, are gradually treated as warranted or not by the situation and hence as accountable to standards of appropriateness: 'Don't get excited, Paul, it's not a horse.'). Of course, it is one-dimensional to think of the adults' role simply in terms of correcting and training, or even as 'scaffolding' linguistic usage (to use Jerome Bruner's famous metaphor). They constantly offer the child linguistic possibilities; they encourage, play and revel in language. They initiate the child into a form of life in which meaning is ubiquitous, and, as I observed above, they invite the child into this form of life by treating her as far more competent than she actually is.

Stage Three: Now we begin to see increasing sophistication in the child's linguistic knowledge. The child not only uses a term in response to certain circumstances, or for certain purposes; she begins to associate the term with criteria for its application. She begins to justify her use of words, and the judgements she expresses in using them, by appeal to such criteria. We need not portray such criteria as comprising a set of necessary and sufficient conditions that, in the case at hand, would specify what properties a substance has to have to count as a horse, properties that can be invoked to explain the meaning of the term 'horse'. Not many predicates have criteria for their use that can be regimented into informative necessary and sufficient conditions, and our understanding of a concept need not take the form of something like a definition. What is critical, however, is that the child begins to justify her thought and talk, and this involves an appreciation of the kind of conceptual connections and inferential relations stressed by conceptual holists: if it is a horse, then it is an animal, four-legged, fond of hay, prone to neighing, trotting, cantering, and so on and so forth. Over time, the child's linguistic knowledge becomes increasingly reflective.

To what extent are these abilities socio-historical in character? First, the child becomes progressively more proficient in the art of giving and taking reasons. She comes to understand that she owes others an explanation of what she says and thinks, just as others have a similar debt to her, and that the kind of explanation expected is a normative one that justifies or vindicates judgement.[22] Second, the criteria with reference to which the appropriateness of the use of substance terms like 'horse' have to be assessed are inherited by individuals from their culture. What counts as a horse and what the word 'horse' means are not up to the individual. Here we see two important dimensions of the *Bildungsprozess*: we learn what Brandom calls 'the game of giving and asking for reasons', and we learn to play it by appeal to standards we inherit from our intellectual tradition.[23]

Stage Four: It is important, however, that even though the child inherits a conception of what a horse is, and what the word 'horse' means, she also inherits this thought: a horse is something that has a nature independent of how we respond to it or interact with it. Horses are creatures of a kind, the nature of which is discoverable by enquiry. So, to put it paradoxically, there is a sense in which someone can know what a horse is without knowing what a horse is; that is, we can have a handle on the criteria a continuant has to meet to count as a horse by our lights, without understanding the real nature of horses, that in virtue of which these animals are representatives of the kind we pick out with the term 'horse'.[24]

It might be argued that we should distinguish two kinds of concepts, those of 'common sense', on the one hand, and something more rigorous, on the other. This is the kind of view Vygotsky takes in *Thought and Language*, where he discusses the transition between 'everyday' and 'scientific' concepts (1934/1986, ch. 6). Vygotsky's insight is that someone interested in concept acquisition and development should not simply focus on the acquisition of the former kind of concept, while ignoring the latter and the transition from the one to the other. I prefer to say, not that there are two kinds of concepts, but that our ability to form thoughts about horses develops in a process with a long, indeed open-ended, developmental trajectory. This stretches the story of a person's conceptual development into adolescence and adulthood.[25]

But whatever view one takes, socio-historical factors will play a significant role. A scientific understanding of horses involves theory set against a considerable amount of background knowledge, much of which we typically acquire only through formal education. The theories in question are parts of an intellectual tradition, just as our practices of enquiry are socially and historically situated. Enculturation into this tradition and these practices gives us the capacity to deploy substance concepts with a proper understanding of what they put us in touch with. Of course, many of us actually lack this understanding and must 'borrow' it from competent authorities, a fact that brings out a further profoundly social dimension to knowledge.[26]

THE CONCEPTUAL AND THE PRACTICAL

The point of our sketch of the development of the child's grasp of one straightforward substance concept is to bring out the many kinds of social influences that must figure in a satisfying rendition of *Bildung*. The account is obviously incomplete, and not just because there is more to *Bildung* than concept mastery. Even in its own terms it is evidently wanting in two respects. First, a fuller story would countenance different kinds of concepts: concepts of artefacts (which are also substances, but markedly different from biological kinds such as horses), abstract entities, moral and aesthetic phenomena, events, actions, psychological notions and (perhaps combining all of the above) the concept of a person. In each of these cases, our understanding of the concept can range from the superficial to the profound, though in many, perhaps all, these cases depth is not found by scientific enquiry disclosing a nature that is hidden from view, but by a variety of other means, and in each case the role of *Bildung* in the path to illumination will be different.

Second, the sketch is one-dimensional: it risks being dismissed as too intellectualistic.[27] At the beginning of *Hard Times*, Dickens describes how the schoolmaster Thomas Gradgrind, who is obsessed with the teaching of facts and only facts, asks two of his pupils to define 'horse'. The first is a girl named Sissy Jupe (or 'girl number twenty', as Gradgrind calls her). Sissy is unable to produce a definition, and is duly ridiculed, though we are to surmise that she really knows a good deal about horses because her father works with them. The second, a boy called Bitzer, pronounces: 'Quadruped. Graminivorous. Forty teeth, namely twenty-four grinders, four eye-teeth, and twelve incisive. Sheds coat in the spring; in marshy countries, sheds hoofs, too. Hoofs hard, but requiring to be shod with iron. Age known by marks in mouth ... .' The satisfied Gradgrind comments, 'Now girl number twenty ... you know what a horse is' (Dickens, 1854/1901, p. 10).

My sketch of the child's developing facility with a substance concept—with its movement from basic recognitional abilities, through increasingly sophisticated and reflexive language skills, to theoretically informed understanding—looks Gradgrindian in that it privileges abstract, verbal, theoretical knowledge and neglects precisely the sort of lived understanding and local knowledge that Sissy possesses. Dickens reminds us that there are other ways of knowing what something is than being able to rattle off a definition or give a theoretical description. Sometimes these other ways are far richer and more meaningful. But the developmental trajectory of the kind of knowledge Sissy possesses is neglected in the sketch I have given. This not only makes for an impoverished view of concepts, it obscures certain important socio-cultural dimensions in the development of mind. Just think of the significance of joint activity and apprenticeship to the development of Sissy's competence.

This is an important objection, both in its own right and because similar complaints have been brought against McDowell's philosophy. Hubert Dreyfus, for example, protests that by placing perception and agency in the domain of the conceptual, McDowell is preoccupied with 'the conceptual upper floors of the edifice of knowledge' and indifferent to 'the embodied coping going on on the ground floor' (Dreyfus, 2005, p. 47).

I have no intention of disparaging the kind of knowledge Sissy possesses. One thing the Russian socio-historical tradition is famous for is its emphasis on *activity*, not just as facilitating knowledge and as facilitated by it, but as embodying and expressing knowledge, and a good deal of work inspired by this tradition is concerned to attack models that portray knowledge as something abstract and theoretical in favour of conceptions that emphasise the situatedness of cognition. The tradition shares with pragmatism a hostility to what Elizabeth Anscombe called modern philosophy's 'incorrigibly contemplative conception of knowledge' (1957, p. 57).

How, then, to accommodate such knowledge in our picture? We could opt to invoke a familiar distinction between theoretical and practical forms of knowledge. This would permit us to say that Sissy has practical knowledge of horses (of how they behave, interact with each other and with humans, what makes them content, what anxious, and so on), even though she cannot fashion the sort of description or definition Gradgrind is after. But she knows what kind of beasts horses are and the kind of lives they lead in that she knows how to act with and around horses; hence the absurdity of the idea that she does not know what a horse is. Bitzer, in contrast, has a sort of theoretical knowledge, or the shell thereof.

At this point, we might be tempted to argue that *conceptual* capacities pertain to the theoretical, not practical, domain. After all, concepts are often portrayed as constituents of thoughts, and thoughts are, or are typically, propositional in structure, but this is not the form taken by practical knowledge (which, one might say, is *know-how*, not *knowledge-that*). Having said that, of course, it would be open to us to note the mutual relations and dependencies between the two kinds of knowledge, emphasising how they complement each other. Bitzer's definition, we may conclude, remains abstract and skeletal so long as it is not enhanced by the sort of knowledge Sissy possesses.

I think this strategy insufficiently radical. It is a mistake to exclude practice from the domain of the conceptual. We should think of conceptual capacities as exercised where we are responsive to reasons, and what Aristotle called 'practical wisdom' (*phronesis*) is unquestionably an aspect of that responsiveness. Such practical judgement, however, does not always find linguistic expression: it may simply be manifest in action. Sissy's appreciation of how to interact with horses is a form of responsiveness to reasons (for example, she takes such-and-such a movement by the horse as a reason to tighten the reins), even though she may be unable to articulate why and how she does what she does. Indeed, the knowledge she displays in riding may be uncodifiable. When Sissy acts as she does, she realises concepts of things to do, concepts realised by *doing* what she does, not by articulating thoughts about it. This is McDowell's response to the charge of 'intellectualism', and it is exactly what we need to say to appreciate how mindedness can be present in our bodily engagement with the world (see McDowell, 2007c/2009b, p. 325).[28]

So the model of conceptual development sketched above must recognise that real facility with a straightforward substance concept, x, must be embedded in a network of (possibly uncodifiable) practical knowledge if a person is to attain a proper appreciation of what an x is. What form that requirement will take will depend on the concept in question. In the case of moral or aesthetic concepts, for example, the practical may be absolutely critical; for instance, you do not know what generosity is unless you know how it is appropriate to act in certain situations. We must also acknowledge that there can be genuine conceptual capacities that find verbal articulation only partly, and perhaps not at all. The nature of the developmental trajectory of such capacities and the role of socio-historical factors therein will depend on the concepts at issue.

CONCLUSION

Focusing on the thought of John McDowell, we have been considering the view that each human individual becomes a minded being only through the emergence and development of conceptual powers that require the appropriation of what is itself an historical object, an intellectual tradition. This account is rather different in character from the kind of transcendental arguments we considered earlier, in the use it makes of the explicitly developmental notion of *Bildung*. I have explored one way we might explicate that concept by considering the socio-cultural influences on the development of a child's mastery of concepts.

The sketch I provided aimed to bring out the kinds of social influences at stake in the *Bildungsprozess*. It will likely be argued that, however successful it is in that regard, it will never be more than a toy theory, even if enhanced and supplemented in the manner suggested in the last section. For it really to explain anything, it will need to be brought into dialogue with empirical research. It is one thing to observe that social influences are important, another to explain the mechanisms of their influence. For the latter we must turn to developmental psychology and cognitive science.[29]

Such a dialogue is beyond the scope of this book. Subsequent chapters will take up the no less important, elucidatory project defined above: exploring the central concepts in which a position like McDowell's is framed—person, agency, freedom, mindedness, the space of reasons, rationality, and so on. Indeed, such exploration is needed to determine how good the prospects are of meaningful dialogue with empirical disciplines. McDowell remarks coyly that he does not 'mean to be objecting to anything in cognitive science' (1994, p. 121). The fact is, however, that he endorses a number of views that are anathema to much scientific thinking about the mind. He maintains, for example, that mental states and processes are attributes of persons, not of brains or sub-personal systems, and that the mental, the realm of thought, has to be understood by deploying a notion of mental content that has no application to sub-personal systems. Indeed, McDowell goes so far as to deny that thoughts are in the head. The idea is that mindedness must be understood as a property of the whole person engaged in interaction with the world.[30] He writes:

> Talk of minds is talk of subjects of mental life, in so far as they are subjects of mental life; ... it is only a prejudice, which we should discard, that mental life must be conceived as taking place in an organ ...
>
> Where mental life takes place need not be pinpointed any more precisely than by saying that it takes place where our lives take place. And then the states and occurrences can be no less intrinsically related to our environment than our lives are. (1992/1998b, p. 281)

It is in light of such remarks that we need to understand McDowell's view of concepts. When McDowell says a concept is an ability, he means it is nothing like a mental representation, as this is typically understood. It is not an *entity* of any kind, but a capacity of a bodily being, situated in an environment, which that being exercises in framing thoughts and manifests in intelligent action.[31] This capacity can be realised in more or less refined ways, as my sketch was designed to bring out. The vocabulary we need to describe this ability is the vocabulary of thoughts, contents and meanings, and, as McDowell has it, this cannot legitimately be applied to the sub-personal systems that underlie thought and that are the legitimate focus of cognitive science.

We can think of *Bildung* as the process of coming to be moved by meanings. As McDowell himself observes, the metaphor of being moved by meanings is a mechanical one. But it would be a vestige of Cartesianism, he suggests, to think

18 *The Formation of Reason*

that explaining how a natural being comes to be moved by meanings requires an account that conceives of itself as explaining the mechanisms of development:

> The idea of a mind's being moved by meanings involves a metaphor from the logical space of mechanical understanding, but it is an idea whose functioning needs to be understood in the contrasting space of reasons. Trying to take the metaphor literally is a form of the basic Cartesian mistake. (1999/2009b, p. 272)

This puts McDowell at some distance from the vast majority of cognitive science and empirical psychology, even those forms tolerant of the idea of the 'extended' or 'embodied' mind, and it makes a cognitive science of the *Bildungsprozess* hard to envisage. A good deal more reflection is required before we even understand the terms in which fruitful dialogue might be possible.

Before we continue to elucidate and develop the kind of position to which McDowell gives voice, I want to consider a more direct approach to the question of socio-cultural character of mind and one at odds with much of what McDowell has to say: social constructionism.

NOTES

1 An earlier version of this chapter was presented at a conference at York University (Toronto) in honour of David Martel Johnson, author of *How History Made the Mind* (2003)—hence my title.
2 The person to whom I owe most is Felix Mikhailov, author of the notable book *The Riddle of the Self* (1964; 1980). It was he who introduced me to the work of Vygotsky and suggested that I focus my studies on the philosopher Evald Ilyenkov, who had died in 1979. Through Mikhailov I met a number of thinkers who generously discussed with me the history of Soviet philosophy and introduced me to the oral culture vital to its existence. Mikhailov also made it possible for me to give a number of seminars to a small group that included V. S. Bibler, V. A. Lektorsky and the psychologist V. V. Davydov. One such seminar, on the concept of a person, has been transcribed, translated and published (Bakhurst, 1995a). The participants' responses to my paper stand as testimony to their oratorical skills and the liveliness of their philosophical world. I presented my research on Ilyenkov's thought and its place in the history of Russian philosophy in *Consciousness and Revolution in Soviet Philosophy* (1991) and many subsequent papers (e.g., Bakhurst, 1997; 2001a; 2005a; 2005b).
3 See Bakhurst and Sypnowich, 1995, for discussion of the 'the social self' in a variety of guises.
4 The rough convention is that the 'rule-following considerations' are at §§138–242 of the *Investigations*, with the private language argument proper at §§243–315. Other important sources include Wittgenstein's *Remarks on the Foundations of Mathematics* (1978), which contains sustained discussion of rule-following, *The Blue and Brown Books* (1958), *The Big Typescript* (2005), and the various volumes on the philosophy of psychology. The literature on these arguments is vast. McDowell's papers on Wittgenstein, collected in McDowell, 1998a, are especially good. I offer a more detailed discussion of Wittgenstein's position in Bakhurst, 1995b.
5 As we saw, Davidson explicitly takes himself to be developing Wittgensteinian insights (especially in Davidson, 1992/2001).
6 When Baker and Hacker argue that there is no reason why a contingently solitary person cannot have language, they mean that there is no *logical* reason; that is, no reason that follows from the very nature of a language. They would happily admit that there may be empirical reasons why, say, a feral child could not develop language.

7 It can be countered, however, that although the purpose of Wittgenstein's arguments is not to establish a constructive account of human beings as essentially social creatures, those arguments nevertheless serve, by removing certain deep philosophical misconceptions about the nature of mind, to draw attention to the significance of considerations about our natural history, including our status as social beings, in any satisfying account of the nature and origin of mind. If we understand Wittgenstein aright, such considerations cease to be merely contingent background factors of no interest to the philosophical imagination. Such a reading is relevant to the discussion of *Bildung* later in this chapter. I consider Wittgenstein on the first-person in Bakhurst, 2001b.

8 Davidson famously attempts to develop Alfred Tarski's semantic theory of truth into a theory of meaning for natural languages. A Tarskian truth theory for a language L gives so-called T-sentences of the form 's is true if and only if *p*', where 's' picks out a sentence of L and '*p*' states the conditions under which the sentence is true. The famous illustration is: (T) ' "Snow is white" is true if and only if snow is white', where the sentence picked out is used to state its own truth-conditions. A theory that yielded a T-sentence for every sentence of L would amount to an extensional definition of truth for that language. Davidson's insight is that, while Tarski helps himself to the notion of meaning and uses the theory to define 'truth', we can work the other way around: if we take the concept of truth as primitive, we can read T-sentences as pairing each sentence of L with its meaning. This strategy can work, however, only if we do not, in constructing such a theory, presuppose an understanding of the meaning of the sentences of L. Davidson therefore proposes that we see a theory of meaning as an empirical theory, constructed in a process of 'radical interpretation' by a theorist who has no prior knowledge of the meaning of the sentences of L or of speakers' mental states. Davidson's view is that radical interpretation is the appropriate model for all linguistic understanding. Every speaker must form a theory of meaning for the utterances of every other speaker with whom she interacts. Each such theory will be unique and speaker-specific. For that reason I call what such theories describe an 'idiolect' (the language of an individual speaker). Davidson argues that an account of mutual understanding does not need to think of idiolects as variations on a conceptually prior shared language ('sociolect'). Indeed, we can do without the latter idea altogether. Hence his provocative conclusion that there is nothing of the kind that philosophers and linguists suppose a language to be. (Davidson's early papers on truth, meaning and radical interpretation are collected in Davidson, 1984; the later papers are principally in Davidson, 2005.)

9 I am grateful to Julia Russell for her insightful remarks on the contrast between Wittgenstein and Davidson.

10 Thornton, 2004, and de Gaynesford, 2004, are helpful book-length introductions to McDowell's thought.

11 What sort of thing is a *reason*? A reason is a consideration that provides a ground for action or belief, a ground which may be cited to justify action or belief. Reasons are often contrasted with causes, but it is possible to think of reasons as a kind of cause (which perhaps we must if we are to speak of 'rational determination'). We can say that citing a reason renders action or belief intelligible by revealing the ground that, through its recognition by the subject, caused her to act as she did or form the belief that she did. More on reasons in chapter 5 below.

12 Putting it this way (as McDowell does, for example, at 1994, p. 26) can mislead, suggesting that the content of experience is propositional in character, a view which is implausible and one that McDowell has recently disavowed. He now argues that perceptual experience presents us with content that is unarticulated. We should still think of this content as conceptual because it can be made discursively explicit in judgements, i.e., thoughts with propositional form. He writes: 'Though they are not discursive, intuitions [i.e., perceptual experiences] have content of a sort that embodies an immediate potential for exploiting that same content in knowledgeable judgments. Intuitions immediately reveal things to be the way they would be judged to be in those judgments' (McDowell, 2007a/2009a, p. 267).

13 To say, as McDowell does, that the world does not lie 'outside an outer boundary that encloses the conceptual sphere' (1994, p. 26) is not to picture reality as a product of our conceptual activity (McDowell, 2007a/2009b, p. 139). His point is rather that perceptual experience yields content that can be articulated into a perceptual judgement *that things are thus and so* and '*that things are thus and so* is also, if one is not misled, an aspect of the layout of the world: it is how things are' (1994, p. 26). In this way, thought can be at one with the world.

McDowell understands the world as all that is the case, the totality of facts. He portrays facts as 'true thinkables', and credits Frege with the best account of what a true thinkable is (McDowell, 2000b, p. 94). The image of the world as 'all that is the case', drawn from Wittgenstein's *Tractatus*, provokes the question of the compatibility of McDowell's conception of reality with Wittgenstein's later philosophy, of which he is much enamoured and on which he frequently draws. In response, McDowell is quick to deny that his conception of a fact is a metaphysically contentious one.

14 See, for example, the Miller translation of Hegel's *Phenomenology* (1807/1977) and the Churton translation of Kant's *On Education* (1803/2003).

15 Illuminating treatments of *Bildung* include Gadamer, 1975, pp. 9–19, and Geuss, 1999, ch. 2. Hegel's conception is nicely discussed in Wood, 1998. Løvlie et al., 2003, is a valuable collection devoted to the significance of the concept to thinking about education; the introduction by Løvlie and Standish is particularly good. The articles by Beiser (2003), Mann (2003) and Munzel (2003)—all in Curren, 2003—provide a composite picture of the place of *Bildung* in German educational thinking. The excellent introduction to Blake et al., 2003, is helpful in locating the notion in educational philosophy more generally. Through the work of von Humboldt and others, the concept had a significant influence on the modern idea of the university, a fact discussed, together with much else of relevance, in the late Bill Readings's book, *The University in Ruins* (1996). Bubner, 2002, is an interesting commentary on McDowell on *Bildung*; McDowell's reply is instructive (2002, pp. 296–7).

16 See, for example, their respective contributions to Dearden et al., 1972. Løvlie and Standish, 2003, pp. 8–19, contains a good discussion of the London School, of the relation of the concept of *Bildung* to the idea of 'liberal education', and of the relevance of Michael Oakeshott's thought.

17 It is important that McDowell appropriates the idea of *Bildung* without commitment to the kind of substantive, normative vision of culture, civilisation and progress that has often informed the notion's use. Although McDowell is drawn to the evocativeness of the idea of *Bildung*, he does not sign up to everything it commonly evokes.

18 In the concluding section of a paper on the theory of meaning, McDowell applauds the German expressivist tradition for assigning 'squarely to the philosophy of language' the task of understanding a key aspect of *Bildung*; namely, 'how the mindedness of a community, embodied in its linguistic institutions, comes to realize itself in an individual consciousness' (McDowell, 1987/1998b, p. 107).

19 Sabina Lovibond comments: '[T]his proleptic or anticipatory mode of relating to babies and children is an essential element in the business of upbringing: we are enabled or helped to make the transition to a fully human mode of behaviour, sensitive to reasons "as such", by the willingness of adults to use their imagination in treating us—sometimes at least—as being further along the path towards this mode of behaviour than is actually the case' (Lovibond, 2006, p. 266; see also McGeer, 2001, p. 123). This is an expression of a thought central to the German idealist tradition. It was first given voice by Fichte, who, as Paul Franks puts it, 'pioneers the idea that a person can come to be through an event of reciprocal recognition, in which a preexisting person summons a latent person to act, thus recognizing that latent person *as* a latent person, and in which the previously latent person becomes an actual person by responding to the summons—positively, negatively or even with indifference—and hence by recognizing both the other and him/herself as persons' (Franks, 2005, p. 174). We shall return to this theme later in the book.

20 It is interesting to observe that although the term *concept* has a venerable pedigree in the history of philosophy and remains ubiquitous in philosophical writing, it does not show up much in everyday discourse. It appears in locutions like, 'That's a weird concept!' (prompted, for example, by a story about a time traveller observing his earlier self), 'He has a great concept for his bathroom', 'I can't stand those 1970 concept albums', or 'The concept cars at the car show were terrific this year'. You are unlikely to hear one parent asking another, 'Does your child have the concept of an aardvark?'. She is more likely to say, 'Does your child know what an aardvark is?' or 'Does she know the meaning of the word "aardvark"?' *Concept* is a technical notion.
21 In what follows, I am interested in stages in a child's mastery of particular concepts. I am not pretending to delineate general stages in children's conceptual or cognitive competence, of the kind familiar from, say, Piagetian theories.
22 There is arguably an intermediate stage at which the child is well aware that certain usages of a term are inappropriate but is unable to give reasons, merely laughing or declaring 'That's silly!' in response to aberrant usage. I am grateful to Willem deVries for suggesting this possibility.
23 It might be argued that, since conceptual holism entails that the child only possesses the concept *horse* if she has a grasp on a range of inferential relations in which the concept figures, the skills described in stages one and two are at best proto-conceptual. In contrast, I prefer to think of these stages as genuinely conceptual in virtue of their role in the developmental process, because of what the child who has them will become. Take this as a reflection, at the level of theory, of the proleptic way we relate to children (see note 19 above). It is also important not to underestimate the holistic dimensions of the child's understanding even at these early stages of development. For example, the child cannot learn to use the word 'horse' unless she has a whole repertoire of recognitional abilities (stage one conceptual skills) of a more general kind. Moreover, we must remember that the child's use of particular words is premised upon a considerable passive understanding of language. So it would be a mistake to take the fact that children's first words appear to emerge one by one to support conceptual atomism.

We need to take a similar approach to McDowell's claim that the intentionality of perceptual experience depends on perceptual episodes being related to a wider world-view (see, e.g., McDowell, 1998c, pp. 435–6 [2009a, p. 7]), a view that also frustrates the idea that the discriminatory and recognitional capacities at stages one and two can be described as conceptual. It would appear to follow that the infant's orientation to her surroundings cannot be properly characterised as experience and that she is incapable of perceptual knowledge. McDowell makes light of this apparent problem. Even though the kind of knowledge afforded by perceptual judgement is 'attributable only to rational animals', we can think of the ability of infants and non-rational animals to 'deal competently with their environments' as manifesting knowledge, only knowledge of a different kind from that available to beings in the space of reasons. For a less easy-going treatment of such issues, as they manifest themselves in Sellars's philosophy, and one informed by developmental literature, see Triplett and deVries, 2007. I return to McDowell's notion of a world-view in chapter 7.
24 I reserve judgement on whether biological species are strictly speaking 'natural kinds'. I simply want to venture the possibility that enquiry might reveal we are radically mistaken about what horses are. Our term 'horse' aspires to pick out a genuine kind whose members are united by a common principle of activity. But we might learn that that is not the case: our best genetic or biological theory might tell us that there are several types of animal here and recommend a different taxonomy from the oh-so-familiar one we are used to. And it might be that, in time, our familiar usage gives way to the more scientifically responsible one. Am I saying that we might discover that there are no such things as horses? Better to say that the term 'horse' might turn out not to be taxonomic. Whether and how the term would survive such a discovery would depend on various contextual considerations.

25 Some philosophers work with a sharp distinction between concept and belief at odds with the position I take here. They would typically adopt minimal criteria for concept possession, either because they embrace a representationalist view of concepts, or because they have an undemanding view of the abilities constitutive of concept possession, so that, for example, someone is said to possess the concept *horse* if she is able to identify and re-identify horses, or, more demandingly, if she can competently use the term 'horse' (or the equivalent in another language). On such an account, two people meeting these criteria would be said to share the same concept even if they had very different understandings of the nature of horses (say, because one is a vet and the other completely unschooled in biology). The difference in their respective understandings is cast exclusively as a difference in what they believe about horses and does not enter into their concepts. Holistic views of concepts, however, cannot sustain a tidy concept/belief distinction, since concepts are defined by their (for example, inferential) relations to other concepts and a subject's grasp on those relations is expressed by her beliefs. Thus holistic views can support the extended view of conceptual development that I favour. Critics complain that holists cannot explain how people can be said to share concepts—differences in their beliefs, after all, will make for differences in their concepts, and disagreement about the nature of x will become impossible: if the disputants differ in beliefs, they will differ in concepts and will not therefore actually be talking about the same thing. I do not find this an impressive objection, in part because the holist can have recourse to overlap between belief sets to explain conceptual convergence and in part because of the significance of singular thoughts to the convergence of belief (i.e., thoughts that, as McDowell puts it, 'would not be available to be thought or expressed if the relevant object, or objects, did not exist' (1982a/1998b, p. 204)). There is, of course, a massive literature on these issues.

26 This last claim recalls Hilary Putnam's famous thesis of 'the division of linguistic labour' (see Putnam, 1988, ch. 2).

I should make clear that even though I have been speaking of the child inheriting the meaning of words, a conception of the boundaries of concepts, standards of correctness in the game of reasons, and so on, I hold that whether something is a horse is not a matter of convention or social construction. What the child inherits are conceptual resources that aspire to be responsive to how things are independent of their exercise. However much weight we place on *Bildung*, what are *gebildet* are the powers that enable us to discern reality, not reality itself. I explore this theme further in the next chapter.

27 I am grateful to Paul Standish for pressing this point, and for invoking the example from *Hard Times*.

28 Theoretical and practical elements are so intimately interwoven in our ability to navigate the world that factoring them neatly into two kinds of knowledge is bound to be artificial, and a source of philosophical illusion. This is an issue of profound educational significance, since in many educational contexts we aspire to cultivate capacities where theoretical knowledge is embodied in practical activity. In nursing or physiotherapy, for example, this is not best seen just as a matter of applying theory, but as acquiring, as it were, 'knowledge in the hands'. We are not helped in understanding this by the trend in contemporary educational theory that would respond to Gradgrind by extolling situated, local and embodied forms of knowledge, and disparaging theoretical knowledge as abstract and decontextualised. What we need, in contrast, is a suitably rich conception of how the practical and the theoretical interpenetrate. I revisit these issues in chapter 6. For an approach to conceptual development that tries to give credence to complex relations of theory and practice, see Ilyenkov's conception of 'the ascent from the abstract to the concrete' (see Ilyenkov, 1956/1997, 1960, and the discussion in Bakhurst, 1991, ch. 5).

29 The relevant literature is vast. Frank Keil offers a particularly rich discussion of conceptual development, though, in keeping with many in the field, he maintains that change is the result of an endogenous process rather than external (environmental or social) factors (particularly

the key transition between concepts organised around characteristic features shared by instances of a kind and concepts organised around characteristics definitive of membership of the kind) (see Keil, 1989, esp. ch. 6). Other relevant classics include Carey, 1985; Perner, 1991; Astington, 1993; Gopnik and Meltzoff, 1996.

30 I discuss the 'personalist' conceptions of mind of McDowell and my Russians in Bakhurst (2008). McDowell's views emerge from a long and complex dialectic, conducted largely in dialogue with analytic philosophers of mind and language. He is cautious about expressing his more outré conclusions, so, as with his conclusions about the significance of *Bildung*, far more time is spent on the journey than at its destination. Nonetheless, these are conclusions of the outmost importance, which deserve a good deal more consideration than they typically receive. I return to the issue in chapter 7.

31 One might say, contrary to what I said earlier, that, for McDowell, *concept* is not a psychological notion, at least as this is normally understood.

2
Social Constructionism

In chapter 1, I began to expound a socio-historical account of mind along lines suggested by John McDowell's *Mind and World*. If McDowell is right that the child develops distinctively human psychological powers as she acquires a range of conceptual capacities, then the child's mindedness issues from *Bildung* to the extent that her developing facility with concepts is significantly mediated by socio-historical influences. I suggested that there is no simple story about the character of this mediation. Its forms are many and varied, depending on the concepts at issue and the phase of the child's development.

In this chapter, I consider a style of thinking that offers a more direct route to a strongly social conception of mind: social constructionism.

SOCIAL CONSTRUCTIONISM INTRODUCED

Social constructionist ideas have been influential in numerous fields—especially science studies, feminist theory, communication and educational theory—and the phenomena that have been described as socially constructed are many and diverse. Ian Hacking opens his influential book, *The Social Construction of What?*, with an alphabetical list that includes Danger, Emotions, Facts, Gender, Literacy, Nature, Quarks and Urban Schooling (Hacking, 1999, p. 1).[1] We can characterise social constructionism in somewhat abstract terms as follows. Those who claim that some X is 'constructed' typically have an ontological purpose.[2] Sometimes they aim to contrast the constructed with the real, either by arguing that X is *un*real—a *mere* construct, or that X is not *robustly* real in the way that, say, physical objects are (X is real but owes its reality to processes of construction). Sometimes the point is not to contrast the constructed and the real, but to question the very notion of reality. The point of calling X a 'construct' is often to emphasise its historical contingency: X is not an immutable feature of the order of things but the product of human practices, modes of categorisation or discourse. This point

The Formation of Reason, First Edition. David Bakhurst.
© 2011 David Bakhurst. Published 2011 by Blackwell Publishing Ltd.

may be supplemented by the thought that what is mutable is open to transformation. What is made can be remade, at least sometimes.[3] Hence constructionist views often have a moral or political dimension, and many present themselves as subversive.

So when someone argues, say, that gender is a social construct, she may be arguing (1) that there is *no such thing* as gender, or (2) that there is such a thing as gender but that in contrast to, say, mass, gender is a product of human practices, or (3) that gender is constructed *just like* mass and everything else. The point is unlikely to be ontological housekeeping for its own sake, but a conclusion about the reality and mutability of gender and gender roles.

In psychology, constructionist themes can be discerned in the work of no less a figure than Jerome Bruner.[4] His *Acts of Meaning* and other later writings contain at least elements of the following views:

1 What we call 'reality' is a social construct, and hence so is mind.
2 Folk psychological forms of description and explanation are cultural resources that construct the states and processes they describe and explain.
3 Certain key psychological categories—such as *intelligence*—are social constructs.

Bruner does not, however, expand these suggestions into a full-blown constructionist account of mind, and the relation of his preferred cultural psychology to social constructionism remains uncertain.

In what follows, I explore how each suggestion has been, or might be, developed. My conclusions will be sceptical about the value of the idea of social construction for illuminating the nature of mind, and in the course of my argument I shall take issue with some more general claims that social constructionists have made. It is important, however, that I do not mean to be dismissive of the idea of social construction as such. It figures in so many views in so many ways that no blanket dismissal would be credible. In any case, I acknowledge the significance of many of the issues constructionism has brought to the forefront of discussion. For any phenomenon under scrutiny, we need to ask whether it possesses the qualities that make it what it is independently of social factors or in virtue of social factors (and if the latter, then how and in what respect, etc.). Otherwise, as Sally Haslanger puts it, we may be 'tracking something social when we think we're tracking something natural' (2005, p. 20). Such issues are profoundly important in educational theory, where we need to be alive to the social processes that create and sustain educational institutions together with conceptions of their purpose and legitimacy; we must attend to the forces that influence how knowledge is created and to the conceptions of knowledge that inform curriculum building and disciplinary distinctions; and we must reflect critically on the concepts we use to categorise and understand people. My criticisms of constructionism do not mean that I am indifferent to questions of this kind. Far from it. What is at issue here is how helpful the metaphor of social construction is for addressing them, especially those that bear on our understanding of mind.

THE SOCIAL CONSTRUCTION OF REALITY

Hacking suggests that no one really holds that reality as such is socially constructed (1999, pp. 24–5). But, for once, Hacking is wrong. Although Bruner himself merely flirts with such 'global' constructionism,[5] recoiling from its more radical implications, a bold statement of the position can be found in the work of American psychologist Kenneth Gergen (1999; 2001).

For Gergen, social constructionism fills the void that remains once we abandon the broadly Cartesian conception of mind and world that emerged in the early-modern period, dominated the Enlightenment and cast its shadow over the subsequent development of philosophy and psychology to the present day. The Cartesian conception has three principal components:

1. The individual human mind represents a self-contained subjective world of experiences, thoughts and other mental phenomena. Each thinking subject, or 'self', is directly aware only of the goings-on in its own mental world, and only it has direct awareness of these goings-on. Our awareness of the world independent of our minds is indirect, via the mediation of mental representations. Our awareness of other minds is doubly indirect: we infer what is going on in the minds of others from observations of their bodily behaviour.
2. Mental and linguistic representations—thoughts and utterances—are able accurately to represent the world beyond the mind. When representations accurately depict—or 'correspond to'—objects and states of affair, they are true. The mind is a mirror to reality.
3. The individual mind is transparent to itself. We are each immediately aware of the contents of our minds, which we know in a special and privileged way, giving us unique authority over what it is we think, mean, want, and so on.

Gergen thinks we should abandon these theses, for familiar reasons. He argues that (1) leads inevitably to scepticism. If I am directly aware only of mental representations, I can never be sure that there even exists a world independent of my mind, let alone verify that these representations accurately depict or correspond to it, as (2) maintains. He embraces a kind of meaning holism (inspired by a curious alliance of Quine and Derrida), according to which we cannot make sense of how sentences considered in isolation represent particular states of affairs or how individual words refer to objects. This further diminishes the plausibility of the idea of correspondence between representation and reality. Finally, Gergen contends that Freud and Wittgenstein have made it impossible to take seriously (3), the idea that the contents of our minds are transparent to us.

Gergen also attacks the Cartesian picture on political grounds. Its confidence in objective knowledge privileges science over other forms of understanding and, moreover, a form of science that sees the natural world as an object to master, thereby legitimating the exploitation of nature. In addition, the extreme individualism of the picture encourages us to see human beings as standing in purely instrumental relation to each other, a view that contributes to the erosion of community.

The consolidation of these conceptions of knowledge and self, it is argued, fosters Western cultural imperialism.

Gergen's constructionist alternative to Cartesianism adopts a conception of language inspired by Wittgenstein. On this view, the meaning of a word or sentence is its role in the discourse or 'language game'. Accordingly, calling something 'true' is represented as a particular kind of discursive move made for certain purposes:

> [W]hen we say that a certain description is 'accurate' (as opposed to 'inaccurate') or 'true' (as opposed to 'false') we are not judging it according to how well it depicts the world. Rather we are saying that the words have come to function as 'truth telling' within the rules of a particular game—or more generally, according to certain conventions of certain groups. (Gergen, 1999, pp. 36–7)
>
> [Truth is] a way of talking or writing which achieves its validity within local forms of life. (p. 38)

For Gergen, 'p is true' means p circulates as true within some community and for p to so circulate is just for p to be generally endorsed or accepted by members of that community. The term 'truth' is used primarily as 'a means for warranting one's own position and discrediting contenders for intelligibility' (Gergen, 1985, p. 268).

This relativistic conception of truth is complemented by a relational or dialogical conception of the self. Gergen urges us to stop conceiving of the mental as a private, inner world and focus instead on the public life of the mind, as expressed in the essentially social medium of language. This presages a radical change in direction for psychology, which must turn away from 'the interior region of the mind to the processes and structure of human interaction' (p. 271): '[F]rom the present standpoint there is no independent territory called "mind" that demands attention' (Gergen, 1999, p. 133; cf. Foster, 1998, p. 110). These claims might be read as congruent with McDowell's position, presented at the end of chapter 1, but where McDowell remains concerned with how best to understand the nature of mind, Gergen would displace that question altogether, urging us instead to view the mind as an artefact of discourse:

> Whether mental concepts are true—whether experience or agency are real, for example—are simply questions that do not require answers. The more important question for the constructionist concerns the consequences in cultural life of placing such terms into motion. (Gergen, 1999, p. 225)

For Gergen, we must focus on the categories we use to create and negotiate the worlds we live in, and consider how we might create better worlds. Since 'the terms in which we understand the world and our self are neither required nor demanded by "what there is"', it follows that 'we are not locked within any convention of understanding' (p. 48). From this, Gergen arrives at a conclusion far more radical than anything envisaged by the philosophers on whom he draws. What there is is a construction of discourse, and since the evolution of that discourse is historically contingent,

> we must suppose that everything we have learned about our world and ourselves—that gravity holds us to the earth, people cannot fly like birds, cancer kills, or that punishment deters bad behavior—could be otherwise. There is nothing about 'what there is' that demands these particular accounts; we could use our language to construct alternative worlds in which there is no gravity or cancer, or in which persons and birds are equivalent, and punishment adored. (p. 47)

Reality is a social construct and, as such, is open to dramatic reconstruction.

WHY BOTHER ABOUT GLOBAL CONSTRUCTIONISM?

It might be thought preferable to consider a more sober version of constructionism, one less sanguine about the transformative potential of discourse. Why worry about so extreme a position? I believe, however, that there are a number of reasons to ponder Gergen's views.

First, ideas of the construction of knowledge and self have been highly influential in educational theory and research, where, according to D. C. Phillips, they have 'become something akin to a secular religion' (Phillips, 1995/2007, p. 398), and Gergen's position encapsulates some of the more radical sources of this influence. In the field of education, constructionist ideas are more than just philosophical pictures of the relation between mind and world. They are thought to have practical relevance to matters of curriculum and teaching practice, challenging our understanding of what learning is and how it takes place. Moreover, social constructionist views are often informed by socio-political commitments that entail significant consequences for education. If human beings are to flourish, it is argued, we must transform our intellectual culture, for the presently dominant conceptions of mind and world, self and science, are constructions that bolster power structures fostering exploitation and the degradation of nature. The significance of the practical issues at stake makes it important to take the more extreme versions of constructionism seriously.

Second, as we have seen, Gergen aspires to transcend the stark opposition of mind and world so characteristic of the Cartesian tradition in favour of a position that expresses the inseparability of self and other. This is an aspiration he shares with many thinkers, including Hegel, Marx, Heidegger, Gadamer, Levinas and—importantly in the present context—McDowell. Gergen's strategy is to attack the very idea of an independent reality, together with the notion of individual 'minds' that supposedly confront it. The radical character of his approach is such that one wonders whether his motivation is in part existential: to counter dark thoughts about the fundamental otherness of the world, and its indifference to human projects and concerns, by casting reality as the outcome of human practices and therefore as something in principle congenial to humanity. The price paid for such a position is an extreme anthropocentrism that places human beings at the centre of the universe. I prefer a very different approach, one effecting a post-Cartesian reconciliation of mind and world that appreciates the profound socio-historical forces at work in shaping both, while preserving the idea of an independent reality and respecting the integrity of individual minds. I believe that this is what McDowell's philosophy can help us attain. It is nonetheless important to be attentive to whether this reconciliation can be achieved without some, possibly problematic, concession to anthropocentrism (certainly some suspect that McDowell's position collapses into a form of idealism that compromises the independence of reality), and whether the existential themes implicit in Gergen's view might not also be at work in more nuanced positions, where their influence is obscured by layers of philosophical detail.

Third, Gergen is an interesting opponent because, paradoxically, the extremity of his views makes them difficult to argue against. After all, the radical constructionist will likely dismiss the standards of soundness invoked by realists as social constructs of an invidious kind. Yet argue against constructionism we must, for I think we stand no chance of developing a plausible socio-historical account of mind unless we accept that we are inhabitants of a world that is, to a significant degree, not of our making; that many real entities and events are independent of us; and that we can acquire genuine knowledge of such entities and events. I shall call my position 'modest realism'. My realism is modest in that it is not committed to a substantive theory of truth (e.g., truth as correspondence or coherence). But it is committed to the 'discourse-independence' of much that is real, and this the global constructionist denies.

AGAINST GLOBAL CONSTRUCTIONISM

In their article, 'Death and Furniture: The Rhetoric, Politics and Theology of Bottom Line Arguments against Relativism', Derek Edwards, Malcolm Ashmore and Jonathan Potter observe that the realist is often tempted to make what they call 'bottom line' arguments against constructionism: 'Surely,' the exasperated realist opines, 'you are not saying that this table, or this rock, are social constructions?!'; 'Don't tell us that 9/11 was a social construction!' Here the realist appeals to what, in her view, are evidently real objects and events, the reality of which cannot be denied or finessed into something semiotic and representational. Of course, the 9/11 example has a moral dimension too: there is a reality to suffering and death that precedes its representation, which we are morally required to recognise.

Edwards et al. respond to such arguments:

> Rocks, trees and furniture are not *already* rebuttals of relativism, but become so precisely at the moment, and for the moment, of their invocation. We term this *the realist's dilemma*. The very act of producing a non-represented, unconstructed external world is inevitably representational, threatening, as soon as it is produced, to turn around and counter the very position it is meant to demonstrate (1995, p. 27).

The idea is that the realist can never have recourse to the brute reality she takes to exist. All she can offer is a discursive act in which something is *represented* as real. But what the realist needs to produce is something unrepresented, uncategorised, uncontaminated by discourse, and that is impossible.

This recalls Berkeley's argument in *Principles* §§22–3, where he challenges the reader to conceive of an unconceived object, and claims triumphantly that it cannot be done (Berkeley, 1710/1998). Berkeley, however, was mistaken. Although I cannot conceive of something without conceiving of it, and hence anything I conceive of is something that exists 'conceived-of', this does not show that I cannot conceive of something, the nature and existence of which does not depend on my conceiving of it. Likewise, though I cannot represent something without representing it, or describe something without using 'discursive techniques', it does not follow that I cannot represent or describe something the nature and existence of which is independent of my representing or describing it.[6]

Consider a mundane case of empirical enquiry. Suppose someone asks how many benches are in the courtyard outside the seminar room in which we are discussing some philosophical issue. We know exactly how to answer this question. We go into the courtyard and count the benches, or we accept the testimony of a reliable witness. In such everyday cases, it is an assumption of enquiry that there is a fact of the matter to be determined, that there is a truth to which we must conform our beliefs. This is not a *mere* assumption of enquiry, but its guiding light. We distinguish sharply between opinion and fact, between what people believe and what is actually the case. We take it that the number of benches is not determined by agreement, but depends on the arrangement of things in the courtyard.

The constructionist will consider these reflections naive. Imagine an argument about whether an elevated slab of stone, on which people habitually sit, is a bench or not. This cannot be settled by appeal to 'reality'; we must aspire to consensus. But that is just to say that consensus determines how many benches there are in the courtyard and this undermines the contrast between fact and opinion. However, in the imagined dispute, the argument is about what is to count as a bench. This is a legitimate matter of controversy, albeit not an exciting one. But even if we grant the constructionist that it is a matter of linguistic convention what falls within the concept *bench* and how benches are to be counted, the question of how many benches there are in the courtyard is not determined by agreement, but by the state of affairs in the courtyard.

Of course, benches are artefacts that would not exist were it not for human practices, and this can make it look as if all facts of the matter pertaining to benches are ultimately up to us. But consider what we would say if the question were: *Is there a child in the courtyard?* Of course, controversy might erupt over who counts as a child. There might be discussion of the historical evolution of the concept of childhood and the contingencies that influence its contemporary use. But imagine that the question is put by a desperate parent frantically searching for her daughter. Now we feel we have a question to be answered by determining how things are. Once conceptual clarification has made certain what we must look for, whether it is there to be found is a matter of brute fact. In such a case the contrasts between fact and opinion, truth and agreement, objectivity and solidarity impress themselves upon us. We want the former of each pair, not the latter. Of course, we usually hope that our attempts to justify belief will issue in consensus, but this is because we seek to base our beliefs on good reasons that others ought to find compelling. We do not seek agreement because it is constitutive of truth.[7]

These reflections are faithful to cognitive norms deeply embedded in our practices of enquiry. I think that global constructionists find it difficult to take these norms at face value because they are implicitly committed to a very strong nominalist thesis: that there is no order, no identity, no regularity independent of our practices of categorisation, conceptualisation, discourse. The constructionist endorses the view Barry Allen expresses when he writes that there are only determinate beings 'because something is, in fact, determined, that is, evaluated, measured, differentiated' (Allen, 1993, p. 178). Apart from such practices, 'there exist no two things in any respect similar or different. Order is nowhere original. Nature does not exist' (p. 149). There is thus nothing for our beliefs to be 'true to'. Better to say that some among our beliefs and utterances 'pass for true' (pp. 4–5); that is, they withstand scrutiny in an economy of knowledge.

A constructionist enamoured of such nominalism faces two principal objections. First, what is the status of the claim that nature as such does not exist—that there is no 'aboriginal reality'—and how are we to understand the process of its construction? Read as an empirical claim, it is either false or unintelligible. So the position must be that the processes that construct reality are antecedent to our empirical interaction with the objects in our environment. But now social constructionism looks like a descendant of Kant's transcendental idealism, holding that the world as we know it emerges out of the interplay of our conceptual scheme—which the constructionist, in contrast to Kant, conceives as something socially established and sustained—and whatever content that conceptual scheme interprets or organises ('sensory input', 'data', 'experience'). This is an awkward conclusion for the constructionist to embrace for a number of reasons. If it is grounded in a strong philosophical thesis about the interplay of scheme and content, it is subject to the telling criticisms that have been brought against scheme-content dualism by the likes of Davidson (1974/1984) and McDowell (1994, lectures 1–2). But even worse, constructionism so conceived risks being charged with rhetorical incoherence. This is because constructionism represents itself as a *post*-philosophical position that turns away from abstract speculation to concern itself with the real life of discourse. But the dualism of scheme and content is a familiar component of the modernist philosophical framework that constructionism overtly disavows.

Second, can we really greet each day with the thought: 'All this owes its determinacy to us'? How, for example, are we to understand our relation to other people? Perhaps I can talk myself into the view that my modes of thought and talk somehow make determinate the physical objects in my environment, but it is less evident that I can persuade myself that my children owe their determinacy to the reality-making powers of naming, categorisation, discourse. This is a crucial point because *social* constructionism surely must embrace the reality of other people, but their reality explodes the idea that 'order is nowhere original'.[8]

MATTERS POLITICAL

Consider now the political dimension to the constructionist's dismissal of realism. Sometimes, social constructionists portray realism as a form of reactionary intellectual authoritarianism. Realists, it is asserted, believe that there is a way things are, and hence that there is one true description of reality. The object of enquiry is to reach this one true description, and the primary purpose of communication is to state the facts. Realists typically think that they are in possession of part of the definitive description, thanks to natural science, which they typically esteem. They are preoccupied with closing debate and intolerant of alternative approaches and contrasting voices. The realist loves the status quo. As Gergen puts it: '[T]he language of objective reality is essentially used as a means of generating hierarchies of inclusion and exclusion' (1999, p. 73). Moreover, it is sometimes suggested that the realist's position is pseudo-theological with the concept of reality figuring as a God-substitute. Or that the realist is guilty of a kind of infantilism, the preoccupation with a stable, unequivocal reality betraying a yearning for the security of the womb.[9] Relativism, in contrast,

> offers an ever available lever of resistance. It is potentially liberating, dangerous, unsettling, with an appeal that is enduringly radical: nothing ever *has to be* taken as merely, obviously, objectively, unconstructedly, true. Reality can only ever be reality-as-known, and therefore, however counter-intuitive it may seem, produced by, not prior to, inquiry. (Edwards et al., 1995, p. 39)

The relativist admits that many find this 'threatening', a reaction that only confirms that realism serves as a comfortable refuge for conservative minds.

This portrait of the realist is misleading. It may be necessary to be a realist to fit this description, but it is certainly not sufficient. The modest realism I outlined above holds only that we are inhabitants of a world that is for the most part not of our making, and that we are capable of knowledge of this world. The modest realist supposes that thought is accountable to reality, in the sense that we are beholden to characterise objects and states of affairs as they are independently of our describing them. This commits the realist to the view that, at least in some contexts, there is a 'way things are' we must aim to discover, but not that there is one description that definitively captures this. Nor need the realist be a dogmatist. On the contrary, realism is consistent with fallibilism, expressing a healthy regard for the difficulty of establishing how things are. There is no obstacle to the realist acknowledging that the formation of belief is influenced by complex social forces. And nothing prevents the realist being a political radical. Conversely, there is no necessary connection between relativism and creativity or progressiveness. Relativism is just as easily combined with a conventionalist conservatism that despairs of criticising alternative conceptions.

It is sometimes supposed that truth, as realism portrays it, is some kind of special commodity, something grand or transcendent. This makes the realist's pretensions to truth appear arrogant. Modest realism, however, has no grand conception of truth.

Social Constructionism 33

On the contrary, the modest realist holds that the concept of truth is so basic and mundane as to be indefinable. The concept is best explicated by Aristotle's remark in the *Metaphysics* (7.27) that: 'To say of what is that it is, or of what is not that it is not, is true.'[10] Aristotle's reference to 'saying' is apt. To understand communication, we must deploy the notion of *utterance*; to understand utterance, we need a notion of *assertion*; assertion brings with it the idea of *telling it like it is*, which in turn introduces the notion of *truth*.[11]

We could say that modest realists reject the idea of 'capital-T Truth' while endorsing a notion of 'plain truth', but it is perhaps better not to speak as if there are different kinds of truth. Truth as such is neither rococo nor plain. Some truths are mundane, some spectacular; some are boring, some thrilling. But what is mundane or spectacular is *what is the case*, not truth itself. In like measure, there are not kinds of falsehood, though some false beliefs are trivial and others momentous. It is easier to disparage talk of truth and reality if such talk looks ostentatious or dogmatic. But it need not be.[12]

THE SOCIAL CONSTRUCTION OF MENTAL STATES

I turn now to the second theme delineated at the outset of this chapter: the idea that mental states are socially constructed. What is at issue here is whether, if the conditions for the attribution of mental states to individuals are essentially social, we should conclude that the very contents of our minds are socially constituted. I shall argue against this conclusion. In so doing, I am not denying that there are profound social preconditions of, and influences upon, our minds; the question is how to understand them aright.

One might wonder how anyone could think that the contents of our minds are socially constructed—how could the doings of others determine what *I* think?—but the ontological status of the mental is so vexed that routes to constructionist answers are not difficult to discern. I shall consider two. The first starts with the idea that psychological explanation is theoretical in kind and proceeds to embrace a social constructionist reading of theoretical entities. The second argues that meaning is the medium of the mental and that meaning is a social construct.[13]

Mental states as theoretical constructs

In *Acts of Meaning*, Bruner argues that every culture has its folk psychology, that is:

> a set of more or less connected, more or less normative descriptions about how human beings 'tick', what our own and other minds are like, what one can expect situated action to be like, what are possible modes of life, how one commits oneself to them, and so on. We learn our culture's folk psychology early, learn it as we learn to use the very language we acquire and to conduct the interpersonal transactions required in communal life. (Bruner, 1990, p. 35)

Bruner adopts the expression 'folk psychology' from the philosophy of mind, where it is used to refer to our everyday modes of psychological description and explanation.[14] Many philosophers and psychologists portray folk psychology as a kind of *theory* that explains behaviour by invoking two kinds of mental state: (i) cognitive states (the paradigm of which is belief) that represent how the world is, and (ii) appetitive states (the paradigm being desire) that aspire to change the world. Action is seen as issuing from the combination of such states: for example, Heather's buying flowers is explained by her desire to please her sister, together with a set of beliefs (that her sister will be pleased by the flowers; that in order to give her flowers, Heather must first buy them, and so on). Such combinations of belief and desire are usually taken to constitute an agent's reasons for action.[15]

It is notable that Bruner takes a broader view than the standard picture, emphasising the contextual dimensions of psychological explanation (1990, ch. 2). To understand why Heather bought the flowers, we need to appreciate the significance of this kind of act, and this requires essential reference to cultural considerations. Moreover, to grasp why she acted on just these beliefs and desires, as opposed to others, we must construct a narrative around her action. Agents strive to act in ways that make sense in light of the lives they are living, and we understand and explain others' behaviour by setting it in the proper context, as every biographer understands. This is a profoundly hermeneutical exercise. Folk psychology is thus a cultural device, part of our cultural 'toolkit' for making sense of ourselves and our lives.

Even though Bruner concludes from this that culture 'is constitutive of mind' (p. 33), we are still some way from a social constructionist model of the mental. Nevertheless, there is plenty for the constructionist to work with, beginning with the idea that folk psychology is a kind of theory.[16]

There is a familiar contrast between realist and instrumentalist accounts of theoretical entities. The realist holds that the entities in question exist independently of the theory that invokes them, and that the theory's claims are true or false depending on the nature of the entities in question, a nature they possess independently of our modes of description and explanation. In contrast, the instrumentalist maintains that theoretical entities are posits introduced to facilitate our understanding of observable phenomena. To say that such items exist is to say no more than that they play a role in our best explanatory theories.

Some philosophers take a realist view of mental states and processes. Of these, some think that folk psychology is essentially a true theory of mind; that is, that there really are beliefs, desires and other such entities that combine to produce behaviour just as the theory says they do. Other realists hold that folk psychology is a false theory and some—the eliminative materialists—envisage the day when our familiar folk modes of psychological explanation will be replaced by something scientifically more respectable (see, e.g., Churchland, 1988). In contrast to the realists, instrumentalists hold that mental states and processes are artefacts of our modes of explanation. To say that someone believes *that today is Tuesday* is just to say that the best explanation of her behaviour attributes such a state to her. This we can say without committing ourselves to the view that there is some identifiable state within her that is *the belief that today is Tuesday*, a state that would figure in a description of what there is independently of our modes of description and explanation.

Social constructionists will naturally be drawn to instrumentalism's idea of mental states as posits. Such a view appears to offer a satisfying alternative to two views the constructionist typically rejects: first, the Cartesian vision of mental phenomena as private objects inhabiting a kind of shadowy mental environment, and, second, the standard physicalist alternative to Cartesianism that portrays mental entities as states and processes occurring in the brain. In response to the notorious problems of any straightforward reduction of the mental to the physical, the constructionist will ask why we even assume that our modes of psychological ascription, which evolved for the explanation of behaviour, will individuate entities that correspond directly to states and processes in the brain, processes that are unobservable to those who use those modes of ascription. Better to think of mental states as constructs rather than 'real' objects, mental or physical. The constructionist's next step is to supplement instrumentalism with an account of the sociality of theory. Theories are not the property of individuals, they are products of culture and mediated by epistemic conventions that determine standards of evidence and argument (what counts as a good question, who counts as an authority, and so on), and all this has a complex cultural and institutional context. Folk theories may be less reliant on institutions than scientific theories, but they are even more obviously products of cultural evolution sustained in a social context. Thus the constructionist can maintain that if mental states are constructs of theories and theories are inherently social, then mental states are social constructs.[17]

Meaning and mental content

The second line of thought proceeds from the idea that meaning is the essence of the mental. Mental states have *content*. In the case of the so-called 'propositional attitudes', this content can be expressed as a proposition: I believe *that it is Tuesday*; I hope *that it isn't raining*. The content of other mental states is not obviously propositional. Though I can express what I see in the form of a proposition (e.g., I see *that he is walking towards me*), the content of my visual experience is not exhausted by the content of that proposition. There is controversy about how best to construe the content of such experiences. McDowell, as we noted in chapter 1, maintains that all mental content is conceptual, while others insist that some content is nonconceptual. Nevertheless, it is safe to say that the preconditions of meaning are preconditions of distinctively human mental states, processes and powers.

The constructionist will maintain, as many do, that no state has meaning intrinsically. No sound, no mark on paper, no configuration of neurons means anything in and of itself. Meaning must be 'made', as Bruner puts it. It is a product of activity, of discourse and interpretation. No physical configuration means anything in itself, and no single person can invest it with meaning unless a community engages in practices of interpretation governed by norms it has established. But if meaning is the medium of the mental and meaning is a social product, it follows that mental states are social constructs.

A position of this kind finds ingenious expression in V. N. Voloshinov's writings from the 1920s (though Mikhail Bakhtin may be the real author of the best known works published under Voloshinov's name).[18] Voloshinov argues that *'The reality of the inner psyche is the same reality as that of the sign'* (Voloshinov, 1929/1973, p. 26). Psychological states are essentially semiotic phenomena. They are forms of utterance (or 'verbal reaction'). This is true not only of mental states that are propositional in character, but also of conscious experience, which *'exists even for the person undergoing it only in the material of signs'* (p. 28). There is no pure experience to which we later give words; the world we confront is already organised by our modes of representation. Hence Voloshinov maintains that *'consciousness itself can arise and become a viable fact only in the material embodiment of signs'* (p. 11). The content of our mental states is determined by the meaning of the signs that comprise them. But signs do not possess meaning in virtue of their intrinsic properties. They take on meaning in the context of communicative practices that are essentially social in nature:

> *The verbal component of behaviour is determined in all the fundamentals and essentials of its content by objective-social factors.*
> The social environment is what has given a person words and what has joined words with specific meanings and value judgements; the same environment continues ceaselessly to determine and control a person's verbal reactions throughout his entire life.
> Therefore, nothing verbal in human behaviour (inner and outward speech equally) can under any circumstances be reckoned to the account of the individual subject in isolation; the verbal is not his property but the property of his *social group* (his social milieu). (Voloshinov, 1927/1976, p. 86)

In making such claims, Voloshinov sometimes runs together two theses. The first concerns the social constitution of the content of particular mental states: how it can be that this utterance has the content it does. The second is the broader thesis that our forms of thinking and reasoning are socially structured. That is, *how* we think is a function of what Bakhtin (1952–3/1986) called the 'speech genres' that predominate in our culture. The questions I think about, the way I think about them, the standards of evidence and argument I deploy, the modes in which I discourse with others, and so on, are all culturally mediated. Although they seem natural and inevitable, as if they embodied trans-historical standards, they are really all inherited from historically evolving cultural traditions of thought and enquiry.[19]

Both theses are at play in the following quotation:

> Between the psyche and ideology there exists, then, a continuous dialectical interplay: the psyche effaces itself, or is obliterated, in the process of becoming ideology, and ideology effaces itself in the process of becoming the psyche. The inner sign must free itself from its absorption by the psychic context (the biological-biographical context), must cease being a subjective experience,

in order to become an ideological sign. The ideological sign must immerse itself in the element of inner, subjective signs; it must ring with subjective tones in order to remain a living sign and not be relegated to the honorary status of an incomprehensible museum piece. (Voloshinov, 1929/1973, p. 39)[20]

It is clear that Voloshinov's view that '[t]he logic of consciousness is the logic of ideological communication, of the semiotic interaction of the social group' (p. 12) is no crass social determinism. His is a vision of the dialectical interplay between the social and the psychological, the outer and the inner, where subjectivity is beholden for its existence to modes of expression in an essentially social medium, a medium that, in turn, gets its life from the creative utterances of individuals.

Voloshinov's position is subtle and elusive, but a core idea is this: once we admit the textuality of the mental, then we must grant that the meaning constitutive of the mental is not determined by the say-so of the thinking subject any more than the meaning of a written text is determined by authorial intention. And it is no more a product of the physical states of our brains than the meaning of an utterance in a television play is determined by the state of the electrical circuitry inside the television. Meaning is essentially social, and so, therefore, is mind.[21]

WHY MENTAL STATES ARE NOT SOCIALLY CONSTRUCTED

In my view, neither line of thought is persuasive.[22] Both offer a distorted vision of our knowledge of the minds of others, our knowledge of our own minds, and of the asymmetry between first- and third-person psychological ascription.

The Cartesian picture of the mind that Gergen rightly derides holds that we know our own minds through introspection, conceived on the model of perception. A person's mental states can be observed directly by her, and only by her, and this mode of observation leaves no room for substantive error. In introspection, the inner eye cannot fail to see what is there to be seen. In virtue of this 'privileged access', subjects' assertions about their own mental states have a special authority. If someone sincerely asserts that she believes such-and-such, or wants so-and-so, then what she says goes.

The Cartesian picture takes as paramount the first-person perspective on the mental. For the Cartesian, each of us knows what a mental state is from his or her own case, and the data for philosophical enquiry into the nature of mind are primarily the deliverances of the first-person perspective. In contrast to the immediate, infallible knowledge we enjoy of our own minds, our access to the minds of others is indirect and fallible. I cannot directly discern what you think or feel, but must infer your thoughts and feelings on the basis of observing your behaviour. In its pure form, such a position has problems explaining how we can even form a concept of other minds. If our concept of the mental is derived in the first instance from our own case, how can we work from there to an idea of a mind that is not our own? As Wittgenstein put it, we will be required to form a conception of, say, a pain that we do not feel on the model of a pain that we do feel, and it is no means obvious how this feat could be accomplished (Wittgenstein, 1953, §302; see the discussion in Dancy, 1985, pp. 70–3).

This and many other problems with the Cartesian picture led to its widespread repudiation in Anglo-American philosophy of mind in the mid-twentieth century. With this, philosophy of mind took a distinctly third-personal turn, abandoning the Cartesian preoccupation with the first-person perspective and focusing instead on the conditions under which we ascribe mental states to other people. Rylean behaviourism was one of the first manifestations of this flight from Cartesianism, but, as the 'cognitive revolution' took hold, it was displaced by the more sophisticated view that mental discourse evolved as a theory for the explanation of behaviour. The latter view rejects the counter-intuitive reductionism of behaviourism and portrays mental phenomena as states 'inside' the subject posited to explain behaviour. We can then ask whether our best sciences of behaviour and brain functioning should invoke the kinds of entities that folk psychology does. This looks like a respectable and tractable question.[23]

This third-person theory-oriented approach—sometimes called 'the theory theory'—has been tremendously influential. Developmental psychologists, for example, are much enamoured of the idea that a child's awareness of other minds emerges around the age of 3, when she acquires a 'theory of mind' that enables her to attribute intentional states to others to explain and predict their behaviour. Much of this literature overtly represents the child as a 'little scientist' trying to construct a theory of how other people tick and making the key breakthrough when she starts ascribing to others unobservable, causally efficacious representational states that she herself does not share.[24] Such theorists would contend that if we offer the kind of account of conceptual development I sketched in chapter 1, the emergence of the child's psychological concepts is a matter of her acquiring a facility with certain ways of theorising about others.

The vast majority of 'theory theorists' do not embrace social constructionism, but it is important to see how the former approach can invite the latter. Under the tacit influence of the Cartesian's perceptual model of self-knowledge, we conclude that the minds of others are 'not visible to the naked eye' and proceed to treat the mental states of others as unobservables. Thereby we cast mental states and episodes as theoretical entities. If we are squeamish about portraying them as real unobservables, we cast them as posits or constructs, and then the way is open to the social constructionist to stress the public character of their construction.

This way of thinking is flawed. It fails to appreciate the many cases where the minds of others are manifest to us. To see this, it helps to bring to the centre of attention cases of intelligent behaviour of an ordinary kind. When I walk with a friend in the woods, much of the mindedness of our behaviour is immanent in what we do. My friend steps over branches, stops to take in the scent of a cedar bush, stoops to pick up fallen leaves. The intelligence in these actions is evident: it is not something I have to work out. We begin talking philosophy and I wax lyrical about the follies of constructionism. It is not that my words are an external manifestation of a shadowy inner process, a kind of overt translation of what I think. My thought is *present in* my speech. I am literally speaking my mind. Similarly, when someone is distraught after the death of a loved one, her grief is manifest in her weeping: it is not something lurking out of sight, lending the behaviour authenticity. Human beings are not fundamentally closed to one another and forced to divine the mental lives of others by hypothesising and projecting. To persist in so thinking is to persevere in the Cartesian view of the mind as an inner realm to which there is no direct access from the third-person perspective.

In my view, we should do our best to understand, as literally as possible, how in joint activity and conversation a meeting of minds is possible. Indeed, we must do this if we are to understand the basic forms of intersubjectivity so critical to the *Bildungsprozess*. As McDowell might put it, to learn a language is to acquire the ability to speak one's mind and the perceptual capacity to hear the meaning in people's speech, a power that enables us to perceive what they are thinking.[25] Of course, there are circumstances in which people's beliefs or motives are not evident, and where we need to work out their true state of mind, just as we sometimes do not say what we think. Indeed, as Wittgenstein observed, another person can be an enigma to us (Wittgenstein, 1953, p. 223). But we should not take cases where we fail to discern what another thinks to define the common factor in all cases of knowledge of other minds. On the contrary, such cases are intelligible only against a background in which human minds are open to one another.[26]

Let us now consider knowledge of our own minds. One curious feature of the theory-centred approach is that, in keeping with the third-person turn in the philosophy of mind, it is inclined to treat third-person psychological ascription as prior to first-person ascription.[27] Thus, Wilfrid Sellars, one of the first to portray mental states as theoretical entities, offers a hypothetical account of the evolution of psychological discourse in which talk of mental states first emerges to explain the behaviour of others and is only later used by individuals to ascribe mental states to themselves (Sellars, 1956/1963, §§56–62; see also deVries, 2005, chs 7–8). Yet this ingenious inversion of the Cartesian picture sits oddly with an important asymmetry between first- and third-person psychological ascription: namely, as Sellars recognises, although we ascribe mental states to others on the basis of observational evidence, in the first-person case, we do not (typically) know what we believe, want, etc. by observation or inference. Sellars takes it that we can acquire the ability to report directly the presence of states that others attribute to us on the basis of behavioural evidence. This is, however, far easier to countenance on a broadly realist construal of mental states. If we treat those states as mere theoretical constructions, it is difficult to see how people might come to report their own states of mind in a way that cuts psychological talk loose from the observational context in which it was given a life.

I believe that we should drop the idea that either the first- or the third-person perspective has priority.[28] It is not that we start with the one and work outward, or inward, to the other. They constitute a unity. A being has a concept of mind only if it is capable of both perspectives on the mental, only if it can report its own states of mind and ascribe states of mind to others. At the same time, however, a being has psychological concepts only if it appreciates the asymmetry between first- and third-person psychological perspectives; that is, only if it understands that psychological predicates are such that they are ascribed to others (and others ascribe them to you) on the basis of observation, while you typically ascribe them to yourself (as others do to themselves) independently of observation, and that this asymmetry reflects no ambiguity in the concepts themselves.[29] So, the psychological predicate 'is grief-stricken' is the sort of thing I can ascribe to another person on the basis of observing his behaviour, and the sort of thing I can ascribe to myself without observation (because of how I feel, not because of what I observe about myself), and if I say, of myself and my wife, that *we* are grief-stricken, then I am ascribing the very same state to us both, even though I ascribe the state to her on a different basis from how I ascribe it to myself.

One critical aspect of the asymmetry between first- and third-person standpoints is 'first-person authority': we credit subjects with a special authority about their own mental states. It is this, I believe, that ultimately undermines social constructionism about the mental. For all Gergen's justified hostility to the Cartesian thesis that the mind is transparent to itself, we should not deny that we know our own minds in a way that others do not, and that we are usually right to take people's sincere assertions about what they think, feel, etc. at face value. While we sometimes have to work out what others are thinking and feeling, this is not generally true in our own case. Although we do speak of a person 'not knowing what she thinks', this is usually a matter of her not yet having formed settled beliefs, not of her having beliefs of which she is unaware. Of course, people's knowledge of their own minds is not infallible: I can be brought to see that I do not believe what I think I believe or that I do not want what I think I want. But these errors are significant departures from the norm. There is nothing odd about my wrongly believing that Peter hopes he will get a tie for his birthday. By contrast, my wrongly believing that *I* hope I will get a tie for my birthday is something that requires special explanation.

A satisfactory account of first-person authority has proved elusive. It is widely believed that we must abandon the Cartesian's introspective model, but with what should we replace it? One option is to deflate first-person authority, either by arguing, as Ryle did, that we know our own minds in the same way as others do—we are just more familiar with the relevant data (Ryle, 1949, ch. 6, especially pp. 160–71). Another is to deny, as Wittgenstein did, that judgements about our own mental states express genuine knowledge at all. Both strategies are hopeless. A different approach is found in Davidson, who portrays first-person authority as a presupposition of interpretation (Davidson, 1984/2001, p. 14). Unless we make the general assumption that a person knows what she believes, we cannot take her sincere assertions as expressions of belief, and this renders interpretation impossible. But this seems too *theoretical* a consideration. Others, such as Richard Rorty and Crispin Wright, treat first-person authority as a kind of licence granted by the community: we allow people's sincere assertions of their beliefs to count as definitive of what they believe. This is a move the social constructionist will likely applaud. But, as Richard Moran argues, it is counter-intuitive to think of first-person authority as *granted* by anyone or anything. That others have this authority is rather 'a normal rational *expectation*' (Moran, 2001, p. 68 (discussing Rorty, 1979, p. 174 and Wright, 1987)).

To put the discussion of self-knowledge on a sounder footing, we need thoroughly to exorcise the perceptual model of self-knowledge and find an entirely different basis for first-person authority. If you ask how I know that Christine believes I will finish my book, I can answer by pointing to evidence. If you ask how *I* know I believe I will finish my book, the answer is: by believing it. Likewise, I know I intend to get up tomorrow before noon by intending it; I know I feel pain by its hurting, and so on. The point is that when I have first-person knowledge of my own mental states, I have it not because I have privileged access to inner objects, but because I *live* these states. In the case of my beliefs and intentions I do not stand to them as objects to be inspected and described, but as positions I have arrived at in deliberation and for which I am answerable.

Moran gives content to such thoughts by appeal to the following consideration (Moran, 2001, chs 1–3; see also Moran, 1994). In third-person psychological ascription the questions *What does Samantha believe?* and *What ought Samantha to believe?* are distinct. Of course, from the position of an interpreter, the questions may be related, since, on the assumption that Samantha is reliable, we may ascribe beliefs to her on the grounds that she usually believes what she ought to, but there is no difficulty in principle in ascribing a false or unjustified belief to her. From the first-person perspective, however, the two questions cannot be held apart when we are considering our present mental states. If someone asks me whether I believe that Kingston is west of Montreal, I answer the question not by inspecting my beliefs, but by asking myself whether Kingston *is* west of Montreal. When I am deliberating about what to think, I cannot disassociate the question of what I believe from the question of what the facts are.[30] If I find that I have the facts wrong, then I have to change my beliefs. Indeed, my so finding *is* my changing my beliefs. I do not stand to my own mental states as a spectator; rather, my relation is *agentive*. I must take responsibility for them: it is up to me to make up my mind about what to think in light of the best reasons for so thinking. This is partly constitutive of what it is to be a rational agent, and it is from this that first-person authority derives. Moran concludes that,

> the primary thought gaining expression in the idea of 'first-person authority' may not be that the person himself must always 'know best' what he thinks about something, but rather that it is *his business* what he thinks about something, that it is up to him. In declaring his belief he does not express himself as an expert witness to a realm of psychological fact, so much as he expresses his rational authority over that realm. (Moran, 2001, pp. 123–4)

Such an approach undermines the very idea of mental states as theoretical constructs. When I form a belief about something, I am not in the business of attributing states to myself to explain and predict my behaviour: I am deciding how the facts stand. This is a crucial point, for 'there would be nothing that counted as agency or deliberation at all if a person could not generally claim the conclusion of his reasoning as making it the case that, as a matter of psychological fact, *this* is his belief about the matter' (p. 120). My self-ascribed belief is thus not a constituent in my theory of myself. And if we grant, as we must, that when I ascribe beliefs to others I ascribe states of the very same kind that I ascribe to myself, then we have to abandon the idea that the states we ascribe to others are theoretical constructs. The first route to constructionism is closed.

A plausible view of first-person authority also undermines the second line of thought: namely, that the content of mental states is socially constructed in interpretative practice. One way in which the textuality of the mental differs from the textuality of literary productions is that the latter are objectified into a product over which the author loses interpretative control: the text is 'out there' to be made something of by others, and the author can plausibly be portrayed as standing to her text as one interpreter among many. But I cannot think of my own present mental states in this way. They are not 'out there' in this way, and not because they are 'in here' in some mental museum to which only I have access. I have interpretative authority over my present mental life because it is *up to me* what I think.[31] We cannot displace this idea without undermining the very idea of persons as rational agents responsible for their thoughts and actions.

It might be suggested that Moran's position should incline us to see mental states as *practical constructs*, as products of deliberative agency, nodes in a normative network in constant flux and transition. I have no objection to such a view, which is, I believe, perfectly compatible with modest realism about the mental. Mental states may be, in Brandom's expression, 'normative standings', but those standings are not bestowed on us by others, nor are they the product of interpretation or social attribution. If mental states are constructed, they are so by those whose states they are. This is so, notwithstanding Bakhtinian insights about the influence of speech genres on the structuring of thought and its expression, and the fact that human beings acquire their distinctive psychological powers only through initiation into a community that deploys psychological discourse as a medium of self-understanding. The latter can be true even if the doctrines of social constructionism are not.[32]

THE SOCIAL CONSTRUCTION OF PSYCHOLOGICAL CATEGORIES

Consider now the thesis that many significant psychological categories are social constructs. Ironically, the most persuasive version of such a view can be derived from the work of one of social constructionism's most articulate critics: Ian Hacking. Hacking describes how certain ways of categorising human beings serve to create the kinds of people they describe: 'numerous kinds of human beings and human acts come into being hand in hand with our invention of the ways to name them' (Hacking, 1986/2002, p. 113). An example is *homosexual*. Invoking Plummer's 1981 collection, *The Making of the Modern Homosexual*, Hacking suggests that homosexuals did not exist prior to their categorisation as such. There was plenty of same-sex sex, but there was no distinct kind of person—the homosexual—before people were so categorised in the nineteenth century. Hacking calls this phenomenon 'making up people'.

Hacking dubs his position 'dynamic nominalism': 'nominalism' because new modes of classification create new kinds of people; 'dynamic' because these 'human kinds' evolve. They are 'interactive kinds'. There is a complex interplay between the existence and evolution of such kinds and human behaviour. These are kinds, the members of which can identify themselves and others as members of the kind. Moreover, the criteria for membership, and the very rationale for the kind itself, can be contested by those who putatively fall under it. Hacking's view of human kinds is compatible with robust realism about many things. Horses, planets and bacilli have the properties they do quite independently of our powers of categorisation. You can only be a 'cancer survivor' in certain cultures, but malignant tumours grow independently of how we describe them. Our ways of representing and understanding ourselves literally create kinds of people, but this is consistent with realism about much of the world.

Hacking's work has great significance for educational theory. His discussions of child abuse (Hacking, 1991; 1999, ch. 5) and autism (Hacking, 1999, pp. 114–22; 2006) are of obvious relevance. Moreover, concepts that define kinds of people circulate in educational institutions all the time. They are central to the way such institutions define their mission. In the theory and practice of education, notions such as *ability, motivation, intelligence, behaviour, aptitude, learning, success, accomplishment* and *maturity* are constantly employed, sometimes loosely, sometimes in highly theorised and even quantified ways. Specialised vocabularies defining learning disabilities are established and evolve over time.[33] These notions all help define kinds of people, as do the categories of the wider intellectual and academic cultures in which many of them figure. As Kurt Danziger reminds us in his study of the evolution of the concepts of psychology, *Naming the Mind* (1997), even such notions as *self, self-consciousness* and *emotion* have a history, taking familiar form only in the early modern period. Educationalists must be alive to the fact that the concepts and categories they deploy to understand educational practice enable certain ways of being and disable others.

I think we can appreciate Hacking's insights while resisting too fervent a view of the powers of categorisation and discourse. It is not as if something that falls under a human kind is merely an artefact of discourse, as if there is nothing more to being, say, a scholar, or a transsexual, or a *garçon de café* than being so categorised. As Hacking brings out so well, numerous forces are at work in making the world such as to afford the categorisation. What had to be the case for people to be identified, or to self-identify, using a particular category and for the category to take root? This question will be answered by appeal to various historical considerations, including social, economic and political factors. The history of discourse is not autonomous. We thus need to appreciate the complex causal forces influencing the deployment of any interactive kind and its effects. This demands detailed study of particular cases of the sort Hacking has undertaken. Sometimes in such cases, the metaphor of construction will have a place, but whether it does and in what respect will depend on the character of the processes at issue. For Hacking, there is no general phenomenon that the term 'social construction' picks out.[34]

It is also important that, while there is a significant element of invention in our use of human kinds, those kinds typically aspire to respond to similarities and differences that are there to be discovered. The kind comes to be in our efforts to capture something we take to be genuinely there to be discerned, even if what is there is a product of historical evolution and known to be such. Using human kinds is not just inventing a type (in the way that deciding to call anything that is either a rabbit or a rat a "rattit" would be). Human kinds have a rationale with respect to which their use is taken to be warranted or not, and on the basis of which they can be criticised as ill-founded or distorting. They are not pure invention, but contain a mixture of invention and discovery typical of the practice of human self-understanding.[35] In this sense, I think Hacking's term 'making up people' can mislead. Numerous historical forces make us what we are, but they do not 'make us up'.

It might be countered that what Hacking's work forces us to acknowledge is that our identities are so profoundly fashioned by our discursive practices that we should think of people as artefacts of culture and history and recognise the elusiveness of our selves, which are not given atoms of personhood, but which are transitory, transitional, decentred and multiple. We should adopt something like Bruner's view that 'it is through narrative that we create and re-create selfhood, that self is a product of our telling and not some essence to be delved for in the recesses of subjectivity' (Bruner, 2002, pp. 85–6). But, if this is the lesson, where does this leave the notion of a 'rational agent', so central to McDowell and Moran, and in which I appear to have so much confidence?[36]

I do not think that we can dispense with the idea of rational agency as it figures in McDowell or Moran.[37] The idea of a rational agent is the idea of a being in command of her thoughts in the sense that it is up to her to determine what to think and do in light of what there is reason to think and do. This is the standing responsibility that governs the lives of beings like us. There is a sense in which, for Moran, agents make themselves through such acts of judgement, but this is the sense of self-creation that comes from taking seriously the idea of agents making up their minds, and this sets constraints on the extent to which we can legitimately view ourselves as constituted by social factors.

A mental life is a unity, and a person is its principle. This is key to the very idea of a first-person perspective. My mental states and processes hang together *as mine*, not as objects I possess, but as states and processes for which I am answerable according to what Davidson calls 'the constitutive ideal of rationality'. The unity of our mental lives is not an artefact of narrative. Quite the reverse. The possibility of personal narratives rests on the fact that unity is implicit in the very idea of a person's mental life.

All this is compatible with a person's feeling that his life lacks coherence, that he is uncertain of his identity, that he needs to 'find himself', or that he has more than one 'persona' in the sense that different, perhaps conflicting, aspects of his personality are expressed when he is among different people or in different contexts, and so on. That such feelings occur in a person's life need not compromise the fundamental unity of that life, nor impugn the rationality of its subject. Of course, mundane failures of rationality *are* common: the idea of the rational agent articulates a norm, an ideal from which human beings often depart.[38] But even where those departures are so dramatic that we are compelled to speak of multiple, fragmented or dislocated selves, the norm is still operative, defining the space that can be occupied by exceptions. It is a norm we affirm, in every act of communication when we address another as 'you'. Only consider the presuppositions and expectations of such acts.

CONCLUSION

The moral of our discussion is that less of the world is made than social constructionists typically suppose, and far more goes into the making of what is made than constructionists typically acknowledge. The story of the *Bildungsprozess* cannot be told without a robust sense of the reality of the natural world and of ourselves as natural beings within it, and without recourse to the notion of rational agents responsible for their thoughts and actions. I appreciate how unpopular this conclusion will be among not just social constructionists, but theorists of education who seek to transcend the limitations of modernism.[39] It is important, however, that the choice before us is not to conceive minds *either* as atomistic, self-contained and self-sufficient mental worlds *or* as shifting constructs of discursive forces. There are other options, as I hope this book will show.

To this end, the next chapter will focus on a concept deployed by many of the philosophers whose work we have considered, and which it seems must have a central place in any account of the socio-historical character of mind: the concept of a person.

NOTES

1 For a careful and sophisticated analysis of the idea of social construction, with particular application to issues of gender and race, see Sally Haslanger's papers (1995; 2005). Although she is keener than I am to redeem the idea and to defend it against critics such as Hacking (on the latter, see Haslanger, 2003), there is much about which we agree.
2 Here I follow Hacking in using 'X' as 'a filler, a generic label for what is constructed' (Hacking, 1999, p. 2).
3 Some social constructionist views are spoiled by the assumption that if something is 'natural' or 'independently real' then it is especially resistant to change. In fact, many aspects of the natural world have been radically altered by human practice—landscapes transformed, diseases eradicated, animals changed by breeding practices, and so on. In contrast, some social phenomena—economic markets, for example—are notoriously difficult to control or manipulate (for example, recent history suggests that it is easier to modify the Earth's climate than it is to alter the behaviour that contributes to climate change). Haslanger stresses this point.
4 See Bruner, 1990, ch. 1, esp. pp. 24–30 and 2002, chs. 3–4. (I discuss Bruner's work in more detail in Bakhurst, 2001c and 2005a.) Bruner deploys the term 'constructivism' rather than 'constructionism', as does Phillips (1995/2007) and Sismondo (1996), reviewing the use of the construction metaphor in education and science studies respectively. Both terms are in common use, and the theories they refer to are so many and varied that no obvious rationalisation of terminology suggests itself. Hacking gives his preferred view of the terrain in his 1999, ch. 2, and Kenneth Gergen provides a helpful typology of varieties of constructionism/constructivism in his 1999, pp. 59–60, n. 30.

In psychology, 'constructivism' is associated more with the (e.g., Piagetian) project of understanding the developmental process in which the individual child builds a conception of the world in contrast to the emphasis on social practices of discourse and categorisation typical of social constructionism. Phillips rightly observes that these two programs are different and are often misleadingly conflated (1995/2007, p. 398; 2003, pp. 239–40). There are, however, routes between the two. Bruner, for instance, is clearly focused on the former project, but his commitment to the view that our conceptual schemes are essentially socio-cultural phenomena, together with his longstanding interest in such philosophers as Nelson Goodman and Richard Rorty, incline him to make pronouncements of a more radically construct*ion*ist kind. A different case is presented by Ernst von Glasersfeld's 'radical constructivism', which begins from the question of how the organism 'builds up' knowledge 'in the attempt to order the as such amorphous flow of experience', but arrives at a conclusion that would appeal to radical construct*ion*ists, namely, the rejection of the realist idea that we can form 'a "true" picture of a "real" world that is supposed to be independent of any knower' (1984, pp. 38–9; see also von Glasersfeld, 1995). Though von Glasersfeld has concerns at odds with those of many social constructionists, I believe that their approaches are informed by certain shared philosophical assumptions, which is why they arrive at similarly sceptical conclusions, as I shall try to show.

Constructivism in moral and political philosophy is another story altogether, only obliquely related to the positions considered in this chapter (though the discussion of Christine Korsgaard's work in chapter 4 below may bring out connections to some of the present themes). Constructivism in philosophy of mathematics is yet another.

5 Applauding some of Quine's more pragmatist pronouncements, Bruner writes: '[O]ur notions of what is real are made to fit our ideas about how we come to know "reality". I'm suggesting that what stories do is like that: we come to conceive of a "real world" in a manner that fits the stories we tell about it, but it is our good philosophical fortune that we are forever tempted to tell different stories about the presumably same events in the presumably real world' (2002, p. 103).

6 Berkeley would be unimpressed by this rebuttal because his arguments rest upon a strongly empiricist theory of mental content. Arguably, social constructionists are heirs to such a view—as they are heirs to a form of nominalism reminiscent of empiricism (of which more later in the chapter)—but it would be uncomfortable for them to admit it because they see themselves as transcending the philosophical traditions of which early-modern empiricism is part. (It is noteworthy that the radical constructivist von Glasersfeld is more at ease with this empiricist heritage and cites Berkeley with approval (see von Glasersfeld, 1995, pp. 4–5, 33–4, 91–3).)

7 The example is one I have used before (Bakhurst, 2002; 2007b). Some constructionists will contend that it misses the point. They will grant that, once the boundaries of the concept *child* are fixed, then it is a 'matter of fact' what answers to it. The key question, they will say, is what fixes those boundaries. Constructionism's insight is that they are not determined by 'reality', but by *us*. However, the realist can counter that although there is a sense in which it is 'up to us' to determine the boundaries of our concepts (they're *our* concepts after all), we have to do this in a way that answers to the character of that which falls under them. This ought to be obvious in the case of natural or biological kinds. But it is also true of concepts like *child* notwithstanding the role played by convention in such cases. The concept *child* is responsive to facts about the human life-form, not just to conventions that, e.g., define who counts as a child for certain purposes (such as who is a child in the eyes of the law). Moreover, such conventions are not arbitrary, but reflect facts about the developing capabilities of maturing human beings, and our conventions can be vindicated or challenged by appeal to such facts. It is thus not wrong to say that it is up to us to ensure that our concept *child* reflects the sort of thing children are.

There are ways in which the concept *child* is akin to a natural or biological kind concept and ways in which it is akin to an artefactual kind concept. This reflects the fact that human beings are objects of self-discovery and self-invention (a theme to which I return at the end of this chapter and in the next). But even in the case of straightforwardly artefactual kinds, the role of convention should not be exaggerated. A crucial difference between artefactual and natural or biological kinds is that, in the case of artefacts, concepts precede their objects, while in the case of natural continuants they do not. (Or as Korsgaard puts it, an artefact concept is a functional concept; it is the name of a solution to a problem [2003/2008, p. 323].) Benches are made to conform to ideas; this is not true of tigers or gold. Certainly this is a simplification, because the idea of an artefact often evolves in tandem with the artefact itself, but it captures the obvious truth that artefacts do not have a nature independent of human practices in the way that (according to the realist) members of natural/biological kinds do. Yet in *both* cases the use of the terms in question is governed by the requirement to be responsive to the world. Benches are a human invention, but once invented, the concept *bench* has to respond to the sort of thing benches have come to be. The use or function of an artefact constrains the norms governing its concept. The use of benches can change, new kinds of benches can be invented, new ways of categorising furniture can evolve, but these are rarely best understood as mere changes of convention. The practice of driving on the right side of the road is a convention, but the practice of distinguishing benches from stools and sofas, pencils and aeroplanes is not.

Is my insistence on the distinction between truth and consensus at odds with Wittgenstein's famous reference to the fundamentality of 'agreement in judgements' (Wittgenstein, 1953, §242)? I do not think so. Wittgenstein's point, as I understand it, is that for normative concepts such as 'truth', 'correctness' and 'rationality' to have application, there must be a background of agreement—human beings must basically 'see things the same way'. Such fundamental agreement cannot be compelled by argument, the dictates of reason, or reality itself. That it exists is just fact. (Of course, one might argue that such agreement in judgement is the outcome of *Bildung*, of being enculturated into a way of seeing things, but then the spotlight falls on what human beings must share if *Bildung* is to be possible.) To acknowledge this is to grant, with Davidson (1997/2001, p. 129), that agreement creates the space in which the concept of truth can operate; it is not to say that there is no more to truth than what people agree to be the case. I return to this issue in chapter 6.

8 As the debate is often portrayed, realism is presented as the 'metaphysical' position, while constructionism is seen as friendly to the ordinary. My argument aspires to invert this picture. As I see things, 'modest realism' has no metaphysical pretensions and is in harmony with norms of enquiry deeply embedded in everyday thought and talk, while constructionism implicitly relies on bold metaphysical theses and is profoundly at odds with much that we ordinarily believe about ourselves and the world.

Readers sympathetic to my arguments against social constructionism should consult Crawford Elder's spirited defence of common-sense ontology against a variety of more mainstream forms of philosophical constructionism. Like me, he discerns the covert influence of transcendental idealism in his opponents' positions and argues that it leads to intolerable paradoxes (see, e.g., Elder 2004, ch. 1; 2011).

9 Bruner, replying to a paper of mine, writes: 'Ontology, to my sceptical way of thinking, is an artefact of epistemology. It is a curious game, making claims about the reality of our proposed realities. I think it a more *grown-up* pursuit just to make claims about their usefulness' (Bruner, 2001, p. 213; my emphasis). The suggestion that realism is a mark of intellectual immaturity is also made by Rorty (1984/1991). McDowell responds in 2000/2009b.

10 In more contemporary terms, familiar from Tarski and Davidson, the character of truth is displayed by the simple disquotational schema: ' "P" is true if and only if p' (famously exemplified by ' "Snow is white" is true if and only if snow is white').

11 The notion of truth, not just 'believing true' or 'passing for true'—the latter ideas are all parasitic on a prior notion of truth.

12 For more on this theme, see Davidson's 'Truth Rehabilitated' (2000/2005).

13 To my knowledge, no one overtly subscribes to the pure form of either position, though elements of one or both are present in the views of a number of thinkers.

14 Daniel Dennett claims to be the first to have given the term 'folk psychology' its current usage (though Dennett, in contrast to many who use the term, denies that folk psychology is a theory). See Dennett, 2007, p. 202, n. 2.
15 Such an account portrays reasons as psychological states (combinations of beliefs and desires). This contrasts with the view given in chapter 1, note 11, where reasons are features of situations that are grounds for action and belief. We will revisit the nature of reasons in chapter 5.
16 Admittedly, many philosophers of mind take the view that folk psychology can be a theory only if its explanations are genuinely *causal* in character (hence Dennett's denial that folk psychology is a theory). They would therefore argue that if folk psychological explanation is as hermeneutical as Bruner suggests, it is not strictly speaking a theory at all. A social constructionist, however, will likely scorn these controversies, preferring to embrace an expansive conception of theory that does not privilege the causal-explanatory strategies of natural science.
17 There is a sense in which social constructionism has an affinity with eliminative materialism. Both positions are agreed that psychological discourse refers to nothing real by standards scientific, but where the eliminitivist argues that we should ultimately replace mental vocabulary by talk of brain states and functions, the constructionist is at ease with the mental as a construct, seeing no promise in a physicalistic alternative that, in the constructionist's view, would be no less a construct.
18 I discuss Voloshinov's position further, and address the question of whether the works in question were actually written by Bakhtin, in Bakhurst, 1990.
19 Here there is some affinity between Bakhtin/Voloshinov's position and Heidegger's thought, notably the latter's famous claim that we do not speak language, language speaks us (see, e.g., Heidegger, 1976, p. 25: 'language is not a work of human beings: language speaks. Humans speak only insofar as they co-respond to language'). See Patterson (1988, ch. 5) for a nice comparison of Heidegger and Bakhtin.
20 For Voloshinov, 'ideology' comprises what might be called socially established beliefs, concepts, theories in the form of science, religion, ethics, literature, etc.—that is, components of what I call historically evolving cultural traditions of thought and enquiry. Voloshinov does not reserve the term 'ideology' for networks of belief that are systematically distorted.
21 Other routes to this conclusion might go via a 'social externalist' view of meaning inspired by Tyler Burge's work (1979/2007), of which more below (note 32), or via Wittgenstein's philosophy, which is also sometimes credited with the idea that meaning is socially constituted. Consider how Richard Gaskin sympathetically expounds Wittgenstein in this passage: 'A subject's beliefs about any subject matter, including his or her own mental states, are necessarily expressible in language, and language is a public phenomenon, in the sense that what words mean is a matter not of the individual's say-so, but of how these words are used by the community ... It follows that no individual has infallible knowledge of what words mean, either in general or on any particular occasion of use, and so no individual has infallible knowledge of the correct way to characterize in words any mental state he or she may be in' (Gaskin, 2006, p. 83). One can see immediately how a social constructionist will applaud this view. In fact, the position Gaskin expresses is ambiguous between the innocuous view that I can be wrong about what I think because I am wrong about the meaning of some of the words in which I frame my thoughts, and the view that what I think is hostage to what 'the community' says I think, a view the constructionist may find attractive, but which has little to recommend it, as I hope the next section will show.
22 Both lines might be thought to converge in Davidson's work, where interpretation, conceived as establishing simultaneously what others mean and what their mental states are, is modelled in terms of the construction of Tarski-style theories of truth. However, Davidson's emphasis on the primacy of idiolect, his scepticism about the notion of shared conventions, and his confidence in the notion of truth put him at considerable distance from social constructionism. Nonetheless, the hermeneutical dimensions of his thought, together with his subtle and elusive view of the

ontology of mind, have sometimes led him to be cast as a postmodern thinker (somewhat to his surprise: see Davidson, 1992/2005, p. 159).
23 The third-person approach dispatched questions about consciousness and phenomenology to the hinterland of the philosophy of mind, from which they have only returned in the past 20 years. It will surely be seen as bizarre that analytic philosophy of mind was long uninterested in occurrent thought, conscious awareness or any phenomenon that resists construal in terms of the propositional attitudes, but so it was. (A notable exception is Wilfrid Sellars, who throughout his career combined path-breaking work on the theoretical-explanatory character of psychological discourse with an interest in sensation, consciousness, and phenomenology.)
24 See, e.g., Gopnik and Meltzoff (1996) and Gopnik et al. (1999). See Hamlyn (1978, pp. 11, 36) for an early expression of scepticism about the image of infants as little scientists.
25 See McDowell, 1984/1998a, p. 253, and 1982b/1998b (the discussion in Thornton, 2004, pp. 45–52, 182–9, is also helpful).

On the subject of perceiving the thoughts of others, Sebastian Rödl writes: 'In the fundamental case, I apprehend the sensible reality of someone else's act of thinking, an intentional action or a speech act, without passing through the observation of something that does not involve recognition of it as an act of thinking' (2007, p. 178; Rödl is discussing McDowell, 1981/1998b). Rödl's position here is directly at odds with a social constructionist view of the mental, for the constructionist has to maintain that mental state attributions require us to put a construction onto events or processes that can be identified and individuated without appeal to psychological notions. Rödl would counter that no way of identifying events and processes in non-psychological terms will disclose the unity of events and processes that manifest thought. It follows that the constructionist must lack an account of what mental states are constructed out of.
26 Someone might protest that, even if, say, grief is sometimes 'on the surface', when we claim of a subject that she is grieving that claim is nonetheless advanced as part of a theory of her behaviour. Grief is a concept holistically related to a range of other psychological concepts that pull together in making sense of what we do. Does that not mean that *grief* is a theoretical concept in a perfectly mundane sense? It is true, of course, that the concept of grief pulls its weight in explanation only in league with other concepts deployed to make overall sense of people, and no harm is done simply by calling this kind of sense-making 'theorising' (though in my view this spreads the notion of theory pretty thin). Mischief is made, however, when the idea that psychological explanation is theoretical is combined with the presumption that mental states are unobservables, for then those with anti-realist proclivities can portray the mental as an artefact of theory and a creature of attribution. By attending to cases in which the minds of others are open to us, we can keep a grip on the sense in which mental states and processes are prior to and independent of our efforts to describe and understand them.
27 This is not true of all developmentalists working in theory of mind. In that field, some persist in the Cartesian assumption that the child has knowledge of her own mind prior to and independently of her understanding that others have minds too. The child is pictured as *discovering* that others have minds. Others would deny that the child has a *concept* of mind, either of her own or other peoples', until she has a concept of a representational state, and this she can be said to possess only when she learns to attribute false beliefs to others. The latter view is compatible, however, with the claim that the child has knowledge of her mind prior to her acquisition of the concept of a representational state in that she can be said to know what she thinks, wants, etc.
28 What I say here is much influenced by P. F. Strawson's discussion of persons in *Individuals* (1959). I consider Strawson's view at greater length in the next chapter.
29 'Typically', because there are some cases of psychological self-ascription that *are* based on evidence and observation, as when a person learns in therapy that he resents his siblings, or someone comes to realise that she is afraid of her father by reflecting on her behaviour. Some self-knowledge issues from the subject's taking a theoretical stance to herself, though such

self-knowledge is different in character from standard cases of first-person psychological ascription. This is a theme in Moran, 2001.

30 I can recognise, of course, that in any act of deliberation I might arrive at the wrong answer, just as I can acknowledge that some belief I held in the past was false. What I cannot do, when considering my present beliefs, is isolate the question of what I *do* believe from the question of what I *should* believe.

31 When an utterance is made, whether in spoken or written form, the utterer retains (defeasible) interpretative authority in so far as the utterance is conceived as a moment in her deliberative practice, and others must defer to the utterer's sincere assertion about what she meant. Having said that, the utterer is responsible for making herself understood, and for the effects of her words on others, including, e.g., unintended effects that might arise from being misunderstood. The utterer's interpretative authority is weakened by the passage of time and other more figurative ways in which she may become distanced from her words, and contextual considerations may override it altogether (for instance, if the utterance is part of a literary or academic text subject to the distinctive interpretative norms of those genres).

32 It might be argued that my discussion has overlooked the kind of 'social externalism' favoured by Andrew Davis (2005), drawing on Putnam and especially Burge. Externalists hold that, at least for certain cases, meaning and mental content are determined by our relations to the environment. This is a view that McDowell himself favours. Social externalists hold that it is the *social* environment that is critical. To take a familiar example, the meaning of 'arthritis' depends on the beliefs and attitudes of suitably placed experts, and, when I use the term, I 'tap into' their competence, just as I can acquire knowledge of the world by relying on testimony and the authority of established traditions of enquiry. This might be thought to redeem the idea of the social construction of the mental because it entails that the content of our thoughts and utterances depends, at least in part, on social factors that obtain independently of individual minds. This is a delicate issue, and one which threatens quickly to be complicated by the introduction of various controversial distinctions such as those between 'word meaning' and 'speaker's meaning', and between 'broad' and 'narrow' content. For simplicity's sake, let us grant that the contents of our thoughts and utterances depend upon the meaning of the words we use to articulate them, and that meaning is not up to us. Moreover, we often frame our thoughts and utterances using concepts that we are not in a position fully to elucidate. I can think and speak meaningfully of electrons, dyslexia and black holes while in considerable ignorance about what I am referring to. For all that, we should nonetheless be cautious about embracing the view that content is determined by social convention or expert opinion. If we consider concepts like *dyslexia* or *Asperger's syndrome*, there is no consensus, even among experts, about the proper scope of the concepts. Such concepts rather loosely collect together varieties of behaviours, and criteria for inclusion are contested and obscure. Something similar might be said about *arthritis* and many, many other concepts. We typically deploy such concepts with the aim of referring to some state or condition. It may be that the concept we have fashioned fails properly to capture what we strive to capture in using it. In which case, we may be referring to nothing at all, or obliquely referring to something else. The key point is that reference depends on our relation to the condition or conditions in question. This is socially mediated (since we can identify the supposed condition only by entering a tradition of thought), but not socially constructed. There are of course many objects, the very existence of which depends on social practices (e.g., Verdi's *Requiem*, the Olympic Games), but in such cases it is the objects that are socially constituted rather than our thoughts about them. I take up some of these themes in the next section. None of this undermines the important idea that sometimes our thoughts and utterances rely on 'borrowed' meaning. But this is consistent with the idea of individual epistemic responsibility central to first-person authority. If I borrow competence, the debt is mine to repay.

33 Davis, 2008, discusses the relevance of Hacking's work to our understanding of learning disabilities.

34 At the outset of this chapter, I remarked on the importance of the question: Does this object possess the qualities that make it a member of a type in virtue of social factors or not? Hacking helps us see that an affirmative answer is not enough to show that the object in question is socially constructed. It remains to be shown that the metaphor of construction can play a genuine explanatory role in the case at hand.
35 As Hacking puts it: 'When it comes to the language that will be used to describe ourselves, each of us ... is a half-breed of imagination and reality' (1995, p. 177).
36 The idea of 'the rational agent' is, of course, one which social constructionists typically reject: see Gergen, 2001, pp. 150–2, 155–6.
37 I am not sure Hacking would agree. He is sceptical about the bearing of his work on philosophical concepts of self or personhood, but this may simply be because he is sceptical about those philosophical concepts as such. He writes: 'We can learn something, perhaps a great deal, about how a group at a certain time represents the self; that would be the philosophical lesson to draw from the varieties of multiple personality. It is not, however, a lesson about the mind or the person or the self, thought of as objective entities about which we wish to know more. If it is a lesson for the philosophy of mind, it is a lesson about what we in the European tradition have called the mind. That mind is a figure in our social arrangements' (1995, p. 178). This is an elusive passage. We might grant that the *understanding* of mind embodied in the European tradition is 'a figure in our social arrangements', while denying that mind *just is* a figure in our social arrangements, thereby leaving it open for philosophical and empirical enquiry to illuminate the sort of things minds are.
38 Of which more in chapter 6.
39 See, e.g., Løvlie (2003), who argues that a postmodern conception of *Bildung* must reject a 'neo-liberal' conception of the individual as a 'free, rational agent firmly centered on his own ego and preferences' and deny that 'the linguistic and historical subject' has 'privileged access to itself as its own property'. He continues: 'The "I" is neither a *homunculus*—the little man or agent within consciousness—nor is it free and independent in its capacity as an ego that plays with its different faces or identities. It seems, indeed, that the subject is not identical with itself in the process of *Bildung*. The subject cannot succeed in its quest for identity because this endeavour is suspended in non-identity, that is, in the impossibility of defining oneself as this person' (p. 157). This passage is insightful, but its conclusion exaggerated.

3
Self and Other

Social constructionism, in its more extreme forms, can be viewed as an attempt to grapple with the problem of self and other. The radical constructionist aspires to cancel the otherness of 'external reality' by conceiving it as a construction of our discursive practices. At the same time, the individual's distance from other people is diminished by the recognition of how profoundly social forces are involved in the construction of self. No man is an island, and together we construct our common reality. Having rejected constructionism, it is incumbent upon me to provide an alternative, and more plausible, vision of the relation of self and other. This chapter begins this task, and those that follow will, I hope, bring it to completion.

PROBLEMS OF SELF AND OTHER

It is important to observe that there is no such thing as *the* problem of self and other. Self and other is a theme incorporating various questions from different areas of philosophy, some of which we have already aired in the first two chapters, while others are yet to make an appearance.

First, there are familiar metaphysical problems about the nature of the self. We are inclined to think of the self as 'the subject of consciousness' and to conceive it as something 'inner'. But what exactly is it? An entity? Or something more like a point of view or perspective? Is talking of my 'self' just a way of talking about *me*, or is my self one of my *parts*? These are difficult questions to answer, and the elusiveness of the self has moved some philosophers to deny its existence. Admittedly, in certain areas of philosophy, and certain fields outside philosophy, people speak and write with breezy confidence that talk of the self has a reference, but it is often by no means obvious that their confidence is warranted. One thing is clear: Any account of the self will require a concomitant conception of the world that the self entertains in thought and experience and of which it is also, presumably, a part. Problems of the self are problems about self and world.

The Formation of Reason, First Edition. David Bakhurst.
© 2011 David Bakhurst. Published 2011 by Blackwell Publishing Ltd.

Epistemological issues are also legion. If selves are anything, they are self-conscious: they are aware of themselves and able to entertain first-person thoughts. It is not easy, however, to say how a subject of experience could form an idea of itself as a subject of experience.[1] And if we can solve that riddle, other epistemic puzzles await. Paramount among these is the concern that is McDowell's focus in *Mind and World*: how can the self make contact with the world in thought and experience? Here the issue is not so much scepticism about whether our beliefs are true, but something more basic: how can a world that is fundamentally other-to-thought be a possible object *of* thought? Such problems pertain not just to the self's relation to 'external objects'. Parallel puzzles relate to other minds. Here again, the concern is not (just) scepticism about their existence. The question concerns how, and in what way, minds can commune with one another.

The latter issue arouses existential concerns. The sense in which each of us is alone in the world can assume philosophical proportions, resulting in a mood of irredeemable metaphysical loneliness.[2] Less dark existential problems are presented by what might be called the phenomenology of personal space, concerning the definition and maintenance of the boundaries of the self.

The problematic of self and other manifests itself in moral philosophy when we ask how altruism and fellow-feeling are possible and explore our ability to view the world from the perspective of another. And recent political philosophy is also no stranger to the dichotomy: only consider the prevailing concern with the recognition of difference and cultural otherness.

It seems that, wherever one looks, issues of self and other are inescapable. This is particularly true of educational theory and practice, which can scarcely avoid commitment, explicit or implicit, to a conception of the self and its relation to the world when adopting views of knowledge, learning and understanding, when thinking about moral education and community, confronting questions of difference and cultural identity in contemporary educational institutions, or exploring the emotional and motivational dimensions of learning. Nor can educators be indifferent to the existential concerns about loneliness, meaninglessness and mortality that can take hold of students, sometimes with devastating effect. It is thus important that educational thinking be informed by a compelling vision of self and world, or at least that it not be distorted by misleading conceptions of their relation.

It is tempting to hope that, though issues of self and other are many and diverse, a single significant readjustment in our thinking will simultaneously illuminate them in a way that will render them tractable. And it is also natural to think, as the social constructionist does, that the focus of this readjustment must lie somewhere in the domains of metaphysics or epistemology, which, it is often held, are prior to moral, existential and political concerns. I share the view that progress in matters metaphysical and epistemic will help us with the existential, moral and political issues, but not because I am optimistic that the correct theoretical solution to the former puzzles will yield solutions to the latter. My approach to the grand metaphysical and epistemic concerns about self and other is largely deflationary. I grant the questions are alluring, but I do not think that we can build satisfying theories that will answer them in their own terms. They need, rather, to be dispelled or dissolved. If we can achieve this dissolution, then the very real moral, political and existential problems of self and other can take proper shape, uninflated by philosophical pretension. Problems of altruism and empathy, for instance, are made much harder by the influence of dubious epistemological concerns about other minds and the limits of mutual understanding. They become easier once those concerns are dispelled (not easy, just easier).[3]

Those who favour dissolving problems often have a general strategy to effect this. They advance a criterion of authenticity that the questions under consideration do not meet, or they offer a narrative about the source of the questions that undermines their legitimacy. It is therefore common to hear the view, influenced perhaps by Richard Rorty's work, that Cartesianism is the source of much mischief in this area. I do not share this approach. I have no general method for identifying and dissolving bogus problems, nor do I think we should lay all the blame at Cartesianism's door.[4] In my view, Cartesianism is not so much the cause of our puzzlement as its symptom. Our problems do not originate in philosophical mistakes. Their real source lies in certain deep features of consciousness, subjectivity and personhood that make it difficult to understand how we can be both objects in the world and minds at critical distance from it. Cartesian and other mistaken views are attempts to accommodate those features. Our task is to find a way to acknowledge them for what they are without causing conceptual havoc, and this requires a sensitive working-through of the issues in all their complexity, rather than the swift application of a technique for downsizing philosophical confusions.

THE PROBLEM OF SELF AND OTHER IN ONE'S OWN PERSON

I shall begin with what I call 'the problem of self and other in one's own person'. In the last chapter, we considered the nature of knowledge of our own minds. I want to say something now about our relation to our own bodies.

Our relation to our bodies is obviously an intimate one, but what exactly is it? Of course, if you think it is identity, then our problem is a non-starter: our relation to our bodies is not a relation to something other—we are our bodies. But many find reasons to deny that we are identical with our bodies.[5] There is clearly a sense in which I can treat my relation to my body as a relation to an object, and when I do, I distinguish myself from it. This is reflected in ways we think and speak about ourselves. We often portray our bodies not as things we *are* but as things we *own*. The relation appears to be possession, not identity. 'You have a lovely body' is a compliment; 'You are a lovely body' less obviously so.

One might respond that the idea that our bodies are distinct from ourselves is just an artefact of the reflexivity of consciousness. That I can 'objectify' my body in thought does not make me separate from it. After all, the self can think about *itself*, thereby making itself its own object, but that does not make it distinct from itself.[6]

However, other considerations quickly present themselves. Some have thought it at least conceivable that we should survive the destruction of our bodies, or exchange bodies with someone. And then there is Leibniz's law: if *A* and *B* are identical, then anything true of *A* is true of *B*. So if Oscar is his body, anything true of Oscar is true of his body and vice versa. Is this plausible? Oscar is witty. Is his body witty? If Oscar loses weight, then there is less of his body than there was, but is there less of Oscar? There is a sense in which there is and a sense in which there is not. Which sense you think primary depends on your philosophical intuitions, but it does seem a stretch to insist that everything true of someone is true of his or her body. After my death, I shall be gone, though my body will remain to be disposed of.

There is also the behaviour of the first-person pronoun. The criteria that govern the identification of bodies are different from those that govern the identity of selves, at least in the first person. From the first-person perspective, I do not have to do anything to keep track of my 'self', and my use of 'I' is immune to error through misidentification. When I say 'I believe it is Thursday', I can be wrong about whether it actually *is* Thursday, but I cannot be mistaken about to whom I am attributing the belief. I can, however, misidentify my body, as when I mistakenly take my body seen in a mirror to be somebody else's.[7]

Finally, there is the following train of thought. We want to say both that we are subjects of experience and that we are objects in the world among other objects. But we find ourselves asking: how *could* anything that is a subject of experience also be an object among other objects? The subject of experience, conceived as that which does the experiencing, does not show up within experience (just as the eye is not present in the visual field). The body, however, is a possible object of experience, so it cannot be the subject of experience. Thus the subject of experience has to be something distinct from the body and its states. If we identify ourselves with subjects of experience, then we seem to be at one stage removed from our bodies, or even to stand to them as to something alien. Or so we may conclude by this sort of reasoning.

In what follows, I approach the issue of self and other in one's own person by drawing on the work of two giants of British philosophy of the past half-century: P. F. Strawson and David Wiggins. I will argue that their respective insights, although they resolve much of the puzzlement about the status of the self, take us only so far. But once they are supplemented by a socio-historical conception of our development as thinking beings, they provide the basis for a satisfying conception of persons and their place in the world.

STRAWSON ON PERSONS

In the third chapter of *Individuals*, Strawson points out that a subject of experience, if it is anything, is something to which conscious states are ascribed. He then reminds us that a feature of our normal ways of thinking is that we take ourselves to ascribe mental states to the *very same thing* to which corporeal characteristics are also ascribed: namely, *persons*. We say of the person in the library that he has red hair and that he is daydreaming about having something nice for supper. The concept of a person is the concept of something to which two different kinds of predicate can legitimately be ascribed. Strawson calls them

'P-predicates' and 'M-predicates' ('P' and 'M' do not stand for 'physical' and 'mental', but for 'person' and 'material'). The latter can also be ascribed to material particulars that are not persons. So, '... is heavy' and '... is located to the left of the door' are M-predicates. P-predicates can be applied only to persons. They include predicates ascribing mental states (e.g. '... is longing for her summer holidays', '... is hoping for a cardigan for Christmas'), but also such predicates as '... is going for a walk', '... is playing at full-back', which, although not themselves mental predicates, may be ascribed only to beings that are conscious, capable of intentional action, and so on.

Strawson maintains that the concept of a person is *primitive*, by which he means that it cannot be analysed into components that are intelligible independently of the concept of a person. We should not treat persons as composites of, say, a material part (body) and a psychological part (self), as if these were separately intelligible ingredients. We *can* coherently think of the self as something purely mental, and even entertain the idea of disembodied persons, but these concepts are abstractions from our normal concept of a person and are parasitic upon it. So Strawson might say that the problem of self and other in one's own person is to be overcome simply by acknowledging the sort of thing persons are. If you understand your own personhood, then you understand that a person is precisely something that is both a subject of experience and a material particular. The puzzle of how anything could be both rests upon isolating the subject of experience and asking how something like *that* could have material properties; but that ignores the fact that the notion of a pure subject of experience is an abstraction from the familiar notion of a person.

The idea that the concept *person* is 'primitive' is designed to block the dichotomising move that would hold apart our mindedness from our embodiment and then demand an explanation of how anything minded could be embodied. 'Primitive' here is not code for 'accept without argument'. Strawson does have an argument about why persons must be the sorts of things to which both M- and P-predicates can be ascribed. It is this: the criteria for the ascription of P-predicates make essential reference to bodily states and behaviour, so persons had better have corporeal characteristics.

Not everyone will be persuaded by this argument. As we have seen, there is an important asymmetry between first- and third-person psychological ascription. Bodily states and behaviour are relevant primarily to the ascription of mental states to *others*, but this is not (usually) true in the case of first-person psychological ascription. I do not take myself to be in pain because I observe my behaviour or the state of my body: I *feel* I am in pain. Likewise, I do not usually assert that I believe it is Thursday on the basis of the observation of my behaviour. Some thinkers take the asymmetry between first- and third-person psychological ascription as a reason to think of the self as distinct from the body. Each of us has knowledge of our own states of mind unmediated by observation of bodily goings-on. As we saw in the previous chapter, some are tempted to understand this as a special relation between the self and the objects of its thought and experience, conceived as inner phenomena that are unavoidably present to consciousness. The outward, bodily, manifestations of mind are then thought of as merely contingently related to such inner happenings. When we try to make sense of the minds of others, these outward manifestations are all we have to go on. It can therefore seem that there is something essentially second rate about third-person psychological ascription, which involves hypothesising and theory-building to work out 'what is going on in there'. In contrast, the circumstances (or lack of them) of first-person psychological ascription are the real McCoy: immediate, unmediated and pretty much infallible. It is tempting to conclude that the first-person context discloses the meaning of psychological predicates: we understand what pain is, and what the predicate '... is in pain' means, from the first-person case and then, using bodily and behavioural evidence, we project such states onto others.

Naturally, Strawson rejects this view of the priority of the first person. But he does not replace it by granting priority to the third-person perspective. Rather, he advances the kind of view commended in the last chapter; namely, that first- and third-person modes of ascription are necessarily linked and each is essential to the intelligibility of the other. You understand what it is you are ascribing to yourself, without appeal to observation, just in case you understand that it is the sort of thing that can be ascribed to others only on the basis of observation. And you do not understand what you are ascribing in the third-person case unless you understand that it is the sort of thing that the person to whom you are ascribing the state could ascribe to himself without observation. It follows that it is a condition of ascribing states of mind to oneself that one should also ascribe them to others. You do not understand 'I am in pain' unless you understand 'He is in pain': neither use is 'self-sufficient'.[8] Thus, you cannot start from either first- or third-person psychological ascription and somehow work towards the other one. If I am to apply psychological predicates to myself, I must understand what it is to apply them to others and I must understand what it is for others to apply them to me. It follows that I must be able to identify others as subjects of experience. Since I cannot identify them as pure egos, they must be the sort of thing to which corporeal characteristics can be ascribed. And I must recognise that this is also true of myself.

So the idea is that selves are subjects of experience and subjects of experience are persons. Persons are essentially such that both P-predicates and M-predicates can be applied to them. Moreover, it is a feature of P-predicates that the very same properties ascribed from the first-person perspective can also be ascribed from the third-person (and vice versa), even though the criteria for ascription from the two standpoints are different. If we accept this, we cannot conceive of the self in one of the ways that generates certain characteristic problems of self and other: namely, as a subject presiding over a self-contained and self-sufficient mental realm, merely contingently related to corporeal things, including its body, situated beyond this realm.

Someone with dichotomising tendencies may yet resist by expressing puzzlement about the nature of P-predicates. How are they possible? How could the same predicate have two such different modes of ascription? Strawson's response to this worry is interesting. He recommends that we focus attention on a certain subset of P-predicates, such as '... is taking a stroll', '... is packing her suitcase', or '... is decorating his study' (see Strawson, 1959, pp. 111–12). We might call these 'predicates of mundane activity'. First-person ascription of such predicates does not rely on inference from observation (we usually know what we are doing, we do not have to work it out[9]), but we are not inclined to think that there is anything special or mysterious about them. We would not take someone seriously who asked how the predicate '... is washing the car' is possible. Here we are at ease with the idea that something that can be known by observation from the third-person perspective can also be known without observation from the first-person. Why think there is anything more mysterious about '... is thinking that today is Tuesday'? After all, P-predicates form a system: the ones we do seem to find puzzling cannot be sealed off from predicates of mundane activity that are not perplexing at all.

Strawson's strategy is ingenious. Yet more remains to be said. One might ask how non-observational knowledge of our own actions is supposed to be possible? Here we can again invoke the work of Richard Moran, whose view of first-person authority about mental states we considered in chapter 2 (see Moran, 2001, pp. 124–34). If a happening is an action, then there is some description of it under which it is intentional.[10] The intentional description of my doing represents it as something done for a reason—as something that is, or could be, the outcome of practical deliberation. If I am a rational agent, acting in light of such deliberation, I must know what it is I am doing, or attempting to do, at least under that intentional description.[11] I know because I am the author of the intention to act, not because I observe something in myself. Hence an agent must have non-observational knowledge of, and accordingly first-person authority with respect to, his own actions. Settling for less would do violence to our conception of rational agency.[12]

Yet as things stand, the dichotomisers will want to know why they should not portray mundane activities, such as washing the car or mowing the lawn, as composites of bodily movements and psychological states. The movements are actions, as opposed to mere happenings, because such states as intentions stand behind them. Intentions exhibit the familiar asymmetry between first- and third-person ascription; but it is not clear that the bodily dimension of action does. Or so they will maintain. So if our approach is to work, we will need a conception of actions as bodily movements that are infused with mindedness. Only this will give the lie to the dichotomising strategy.

Accordingly, we also need a richer conception of what a person is. Strawson's strategy is mainly negative: to counter tendencies to portray the authentic self as a pure ego set apart from the material. To this end, he counsels us not to draw the boundaries of the self around something purely psychological. The point of the appeal to predicates of mundane activity is to force recognition of the fact that the self's non-observational awareness of its own states extends into the bodily realm. Here there is a glimpse of a positive conception of the self as genuinely in and of the world. But only a glimpse. We want a fuller picture of the intimate connection of the spiritual and the physical in our nature, and that requires more than tracing connections between predicates.[13]

WIGGINS ON PERSONS AND HUMAN NATURE

What more can we say about the nature of persons? It is common in philosophy to suppose that if you want to know what something is you should look into its identity conditions. Discussions of personal identity are, however, fraught with just those dichotomising tendencies that give life to the problem of self and other in one's own person. The classic literature presents a choice between theories that treat personal identity in terms of psychological continuity (*A* is the same person as *B* if and only if *A* has the same memory and character as *B* (or if and only if *A*'s mental states stand in the appropriate relation of continuity to *B*'s mental states)) and those that think it resides in bodily continuity (*A* is the same person as *B* if and only if *A* has the same body as *B* (or if and only if *A*'s physical states—or some subset thereof—stand in the appropriate relation of continuity to *B*'s physical states)). Both kinds of theory appear so obviously prey to counter-examples that one suspects an antimony. We need to break out of the dualistic framework of the debate.[14]

Someone who appreciates this, and whose work attempts to remedy it, is David Wiggins. Wiggins's view of personal identity, which has evolved over many years, deploys the concept *human being*: although 'person' and 'human being' differ in sense, they assign the same underlying principle of individuation, so *A* is not the same person as *B* unless *A* is the same human being as *B*.[15] It is easy to miss what Wiggins is up to because his view provokes an obvious objection. Cannot we imagine intelligent beings who are persons, but not human? Star Trek and Doctor Who provide numerous examples of such imaginings. But we need not resort to science fiction. It is a contingent fact that only *Homo sapiens* evolved to be persons. We might have had to share the planet with some other intelligent, language-using primates. But to harp on this is to misunderstand the point and subtlety of Wiggins's position. His is not really the view that nothing non-human can be a person. It is that the concept *person* derives its criteria of individuation from the concept *human being* and that, for beings like us, our personhood is allied to our being human. So if we consider thought experiments about brain transplants or 'memory swaps', the relevant criterion of identity is: *same human being, same person*. Our stereotype of a person is a human being (cf. Williams, 1970a/1973). The concept could be extended to something non-human, if it were sufficiently like that stereotype.

Wiggins's point is to break the either/or of the traditional debate. He thinks that Locke was right to portray the integrity of our mental lives as crucial to our identity, but he challenges the idea that we can represent continuity of consciousness as anything other than an expression of the vital functions of a creature engaged, as we are, with the world and other such creatures. It is not that personal identity consists in continuity of *either* mind *or* body. What is at issue is the continued active existence of an embodied, minded being; moreover, of a being whose mindedness and whose embodiment are not two independently intelligible phenomena.[16] Our mental lives are a mode of expression of our animal nature and Wiggins looks to the concept *human being* to capture this.

Wiggins rightly rejects constructionist treatments, according to which the criteria for the concept *person* are determined by convention and personal identity puzzle cases are to be answered by decision.[17] For him, the concept *person* has a *depth* that transcends convention. The nature of personhood is to be discovered, not invented, and the discovery will yield determinate answers to the notorious puzzle cases. So far so good, but then Wiggins strikes a wrong chord. He takes as his paradigm of a concept with the right kind of depth a natural kind concept. *Person*, he admits, is not itself a natural kind concept, but *human being* is, and that is part of the attraction for Wiggins of linking *person* to *human being*. The problem, however, is that Wiggins holds that the depth of a natural kind concept is to be plumbed by scientific means, but, by his own admission, appeal to the biological essence of human beings will not disclose the depth of the concept *person*.

In his original statement of what he then called 'the animal attribute view', Wiggins identifies a 'systemic' component to the concept *person*. Persons are animals

> of a kind whose typical members perceive, feel, remember, imagine, desire, make projects, move themselves at will, speak, carry out projects, acquire a character as they age, are happy or miserable, are susceptible to concern for members of their own or like species ... [note carefully these and subsequent dots], conceive of themselves as perceiving, feeling, remembering, imagining, desiring, making projects, speaking ... , have, and conceive of themselves as having, a past accessible in experience-memory and a future accessible in intention ... , etc. (Wiggins, 1980, p. 171; the parenthetical injunction is Wiggins's own)

Wiggins has always insisted there is no prospect of a scientific, law-like explanation of the psychological qualities enumerated in the quotation. Understanding people as minded beings involves a different mode of intelligibility. It is a matter of interpretation, rather than (purely) causal explanation. As Wiggins himself has put it, the marks of personhood are revealed by reflecting on what it is for something to be 'a fit subject of our interpretation and reciprocity' (1996, pp. 244–5).

We might now ask why a 'rationalist' position is not a viable alternative to Wiggins's biologistic 'human being approach'. Why not portray these 'systemic' features as an exhaustive characterisation of personhood, rather than as a mere component of the concept? These features capture our responsiveness to reasons. Surely this is the core of personhood as such—this explains why non-human persons are so easy to imagine. Why not say that the depth of the concept *person* derives from the depth of our rational nature? Admittedly, Wiggins is right that to fill in the dots in his description we naturally focus on persons as we encounter them, but what we attend to is their rationality, not their animality. Facts about biology may enter the picture as conditions of rationality, enabling or limiting, but such facts will not be constitutive of personhood.

THE SIGNIFICANCE OF SECOND NATURE

Wiggins confronts a familiar challenge: how to embrace the explanatory autonomy of the rational without bifurcating our nature into rational and animal components in a way that invites us to identify personhood exclusively with the former. What is required is an argument that reveals how the psychological characteristics enumerated above are not just 'matter-involving', but are matter-involving in a way that includes our humanity. To this end, an appeal to the supervenience of the psychological on the physical is surely inadequate, as are Wiggins's many perceptive remarks about the causal and situational elements of perception, memory and other psychological capacities (Wiggins, 1980, pp. 182–3).[18] These might show that persons must be somehow embodied, but not that they must be, or be very like, human beings.

In Wiggins's writings, the concept closest to supplying the desired ingredient is *interpretation* (see Wiggins, 1980, Longer Note 6.36; 1987, pp. 70–2; 2001, pp. 198–9). He maintains that it is in the practice of making sense of one another in accord with norms of rationality that we are furnished with our stereotype of personhood. It is important that, despite its Davidsonian pedigree, Wiggins's view of interpretation is considerably richer than Davidson's austere conception of the coordination of idiolects.[19] Wiggins stresses how in interpretation we must 'find our feet' with one another, get on each other's 'wavelength'. For him, the alpha and omega of interpretation is a mutual recognition and reciprocal attunement that reflect the parties' common form of life.[20] Thus we cannot properly separate the mindedness of the beings we confront from the embodied activity of the living animals that expresses or realises it (or rather, we can achieve the separation in thought only by exercises of abstraction and imagination). To think that it is merely contingent that we find the marks of personhood in the activity of human beings, as if what finds human expression in this context might readily be given alternative realisation, underestimates the *intimacy* of the connection between our mindedness and the mode of its expression in our activity. For example, the norms of rationality that mediate interpretation are not purely abstract and universal. We are required to consider the rationality of others' ends, and this cannot be assessed in abstraction from the kind of beings that they are, from considerations about how human beings live, and, indeed, about how it is fitting for them to live (Wiggins, 1996, p. 245).

At this point I think it essential to reintroduce the idea of *second nature*, which we met in chapter 1. Though this notion finds scant expression in Wiggins's writings on identity, it is invoked in his 2006 book *Ethics*, and it figures in the work of thinkers he admires, most notably McDowell.[21] McDowell deploys the term to refer to those propensities a creature acquires by 'education, habituation, or training', rather than as a result of 'merely biological maturation' (2008, p. 220). As far as this goes, 'second nature' characterises aspects of the life activity of many animals. But in the case of human beings, its acquisition equips us with powers unique to us. For McDowell, our second nature includes those conceptual capacities and moral sensibilities which make us inhabitants of the space of reasons, able to entertain the world in experience and thought (McDowell, 1994, p. 125). With this, we are not talking merely of the transmission of knowledge and skills across generations, but of the very formation of children's minds and characters through enculturation, a process that is a precondition of the individual inheriting the collective wisdom of past generations. As McDowell puts it, human beings are born 'mere animals' and our very mindedness is a product of *Bildung*. Such an approach invites us to see personhood itself as an aspect of second nature, at one and the same time the outcome of the natural maturation of human beings and the work of culture.

It might be suggested that invoking second nature merely plays into a rationalistic view of personhood. If we identify persons with inhabitants of the space of reasons, why does their status as flesh-and-blood human beings matter? Yet reflecting on the character of *Bildung* facilitates recognition of the affinity between our personhood and our humanity. A child's attainment of personhood depends on her attunement to those around her: on the creation of an evolving intersubjectivity. This is not reciprocity between two *given* subjects, as in the standard depictions of interpretation. The infant's elders must see in her the potential for reason. Where are they to find it except in the form taken by the child's animal being?[22] What they must find meaning in is precisely her physical engagement with her surroundings. Reflection on the interaction of infant and parent, in search of a meeting of minds, makes evident how artificial it is to separate the child's emerging mindedness from the specific character of her bodily presence in the world.[23] This enables us to see personhood as a fundamental modification of the mode of life activity of an animal, a human being. The child's becoming a person, however, in no way cancels her animal status, as if *Bildung* could somehow transport her out of nature. As McDowell insists, though the rational powers partly constitutive of personhood resist explanation by natural-scientific means, 'the second-natural is no less natural than the first-natural' (2008, p. 221). It is in the nature of human beings that their development is open to the transformative potential of their initiation into culture.[24]

Wiggins (2005) has reservations about my deploying the idea of second nature to this end. He worries that we will find ourselves, for instance, saying of *A* that he is less of a person than *B*, but still more of a person than he used to be. Such claims, if taken literally, raise a host of problems, moral and metaphysical. Not only do they compromise the clarity of Wiggins's account of personal identity, which relies on the congruence between the concepts *person* and *human being*; they threaten to disturb our moral intuitions about the equal moral worth of all persons. In light of this, it is surely preferable, Wiggins suggests, to say (i) that persons have the capacity to develop a rational nature, rather than (ii) that human beings have the capacity to develop into persons.[25]

These concerns deserve careful consideration. I agree with Wiggins that talk of personhood admitting of degrees cannot be taken literally. Nevertheless, I believe that the idea of the emergence of personhood and its loss do have resonance for us. We do no violence to the concept when we think of the infant as entering personhood or lament of someone severely impaired by a devastating stroke that he is a person no longer.[26] Indeed, sometimes we feel compelled to speak in this way. At the same time, this stance coexists with the propensity to extend the concept person to *all* human beings regardless of their rational capacity. This we do, I believe, in recognition of the fact that human beings are creatures *of a kind*, whose nature is to develop the rational powers constitutive of personhood, even if those powers are as yet undeveloped, or diminished or destroyed by injury or disability. Extending the concept in this way preserves both the congruence of the concepts *person* and *human being* so crucial to Wiggins's account of personal identity, and the intuition that the moral regard owed to all human beings is linked to their status as persons. There is thus a kind of dialectical tension between theses (i) and (ii). To resolve it, we can say that the locus of personhood resides in the rational capacities that human beings acquire through the acquisition of a second nature—if human beings were not of a kind to develop such capacities, there would be no persons—but given that human beings are of that kind, the concept *person* may happily embrace all human beings in recognition of their membership of the kind, even in circumstances where the development of their rational powers is thwarted or their integrity undermined. In this way we capture a truth that both theses partially articulate.

These are deep waters with strong currents, but what is vital in the present context is just the thought that to take seriously a strongly developmental account of the emergence of rational capacity is to see the child's emerging rationality as present in her activity with which others can directly engage and work upon. This consolidates the idea of the self's presence in the world, thereby undermining the problem of self and other in our own person.

Among the reasons that the notions of *Bildung* and second nature are so attractive is that they throw into relief the significance of the second-person perspective. The second person has been almost entirely obscured in discussions of psychological ascription, which tend to be preoccupied with the contrast between first- and third-person standpoints. That contrast, as it is typically conceived, embodies a stark self–other dichotomy that generates familiar problems: from the first-person perspective we have difficulty countenancing the subject's status as a bodily object, while from the third-person perspective we have difficulty explaining the subjectivity of others. Things look rather different when we consider what it is to relate to another being as *you*. The second-person perspective already embodies recognition of the subjectivity of the other and, it might be argued, simultaneously contains the presentation of self in a way that warrants reciprocal recognition from the other person. Implicit in addressing another as 'you' is the recognition of him or her as a rational agent, an inhabitant of the space of reasons. *Bildung* brings this vividly into view, in part because the reciprocal recognition of subjectivity contained in the second-person perspective is a precondition of the possibility of education, in the fullest sense of that word, and in part because at the earliest stages of the *Bildungsprozess* the elders' commitment to the recognition of mutual subjectivity is so obviously an assumption warranted by the child's potentiality rather than his or her actual capacity. At this stage, the child is addressed as a 'you' so that he or she might become an 'I' that can return the compliment (see chapter 1, note 19). Of course, the assumption of rationality is made of the child as a human being, a bodily presence. This being is the referent of 'you' and it is this being to which the elders accord the responsibilities of rationality and to which they direct their love and concern. Thus the idea of *Bildung* draws our attention to the dynamics of the second-person perspective, so sadly neglected in discussions of personhood, and reflection on the *Bildungsprozess* illuminates just what it is to treat others as rational beings, as subjects of a life of their own.[27]

FURTHER POSITIVES

Let us take stock. I have been considering one strand in the problematic of self and other: the problem of self and other in one's own person. How can I, a subject of conscious experience, also be something bodily, part of the object world? Strawson's account of persons helps us see our way out of this puzzlement, inviting us to focus on the concept of a person and recognise that persons are essentially the sorts of things to which both M-predicates and P-predicates can be applied. This cure will not take, however, unless we wean ourselves off the idea that the self is something purely inner and psychological. Strawson does his best to show that we do not really think that way, nor can we if we are to understand the possibility of psychological ascription. But his opponent can deploy the asymmetry between first- and third-person psychological ascription to keep the dichotomy between inner self and outer world. Strawson counters this by bringing predicates of mundane activity to centre stage.

Strawson's strategy can work only if we complement his view with a plausible conception of persons and an authentic account of bodily agency. For the former, I turned to Wiggins's account of personal identity. Although Wiggins intends to capture how our rationality and our animality are intrinsically interwoven, his account falls short. I argued, however, that his position can be enhanced by a conception of second nature, inspired by the work of McDowell, which represents emerging rationality as an expression of, and transformation of, our animal nature. Attention to the circumstances of *Bildung*, and accordingly to the second-person perspective, brings into view the intimate connection between the rational and the animal in our nature.

McDowell's view also helps install an account of bodily agency that complements Strawson's position. Earlier I wrote of the need to supplement Strawson's appeal to predicates of activity with a suitably rich account of action. We must be comfortable not just with the claim that our mindedness is an aspect of our animal nature, but also with the idea of the presence of mind in activity. We require a view of rationality as present in action, rather than simply standing behind bodily movement. Interestingly, McDowell has evoked the notion of second nature to this end (1994, pp. 89–91).

The concept of second nature requires us to work with a richer conception of the natural world than that typically countenanced by the natural sciences. We are to reject those forms of naturalism that leave nature 'disenchanted' for a view of the world as containing phenomena that, though genuinely natural, cannot be explained by scientific methods. This richer conception includes the rational capacities that human beings acquire through enculturation—the capacities that make responsiveness to reasons 'second nature' to us—as well as those features of the world that our rational capacities enable them to respond to, such as reasons, values, norms, and meanings. As McDowell puts it:

> [S]econd nature acts in a world in which it finds more than what is open to view from the dehumanized stance that the natural sciences, rightly for their purposes, adopt. And there is nothing against bringing this richer reality under the rubric of nature too. The natural sciences do not have exclusive rights to that notion; and the added richness comes into view, not through the operations of some mysteriously extra-natural power, but because human beings come to possess a second nature.
>
> Nature, on this richer conception, is to some extent autonomous with respect to nature on the natural-scientific conception. Correctness in judgements about its layout is not constituted by the availability of a grounding for them in facts of first nature; it is a matter of their coming up to scratch by standards internal to the formed second nature that is practical *logos*. (1996/1998a, pp. 192–3)

The passage occurs in the context of a discussion of practical reason in a broadly moral context, but the point it makes is of wider significance. To understand our rational responsiveness and everything that responsiveness discloses to us, we must operate with a less austere conception of reality than that countenanced by natural science.[28]

Consider the effect this should have on our conception of action. If we embrace a conception of nature as disenchanted, then the difference between action and mere bodily movement can be marked only by the presence or absence of something mental—an intention or an act of will—conceived as an event in some inner realm. What is in the world—the movement of limbs—is the same in both cases. McDowell complains that such a picture robs us of 'any authentic understanding of bodily agency' (1994, p. 91). The alternative is to think of agency as *in* nature, present in the agent's movements, so that those movements are 'imbued with intentionality' and intention, will, meaning and rationality are there in the deportment of the body. This is surely phenomenologically accurate. I do not think of myself as controlling my body at any kind of distance like a puppeteer. I feel myself biting the food, or reaching into the drawer, or rising to head the ball, or holding hands with my spouse. It is also hermeneutically accurate, so to speak, since it acknowledges—in harmony with the view of the publicity of the mental ventured in the previous chapter—that the agency of others can be there for us to see.

It is worth noting other happy consequences of McDowell's stance. For example, he has important things to say about the metaphysics of self (1994, pp. 99–104). He concurs with Strawson (1966, pp. 162–70) that if we seek the self purely in the domain of consciousness, the fact that self-identification is immune to error through misidentification will incline anyone who thinks the self is something substantial to portray it as simple and undifferentiated, like a Cartesian ego. The only alternative appears to be to deny the substantiality of the self and to treat it, as Kant did, as something purely formal: as the principle of the unity of consciousness. Thus we confront a dilemma: if the self is not an occult entity, it shrinks to a mere perspective. But a workable conception of second nature allows us to deny that the self

66   *The Formation of Reason*

inhabits only the realm of consciousness, and to identify it with the person, that is with a subject of experience who is in the world. This makes it possible to see a series of events in consciousness (a series of representations, as Kant would say) as a sequence of events in the life of a human being, events no more self-sufficient than, as McDowell pithily observes, a set of digestive events could be. The 'I think' that can accompany all my representations is displaced by the I whose representations they are: namely this human being, David Bakhurst. Once the philosopher has achieved a sense of our bodily presence as imbued with intentionality, then she can say, in a way faithful to common sense, that what one sees in the mirror is oneself, not simply the outer bodily shell of the authentic inner being.

Much of our discussion has focused on matters metaphysical. What of the epistemological dimensions of self and other? McDowell makes his appeal to second nature as part of a story about how thought can make genuine contact with reality, a story that dispels the appearance of an epistemological gap between mind and world. Moreover, the emphasis on *Bildung* acknowledges the relevance of the interaction of subjectivities from the outset of development. If 'through others we become ourselves', as Vygotsky once wrote (1997, p. 105), a gulf between minds is not built into the very idea of interpersonal relations. Of course, all this is speculative and largely negative in orientation. The arguments are directed to *what not to think* (do not let the self take up refuge in pure consciousness; do not split the mental and the bodily into different realms; do not identify nature with disenchanted reality). But if one heeds this advice, space emerges for a compelling picture of a self 'at home in the world'.

At the outset of this chapter, I suggested that educational theory and practice need to be informed by a satisfying vision of the relation of self and other. On the view we have endorsed, selves are persons—flesh-and-blood human beings who have acquired a second nature through initiation into culture.[29] Persons are open to the world in experience and thought, capable of knowledge and of rational action, and open to each other, their mindedness manifest in their life activity. Such a vision provides a helpful framework in which to frame issues of education. But more than this, education is a vital constituent of the vision itself, in virtue of the role it plays in the acquisition of the second nature essential to our community with the world and with other minded beings.

CONCLUSION: TWO CAUTIONARY NOTES

In concluding, I want to dampen the congratulatory tone of the previous section by sounding two cautionary notes. First, we should observe that although much ground has been gained, philosophical reflection on the problem of self and other can only take us so far. It is one thing to provide a satisfying framework in which issues of education may be cast, another to resolve those issues in a way that enhances the real life of education; one thing to give credibility to a conception of knowledge, another to consider what an educated person needs to know; one thing to show that minds can meet, another to consider how to facilitate their meeting. We will make a start (but only a start) on such issues in chapters 6 and 7. Similarly, even if no unbridgeable gulf between persons is built into the very idea of interpersonal relations, there are plenty of more mundane differences between people and failures of understanding that need to be overcome. The moral and political dimensions of the self–other problematic are not resolved just by the removal of bad philosophical reasons for thinking that interpersonal understanding and fellow-feeling are impossible. The contingent, this-worldly reasons for failing to find our feet with one another remain.

Similar remarks are relevant to our understanding our relation to the body. It is commonly complained that modern philosophy makes it impossible to get a satisfying view of this relation. This may be so, but do not think that such a conception naturally emerges once the follies of modern philosophy are dispelled. An illustration. An 11-year-old boy of my acquaintance, call him Sam, went through a period where he was 'grossed out' to the point of distress by his physicality. The thought that his body was flesh, meat, made him anxious. He was not so much afraid of being eaten, as of being the sort of thing that could be eaten. Sam's anxiety was certainly philosophical in character, though he was not saddled with it by having done philosophy: the problem of self and other in his own person was just there for him, as it were. He recoiled from the idea that he *is* a body, and he consoled himself with the thought that he was actually distinct from his body, at some remove from his fleshiness.

How might the present discussion help Sam with his predicament? What light has this chapter cast on the question we raised at the beginning: 'Are we our bodies?'? We might say that selves are persons and that persons are living human beings, where a living human being is an animal that has a certain characteristic mode of activity, one that involves coming to live a life in the space of reasons. Thus, when it comes to questions of survival, what is essential from the perspective of a person is the continuation of the life of the human being who the person is. We can say this without identifying person and body (just as we don't need to identify a house with the bricks and mortar that make it up (McDowell, 1997/1998a, p. 378)). But what is at issue is still the life of an animal, and that is likely to be too fleshy for Sam.

The point I want to stress is that dispelling false philosophical pictures of our relation to our bodies does not automatically reconcile us to our embodiment. If we are bodies, or are constituted by our bodies, what is the appropriate attitude to this fact? Is Sam wrong to feel fear, loathing and disgust? What standards of appropriateness should we deploy, and whence are we to derive them? Showing that we can be at home in the world, in McDowell's sense, does not guarantee that we will feel at home in our skins, or, for that matter, that we are at ease with others, appropriately sensitive to them, or any less lonely and bereft. Cures for philosophical pathologies do not treat more ordinary forms of distress, alienation, loneliness, wickedness, callousness, lack of compassion, and so on. Perhaps the best we can do is to stop philosophical distortion from making those concerns look more menacing than they are, but there is no guarantee that their proportions will be manageable. And when they are not, what we face are real problems in familial, educational and other contexts of everyday life that we need to address by more-than-philosophical means.[30]

My second note of caution returns us to matters theoretical. I have argued that, in order to attain what McDowell describes as 'a firm and integrated conception of ourselves as rational animals' (1997/1998a, p. 382), we must deploy what he elsewhere calls 'a seriously exploitable notion of second nature' (1994, p. 104).

However, a number of commentators, sympathetic and otherwise, maintain that McDowell's notion of second nature stands in need of development (see, e.g., Gubeljic et al., 2000; Gaskin, 2006, ch. 2, especially pp. 37–44; Fink, 2008; Halbig, 2008). Graham Macdonald, for example, argues that it would take some 'heavy-duty metaphysics' to justify McDowell's claim that exercises of rationality cannot be explained by the resources of natural science, especially once the latter are taken to encompass the functional explanations of evolutionary biology (Macdonald, 2006, p. 233). Other commentators recommend a different strategy, fearing that the more McDowell succeeds in establishing the *sui generis* character of the rational, the more counter-intuitive will be the idea that second nature is no less natural than first nature. Richard Bernstein, for example, argues that scientific naturalism, on the one hand, and McDowell's 'naturalism of second nature', on the other, represent two rival conceptions of nature. If calling second nature 'natural' is to be more than a verbal trick, the two conceptions must be reconciled to establish 'genuine continuity in the realm of nature'. Bernstein suggests that this project would entail the kind of conceptual revolution begun by C. S. Peirce in his quest for a thorough-going evolutionary naturalism (Bernstein, 2002, p. 23, n. 11). If these commentators are right, McDowell owes us nothing less than a constructive philosophy of nature.

In harmony with his minimalist approach to the characterisation of *Bildung*, McDowell contests this diagnosis, arguing that it misrepresents the role of second nature in his thinking. The point is to enable the thought that there is nothing contrary to nature about human rational powers just because they elude explanation by scientific means:

> [B]y dint of exploiting, in an utterly intuitive way, ideas like that of the patterns characteristic of the life of animals of a certain kind, we can insist that such phenomena [that exemplify free responsiveness to reasons], even though they are beyond the reach of natural-scientific understanding, are perfectly real, without thereby relegating them to the sphere of the occult or the supernatural. We can accept that a distinctively human life is characterized by a freedom that exempts its distinctive phenomena from natural-scientific intelligibility, without thereby being required to push it back into the region of darkness, the region supposedly occupied by phenomena that resist the light cast by natural science because they are occult or supernatural. (McDowell, 2008, p. 217)

Only if we make a present of the concept of nature to natural science do we force the burden of proof onto those who would claim that something can be both natural and escape natural-scientific explanation. But the burden of proof is not something we need to shoulder, by proving that reason is *sui generis*, on the one hand, and then 'unifying' reason and nature, on the other. This is to play by rules set by the scientific naturalist. Why not say instead that the explanatory resources of natural science, outstandingly good for so many purposes, are not compromised by the fact that we must draw on different resources to understand human responsiveness to reasons. Reality is one, but it is diverse, and it takes diverse means to render it intelligible in all its aspects.[31]

Although many find McDowell's reluctance to theorise second nature unsatisfactory, I have considerable sympathy with his stance.³² Nevertheless, as we saw in chapter 1, part of the attraction of McDowell's view in philosophy of education is the prominence it gives to *Bildung*, which is, after all, the process of the acquisition and refinement of second nature. And in that context, we surely cannot avoid questions about how to characterise the *Bildungsprozess*. In chapter 1, I took some small steps in the direction of such a characterisation, restricting myself to speculative reflection on facts in plain view. Even that is contentious enough, but it is far from the project of constructing a serious account of human development consistent with McDowell's insights. The latter project, though beyond the purview of this book, will demand that we address the respective contributions of first and second nature in development, and their interaction. Not that the project would compel the kind of philosophical projects McDowell's commentators want to force upon him, but it would require a willingness to say more about the formation of reason than McDowell is inclined to.

Yet although McDowell disavows the need to theorise second nature as such, it is not that we lack resources to elucidate the notion: we can explore those cognate ideas from which it draws its intelligibility. McDowell writes that 'human beings are unique among living things—outside the reach of the sort of understanding achievable by a scientific biology—in virtue of the freedom that belongs with our responsiveness to reasons as such' (2006b, p. 237). To understand the character of our second nature, we can do no better than to address the two key notions in this passage: freedom and responsiveness to reasons. This is a demanding task. It is one thing to counter those philosophical tendencies that act to pull apart the rational and the animal in our nature, as we have sought to do in this chapter. It is another to provide a rich and compelling portrait of rational agents. For McDowell, freedom and rationality are one. A rational agent is a source of judgement and action. She is in control of her thoughts and deeds. Rational agents are responsible, epistemically and morally, and they can be so precisely because there is a sense in which it is 'up to them' what to think and do. Yet there is something elusive about the relation of freedom and reason. We are most comfortable with the idea of freedom in situations where there is choice, where it is open to the agent to do one thing or another. But rationality often leaves us no choice about what to think or do. Indeed, rationality requires that we think and do precisely what is dictated by the best reasons. So how can it be that our freedom is exemplified in the exercise of rationality? This is the topic of the next chapter.

NOTES

1 P. F. Strawson explains: 'For [a subject] to have the idea [of himself as a subject of experience], it seems that it must be an idea of some particular thing of which he has experience, and which is set over against or contrasted with other things of which he has experience, but which are not himself. But if it is just an item *within* experience of which he has this idea, how can it be the idea of that which *has* all the experiences?' Strawson introduces this problem in a discussion of the conceptual scheme of an inhabitant of a purely auditory world, but he claims that the problem is 'completely general', applying 'as much to the ordinary as to the auditory world' (1959, p. 89).

2 As Cyril Connolly put it in *The Unquiet Grave*, 'We are all serving a life-sentence in the dungeon of self' (1944/2002, p. 199).
3 Social constructionists such as Gergen also represent themselves as dissolving or deconstructing the problems of traditional philosophy. But as I argued in chapter 2, it is hard to see constructionism of this kind as a genuinely post-philosophical position. If its more radical claims are not to be dismissed as empirical falsehoods, they must draw intelligibility from substantive philosophical commitments.
4 There was a time when I was quicker to trace all philosophical evils to Cartesianism. See, e.g., Bakhurst, 1991, pp. 200–12, 236–44, and Bakhurst and Dancy, 1988.
5 See Williams (1970a/1973) for an excellent (and critical) discussion of such reasons.
6 The Russian philosophers mentioned at the opening of chapter 1 might disagree. The fact that we can make ourselves objects of our own consciousness and transform ourselves in that light means that persons are always moving targets of their own self-understanding and thus cannot be identified with any static states of body or mind. In dialectical mood, this insight is expressed as the thesis that human beings are 'not identical with themselves' (in contrast to non-human animals that are said to be 'identical with their life activity'). The source of the insight is the section on alienated labour in Marx's *Economic and Philosophical Manuscripts* (1844/1977), which is in turn inspired by Hegel.
7 See Bakhurst, 2001b, for further treatment of this issue, and references to the relevant literature.
8 Indeed, in *The Bounds of Sense*, Strawson claims that when 'I' is used without need of empirical criteria of subject-identity (i.e., in the first-person case), it refers to a subject only because there are 'links' to those empirical criteria (1966, p. 165). The person who uses 'I' recognises that others identify her as the person she is only by the application of such empirical criteria.
9 The same is also true, of course, of the position of our limbs, which is usually known to us without observation.
10 As Davidson puts it, 'a man is the agent of an act if what he does can be described under an aspect that makes it intentional' (1971/1980, p. 46).
11 Of course, sometimes rational agents behave irrationally, but in such cases it is still true that there is some description of their action under which they know what they are doing.
12 Moran draws on Anscombe's work, rather than Strawson's, to make this point, but the latter would surely have approved. Moran's position also helps explain the immunity of the first-person pronoun to error through misidentification. When, in a process of deliberation, I form an intention to do so-and-so, I have unmediated first-person knowledge of my intention that leaves no room for the thought: Someone has formed an intention, but is it me?
13 A similar objection is made, rather more aggressively, by Sebastian Rödl (2007, p. 128, n. 24) (though he would likely complain that what I say in the next section misses the point no less than Strawson does).
14 It is surprising that in 1966 Strawson could write: 'The topic of personal identity has been well discussed in recent philosophy. I shall take the matter as understood' (1966, p. 164, n. 1). Soon thereafter, there was an explosion of literature on the subject that included many of the papers now considered classics (e.g., Williams (1970c/1973) and Parfit (1971)).
15 To chart the development of Wiggins's view, see Wiggins 1967; 1980, ch. 6; 1987; 1996; 2001, ch. 7. The material in this section and the next is drawn from Bakhurst, 2005c.
16 McDowell concurs and cites Wiggins with approval (McDowell, 1997/1998a, pp. 360–1).
17 Wiggins's target includes social constructionism, but he has in mind any view that thinks it is somehow up to us how to draw the boundaries of the concept *person*.
18 To say that the psychological 'supervenes' on the physical is to say (a) that any two creatures identical in physical respects will be identical in psychological respects, and (b) a creature's psychological properties cannot change without a change in its physical properties. Although philosophers of mind tend to agree that the mental supervenes on the physical, there is much less

Self and Other   71

   consensus about the metaphysics of supervenience and how the supervenience-relation is to be distinguished from the relation of identity.
19 See the discussion of Davidson in chapter 1 above.
20 Of course, interpretation is sometimes a one-way process. When I make sense of what someone is doing on film, or seek to understand a text, there is no possibility of reciprocal understanding. I seek to attune myself to someone or something that cannot attune itself to me. However, I think we do better if we construe interpretation in such cases on the model of engagement with an interlocutor (we take our interpretation to be responsible to what the person on film, or the author, *might have said* in response), rather than treat unidirectional interpretation as the paradigm from which conversation is a departure, as if it were a merely contingent complexity that sometimes the object of interpretation is itself an interpreter.
21 See, e.g., Wiggins, 2006, pp. 119–20, 132 and 137, where he explicitly deploys the term, and 336, n. 15, where he calls for an 'effort to reconstruct a natural history of the grasping of ethical concepts and the elaboration and handing down of the language in which they are expressed'.

   Although it is natural to associate the idea of second nature with Aristotle (McDowell illustrates the notion by invoking Aristotle's view of moral development), the term does not actually figure in Aristotle's works (McDowell (1996/1998a, p. 184) writes that it is 'all but explicit' in Aristotle). As Gubeljic et al. observe in their excellent discussion, the term does appear in Augustine's writings, but there it has negative connotations, representing a corruption of God's first nature. It is only with Hegel that a positive view of second nature emerges. See Gubeljic et al., 2000; Halbig, 2008; and McDowell's responses, 2000b, pp. 97–9, and 2008, pp. 219–25).
22 It is sometimes supposed that to speak of the human infant as an animal falsely implies that the infant is self-sufficient. John Macmurray, for example, complains that the fact that a baby cannot act intentionally and think for himself does not signify 'that he is merely an animal organism; if it did it would mean that he could live by the satisfaction of organic impulse, by reaction to stimulus, by instinctive adaptation to his natural environment. But this is totally untrue' (Macmurray, 1961, p. 51). However, my reference to the child's animal nature carries no such implication of self-sufficiency. On the contrary, I hold that it is a feature of the kind of animals that human beings are that they, in Macmurray's words, 'can live only through other people and in dynamic relation with them', and I agree wholeheartedly with him that 'the human infant is not in direct relation to nature. His environment is a home, which is not a natural habitat, but a human creation, an institution providing in advance for human needs, biological and personal, through human foresight and artifice ... [The human infant] cannot, even theoretically, live an isolated existence; ... he is not an independent individual. He lives a common life as one term in a personal relation. Only in the process of development does he learn to achieve a relative independence, and that only by appropriating the techniques of a rational social tradition. All the infant's activities in maintaining his existence are shared and co-operative. ... His rationality is already present, though only germinally, in the fact that he lives and can only live by communication. His essential natural endowment is the impulse to communicate with another human being. Perhaps his cry of distress when he awakens alone in the night in his cot in the nursery has no meaning for *him*, but for the mother it has' (pp. 49–51). These wonderful passages reveal something important about us as animals. To deny this is to set up a false dichotomy between the animal and the rational, the organic and the personal. I am grateful to Andrew Davis for drawing my attention to Macmurray.
23 Relevant here is the following marvellous passage from the *Philosophical Investigations*: 'But can't I imagine that the people around me are automata, lack consciousness, even though they behave in the same way as usual?—If I imagine it now—alone in my room—I see people with fixed looks (as in a trance) going about their business—the idea is perhaps a little uncanny. But just try to keep hold of this idea in the midst of your ordinary intercourse with others, in the street, say! Say to yourself, for example: "The children over there are mere automata; all their

liveliness is mere automatism." And you will either find these words becoming quite meaningless; or you will produce in yourself some kind of uncanny feeling, or something of the sort.

'Seeing a living human being as an automaton is analogous to seeing one figure as a limiting case or variant of another; the cross-pieces of a window as a swastika, for example.' (Wittgenstein, 1953, §420).

24 As I have observed, McDowell stresses that the notion of second nature has application to non-human animals. They too can acquire propensities though 'education, habituation, or training', a point he illustrates with reference to dogs and cats (see, e.g., McDowell, 2008—though it is noteworthy that these are domestic animals, trained in the circumstances of a human community where second nature is operative). It is important, however, to note a number of significant differences between the second natures of human and non-human animals, over and above the fact that human beings are distinguished by the acquisition of rational powers. First, as the term 'second nature' is used in everyday discourse, it suggests acquired behaviour that is so integrated into a creature's spontaneous activity that it is as-if instinctual. There is an obvious sense in which this is true of human conceptual capacities, especially in the way that they are brought into play in experience. But at the same time it is vital to McDowell's account that the exercise of human conceptual capacities is in principle open to rational scrutiny. Indeed, we are under a standing obligation to subject their exercise to critical reflection. Second, although, as McDowell makes clear, *Bildung* does not bring about 'a transfiguration ... of everything that happens in a human life' (1994, p. 183), the acquisition of a second nature in the human case is *pervasive* in a way that has no parallel in the case of non-human animals. Our rational capacities make it possible for us to take an attitude to every aspect of our lives, and at least to this extent human second nature leaves nothing untouched.

25 'Is it not better to conceive of a human person as a creature with a *natural capacity*, which may or may not be realized, for reason, morality, Bildung ... and better to say that these achievements *fulfil the potentialities* of human beinghood/personhood?' (Wiggins, 2005, p. 475; his ellipsis).

26 Accordingly, we will need to countenance transitional or twilight states where the question of whether *N* is a person has no sharp answer. But this is not to grant that, where the foothold of the concept *person* is firm, personhood admits of degrees.

27 A sea-change may be about to occur within the broadly analytic tradition. Sebastian Rödl's fascinating book *Self-Consciousness* (2007) concludes with a chapter on second-person thought, and in moral philosophy there is growing interest in distinctively 'second-personal reasons', notably in the work of Stephen Darwall (2006). Beyond the confines of the analytic tradition, the second person has received more attention. A good example is Martin Buber's influential *I and Thou*, which maintains that 'a person makes his appearance by entering into relation with other persons' (1923/1959, p. 62). Such themes are modified and intensified by Emmanuel Levinas, for whom the idea that we are always already addressed by the other is central to his understanding of the human condition (hence the slogan 'ethics before ontology') (see, e.g., Levinas, 1958/1989 and 1984/1989). I must also mention Felix Mikhailov, whose writings contain many interesting reflections on the development of intersubjectivity. Mikhailov deploys the notion of *obrashchenie*, which translates clumsily as 'addressivity', but which embodies the (ultimately Fichtean) idea of mutual recognition contained in the meeting of subjectivities in second-personal interaction (see Mikhailov, 2003; cf. Franks, 2005, cited in chapter 1 above, note 19). Another relevant thinker, now often overlooked, is Macmurray, who writes: 'Any agent is necessarily in relation to the Other. Apart from this essential relation he does not exist. But, further, the Other in this constitutive relation must itself be personal. Persons, therefore, are constituted by their mutual relation to one another. "I" exist only as one element in the complex "You and I"' (Macmurray, 1961, p. 24).

28 Some read McDowell as including under the concept of second nature both the rational capacities of human beings *and* such features of reality—e.g., ethical reasons, meanings, values,

Self and Other 73

etc.—which those rational capacities enable us to discern and which cannot be reduced to, or otherwise grounded in, first-natural facts (see, e.g., Halbig, 2008). This is an inviting reading, since McDowell contrasts both with first nature. But McDowell himself rejects this interpretation, insisting that 'second nature' should be reserved for 'a region of the nature of human beings (and less interestingly, other animals) themselves', rather than for 'an evaluative and normative level in the reality that human beings confront' (McDowell, 2008, p. 223). Several considerations may motivate McDowell's insistence on this point. First, he resists the amalgamation of all the scientifically intractable features of reality into a single category in a way that would warrant the claim that reality has a two-level structure (2008, p. 222) or that the second-natural is 'an ontologically distinct compartment of reality' (p. 221). Second, while McDowell portrays second nature as 'a cultural product' (1996/1998a, p. 194), he is not committed to a culturalist view of everything that resists explanation in natural-scientific terms. We will revisit these issues in chapter 5.

29 Indeed, it might be said that our picture enables us to displace the concept *self* in favour of the concept *person*, and this is a salutary consequence.

30 Smeyers et al. (2007) are more optimistic that, where philosophical puzzlement is a reflection of concerns and anxieties deep in the human condition, a form of philosophy suitably inspired by Wittgenstein's therapeutic approach might speak not only to the philosophical problems themselves, but also to their sources. They argue that philosophy so conceived might have an important educative role: 'Such a philosophy would not, of course, be the preserve of a professionalized discipline ... but something closer, as Cavell puts this, to the "education of grownups" ... Our account of the qualities of such an education [involves] modulations of the theme of return—of turning away from the extravagances of wonder, or the false securities of metaphysics, or fake identities or phoney happiness, and, by a number of routes, towards the ordinary' (p. 235). I do not mean to preclude such a conception of a 'mature philosophy'. My concern is just that it is one thing for philosophy to return us to the ordinary, another for philosophy to redeem what it finds there.

31 McDowell goes so far as to say that 'the only unity there needs to be in the idea of the natural, as it applies, on the one hand, to the intelligibility of physical and merely biological phenomena (themselves needing to be differentiated for some purposes ...), and, on the other, to the intelligibility of rational activity, is captured by a contrast with the idea of the supernatural—the spooky or the occult' (2000b, p. 99). I think this is too extreme an assertion, in tension with the moral of this chapter. To address the problem of self and other in our own person, we need to understand ourselves as a unity of the biological and the rational. As I tried to show above, the notion of second nature, properly deployed, helps us achieve this. McDowell is right that this achievement does not need to be underwritten by a substantive philosophy of nature. Better to add, however, that if there seems to be a pressing philosophical issue over unity, then our account of second nature may have gone awry, than to try to shrug off the problem of unity altogether. Persons, after all, are living expressions of the supposedly-problematic unity and that unity is visible in their development once we give ourselves the chance to see it aright.

32 As might be expected, in light of my remarks at the outset of this chapter about the need to dissolve the grand problems of self and other, rather than to address them by constructive philosophical theorising.

4
Freedom, Reflection and the Sources of Normativity

In light of the role played by *Bildung* in the formation of our rational capacities, and the intimate relation between reason and freedom, we can describe *Bildung*'s proper end as freedom: the formation of an autonomous subject, creative, critical and in control of herself and her life.

There may appear to be an air of paradox about this position, for there is often thought to be a tension between views that stress the depth of our connectedness to others and those that emphasise the value of autonomy. For example, when Ilyenkov argued that initiation into culture is a precondition of our attaining the status of rational animals, he was sometimes criticised for representing individuals as 'products' of society. His opponents took such views to play into Stalinist myths about the creation of a 'New Soviet Man' and to legitimate education as social engineering. These critics sought an antidote by portraying autonomy as a quality possessed by individuals prior to and independently of social interaction, as a fact of individual human nature. Yet Ilyenkov, and like-minded thinkers such as Vygotsky and Mikhailov, saw initiation into culture as a precondition of the emergence of *self-determining* individuals, so their appeal to the formative influence of enculturation was no slight to autonomy or individuality. There may be a kind of pleasing irony in the fact that our dependence upon others is a precondition of our independence of mind, but there is no deep conflict between *Bildung* and the ideal of autonomy.

There is, however, much that needs to be said about the freedom that *Bildung* makes possible. We are accustomed to construing notions such as freedom and autonomy in terms of choice and decision. I am free in so far as I can choose what to do and act in light of that choice.[1] Much philosophical discussion about freedom and autonomy therefore concerns the conditions of free action. Yet the self-determination that is *Bildung*'s end is a far richer and more controversial notion. It governs not only free action, but the exercise of thought. And in the latter is included not just the play of the imagination, but all exercises of the intellect, including judgement about what is the case.

The Formation of Reason, First Edition. David Bakhurst.
© 2011 David Bakhurst. Published 2011 by Blackwell Publishing Ltd.

Such a view has resonance for educational theory and practice. It enables us to think of freedom as an educational ideal, and, moreover, freedom understood as manifest not just in unconstrained acts of will, but in rational agency and spontaneity of mind. Of course, the view that there is an essential connection between education and freedom is longstanding. The idea that education should bring liberation through the acquisition of knowledge and the cultivation of virtue goes back to antiquity, and in recent philosophy of education emphasis has often been placed on personal autonomy understood as the ability to make informed choices.[2] It is important that the conception of autonomy under consideration here is more ambitious. What is at issue is the cultivation of a certain kind of being, one that is autonomous in the sense of being the author of its life. Such a being is, as McDowell might put it, an inhabitant of the realm of freedom, and its freedom is manifest not just in acts of choice, but in all its rational activity, including thinking and judging.[3]

This last view is certainly contentious. Can it really be correct to speak of freedom when considering the domain of belief? After all, many judgements are forced upon us by evidence or wrung from us by experience. In what sense, then, are they freely made? One reason to maintain that thinking must essentially involve an element of freedom is that we hold people responsible for what they think. We blame people for forming opinions on inadequate grounds, praise them for their insightful, well-founded beliefs, and such praise and blame would not be appropriate, it is argued, unless thinkers were in control of what they think. But how are we to understand the relevant sense of control?

McDOWELL ON JUDGEMENT

Let us begin with a quotation from McDowell. He writes:

> [J]udging, making up our minds what to think, is something for which we are, in principle, responsible—something we freely do, as opposed to something that merely happens in our lives. Of course, a belief is not always, or even typically, a result of our exercising this freedom to decide what to think. But even when a belief is not freely adopted, it is an actualization of capacities of a kind, the conceptual, whose paradigmatic mode of actualization is in the exercise of freedom that judging is. This freedom, exemplified in responsible acts of judging, is essentially a matter of being answerable to criticism in the light of rationally relevant considerations. So the realm of freedom, at least the realm of freedom of judging, can be identified with the space of reasons. (1998c, p. 434 [2009a, p. 6])

There are four—no doubt related—notions of intellectual freedom that might be discerned in this passage:

1 The emphasis on the mental act of *judgement* evokes the Kantian idea that the spontaneity of the intellect is manifest in acts of judgement because judgement involves the active deployment of concepts to form a thought.
2 Intellectual freedom is 'freedom to decide what to think'.

3 Intellectual freedom is 'essentially a matter of being answerable to criticism in the light of rationally relevant considerations'.
4 The final sentence of the passage evokes the Kantian doctrine that freedom is essentially related to, or is to be identified with, rational necessitation; we are free because we are, and in so far as we are, responsive to reasons, even where those reasons necessitate what we must think or do.

I will say nothing about the first notion, and postpone discussion of the fourth until later. For now, let us consider (2) and (3).

McDowell tells us that judgements are decisions about what to think, for which we are accountable precisely because they are freely made. Sometimes, of course, we form beliefs without deliberation: we look out the window and see it is raining. But even in such cases, we exercise the same conceptual capacities that we employ in making judgements on the basis of deliberation and reasoning. These are the capacities that empower us to make up our mind when we need to, and their deployment can be seen as expressive of our freedom even when belief formation is immediate.

It is clear, however, that the idea of 'deciding what to think' needs elucidation. Deciding what to think is very unlike, say, deciding where to eat dinner, for the reason that belief is not under the control of the will. Even in cases where our coming to believe is the result of extensive deliberation and enquiry, belief formation is not the outcome of choice, for rationality requires us to believe what we find we have compelling grounds to believe. If I am a judge trying to decide whether the accused is guilty, I deliberate to establish what I must believe in light of the evidence. It is 'up to me' whether the accused is guilty only in the sense that it is my responsibility to pronounce a verdict. What is not up to me is whether he committed the crime, and whether, if the evidence so suggests, I should believe that he did. Belief aims at truth—at conformity with the facts—and 'deciding what to think' cannot be a matter of choosing what to believe, but of finding a perspective from which there is one and only one thing to believe.[4]

McDowell's claim that intellectual freedom is 'essentially a matter of being answerable to criticism' can also seem curious. Perhaps the existence of intellectual freedom is a precondition of what we might call 'cognitive accountability', but it can be hard to see how it can *consist* in this. The point, however, is that we can exercise control over what we believe by subjecting our beliefs to critical scrutiny. An epistemically responsible subject recognises a standing obligation to ensure her conception of the world is in good order by being ever ready to reflect upon the grounds of her beliefs. Reflection and freedom are related not just because the critical examination of our beliefs requires agency, but because reflection ensures that our beliefs are held by us because we do (or could) endorse them in light of the grounds for so doing. This idea of reflective endorsement captures part of the idea of 'deciding what to think', just as reflection suggests a form of control over our mental lives that is not control by the will. Reflection, thus understood, is a central ingredient of the idea of the self-conscious rational subject, in control of her mental life.[5]

OWENS'S CRITIQUE

The idea that reflection is the source of intellectual freedom has been attacked by David Owens in *Reason without Freedom* (2000), a book that targets McDowell and other supposedly like-minded philosophers, such as Christine Korsgaard.

Owens endorses a broadly internalist view of justification, according to which a subject's beliefs are justified by reasons, and reasons are states of which subjects are, or can be, aware. It follows that a rational subject must be able to think about her reasons and be prepared to endorse them. Owens denies, however, that such reflection empowers us to control our beliefs in a way that would license talk of epistemic freedom.

Since the proper aim of first-order deliberation is simply the conformity of belief to evidence, Owens concludes that the supposed instrument of reflective control must be higher-order judgements about what we ought to believe, judgements made by reflecting on the quality of our reasons and their fidelity to sound epistemic norms. But such higher-order judgements would permit a subject to control her beliefs only if they are able rationally to motivate belief. On such a picture, I reflect on my grounds for belief and make a judgement, 'I ought to believe that p', and having made that judgement, I am rational only if I believe that p. Such judgements would enable us to control our beliefs because they would fix what it is rational for us to believe. But, Owens argues, the picture is flawed. It is always our non-reflective awareness of the considerations in favour of believing that rationally motivates belief, not higher-order reflection upon those reasons.

This might seem plausible in, say, cases of perception where belief is simply compelled by evidence, but is there not an efficacious role for reflective judgement in cases where the results of first-order deliberation do not so rigidly determine what we should believe? Owens does not think so. He maintains that I can form a belief only if I take myself to have conclusive grounds; that is, grounds that establish its truth. This is because knowledge requires conclusive grounds, and I cannot believe that p unless I think I know that p. But if I think I have conclusive grounds, then those grounds rationally compel my belief, and reflective judgement is redundant; and if I think I lack conclusive grounds, then reflective judgement about what I ought to believe will be impotent (Owens, 2000, p. 111). So the notion of reflective control is empty.

But might not the thought that I have conclusive grounds *itself* be a product of reflection? Owens denies this. We form beliefs when we get the impression that we have conclusive grounds, but what creates that impression is not reflection, but our awareness of the evidence that favours belief in combination with various pragmatic considerations (e.g., how much time there is to deliberate, how important the issue is, how costly it would be to enquire further, and so on). Pragmatic considerations are necessary because the evidence before us is almost always *in*conclusive. We will not believe unless we think there is sufficient evidence to compel belief, but what counts as sufficient in any case is determined by matters pragmatic. But, if this is so, reflection will be powerless, because no amount of reflection on inconclusive evidence or on pragmatic considerations can rationally motivate belief (Owens, 2000, p. 45).

This is not intended as a sceptical point. Owens is not saying that reflection threatens to destroy our beliefs by exposing the fact that that they are based on inconclusive evidence supplemented by pragmatic considerations. We can acknowledge that adherence to fallibilist and pragmatic epistemic norms is perfectly reasonable. His point is that what we believe is simply not under our control; as he puts it, 'In the end, it is *the world* which determines what (and whether) I believe, not *me*' (p. 12). So when it comes to rationally influencing belief, reflection is neither here nor there: it does not motivate belief, and it does not undermine it either.[6]

If intellectual freedom is a chimera, what would Owens have us say of epistemic responsibility? Owens argues that epistemologists typically adopt a 'juridical' theory of responsibility, according to which we can be held to account only for things over which we can or should exercise control. Expressed in a slogan, '*nothing is down to you unless it is also up to you*' (p. 21). But the juridical theory is false. We rightly hold people responsible for their moral character—praise them for their virtues and blame them for their vices—even though such traits are not under their direct control. Owens suggests we apply the same model to epistemology. There are epistemic virtues, such as wisdom, judiciousness, sharpness; and vices, like dogmatism or gullibility. These virtues and vices directly affect the degree and character of our responsiveness to reasons, and we are appropriately praised or blamed when we manifest them, even though they cannot be controlled by the will or by reflection. If we put the notion of responsiveness to reasons, rather than agency or control, at the centre of our theory of responsibility, we can abandon intellectual freedom while preserving epistemic responsibility.

Owens thinks that the notion of intellectual freedom is part of the doctrine of epistemic self-reliance that, since the early-modern period, has had so powerful an influence on epistemology and, we might add, on educational theory and practice. On this view, each individual thinking subject, if she is to be entitled to her beliefs, must be able to authenticate them herself. Unless subjects are in a position to make transparent their grounds for belief, they are not in control of their mental lives, and if such control were not possible they could not be responsible for their convictions. Owens maintains that if we abandon this obsession with control, we can combine a broadly internalist view of justification with a much more psychologically realistic account of belief—one that makes it possible, for example, to explain the epistemology of memory and testimony, which have always thwarted traditional internalist accounts.[7]

DEFENDING INTELLECTUAL FREEDOM

Owens's argument is nicely constructed, but much of what he says does not ring true as a criticism of McDowell. McDowell is committed to the idea that persons are in control of their mental lives, in the sense that persons stand to their own beliefs as agents rather than spectators, agents who are under a standing obligation to keep their epistemic houses in order. It is up to each of us to ensure that our beliefs are not inconsistent or ill-founded, that our desires and intentions are reasonable, and so on. This is what it is to be a rational agent. In chapter 2, I drew on Moran's work to argue that such a conception is key to a proper understanding of first-person authority. The relevant notion of control to which this view is committed is significantly weaker than that presupposed by the idea of the epistemically self-reliant individual that Owens attacks.

In his writings on epistemology, McDowell explicitly argues that our 'powers of acquiring and retaining knowledge that common sense has no hesitation in ascribing to us are at the mercy of factors that cannot be made subject to our rational control' (McDowell, 1993/1998b, pp. 442–3). In everyday discourse, we would have no compunction about crediting someone with knowledge that there is a cat on the mat in virtue of her seeing, or remembering, or hearing from a competent authority that there is a cat on the mat. In each such case, the subject's knowing depends on the obtaining of factors that are not under her control (e.g., she must not have been the victim of an optical illusion, the informant must not have made a mistake, and so on). Knowledge is, as McDowell puts it, a 'standing in the space of reasons' and whether a person enjoys that standing can depend on luck, on the world 'doing her the favour' of being as it seems to be (see McDowell, 1995/1998b, p. 396).

McDowell is as critical as Owens about standard internalist epistemologies that would restrict questions of justification to an internal domain over which the subject supposedly possesses full control: namely, how she *takes* things to be (i.e., the domain of her beliefs and perceptual appearances). Since nothing can guarantee that how a subject takes things to be is how they actually are, scepticism is a constant threat to such positions. McDowell also disparages externalist alternatives according to which whether the subject knows depends on causal factors operating independently of the subject's standing in the space of reasons (e.g., on whether the fact that *p* obtains and stands in appropriate causal relations to the subject's belief that *p*, etc.). The effect of externalism, he argues, is to deny that knowledge is a standing in the space of reasons at all.[8] McDowell complains that epistemology overlooks the position he favours precisely because it is in the grip of the 'fantasy' that reason has 'a sphere of operation within which it is capable of ensuring, without being beholden to the world, that one's postures are all right' (1995/1998b, p. 405). The fact is that 'we are vulnerable to the world's playing us false; and when the world does not play us false we are indebted to it. But that is something we must learn to live with, rather than recoiling into the fantasy of a sphere in which our control is total' (pp. 407–8). To reject the fantasy of total control, however, is not to foreswear the more modest notion of control that is central to the idea that a person is a subject of a mental life, responsible for her beliefs. Indeed, the very idea of a standing in the space of reasons presupposes the notion of epistemic responsibility, which in turn assumes the idea of a subject in control (but not total control) of her thoughts (see McDowell, 1993/1998b, p. 430). Knowledge is a standing that can be had only by a being capable of epistemic responsibility, even if it is a standing that ineradicably depends on cooperation from the world.

Owens would no doubt question whether there is room for the supposedly more modest notion of control McDowell wants. Here McDowell's conception of reflection carries much of the explanatory burden. The primary idea is simply openness to criticism: the standing willingness to be alive to considerations that might bring one's beliefs into question. In one way, this idea of reflection is more ambitious than the one Owens targets, because McDowell envisages reflection asking difficult questions about the adequacy of our empirical concepts and methods of thinking (McDowell, 1994, p. 40). But in another respect, it is less ambitious, for there is no suggestion that reflection issues in higher-order judgements that possess intrinsic authority over what we must believe. On such a view, reflection is not a supplement to our responsiveness to reasons, so much as a component of it—a feature of the distinctive kind of responsiveness to reasons exhibited by self-conscious rational beings.[9]

Owens would likely protest that reflection so conceived is simply the capacity to ponder and evaluate epistemic reasons. How does such a capacity enable us to control what we believe? The answer is this. We can say that although reflection does not control what we have a *right* to believe—which is determined by the evidence—there is a perfectly straightforward sense in which it helps us control whether we allow ourselves to err, whether we are guilty of poor judgement, jumping to conclusions, prejudice, and so on. This might seem to make reflective control purely retrospective, especially if we focus on such classic epistemological examples as acquiring the belief that it is raining by looking out of the window. In such cases, reflection is confined to retrospective questioning (Do these spots on the window really mean rain?). But consider a more complex, though no less ordinary, case of enquiry, or what McDowell calls 'active empirical thinking' or deliberation (1994, p. 12). Suppose I ask myself whether one of my acquaintances is trustworthy. Here it seems entirely appropriate to describe me as trying to 'decide what to think' about him. And in this process, reflection figures as a precondition of responsible judgement. I need to evaluate evidence carefully and critically. I need to consider the judgement of others, alive to the possibility of prejudice or deceit. I may need to ponder whether the conceptions of trust current in our culture are adequate. I must also worry about the extent to which it is appropriate to press reflective questions, and this involves asking whether there are legitimate grounds to call into question my settled beliefs on the subject. The answer is clearly a matter of judgement. Of course, I cannot control whether I should believe this person to be trustworthy. That is for the evidence to decide. But I can control whether I allow the evidence to decide the matter and whether I remain alive to fallibility. Such control is not purely retrospective; it is as necessary when we set out to form a view as when we scrutinise beliefs we find ourselves saddled with.[10]

Owens's view is distorted by his conviction that we cannot believe unless we are willing to claim knowledge. Surely, I might conclude that I must think of my acquaintance as a shifty character, without claiming to know that he is one, because I have good, yet not conclusive, grounds for this belief. There can be a significant gap between what it is rational to believe and what it is permissible to claim to know.[11] This is in part because pragmatic considerations often operate in far less subterranean ways than Owens suggests. We make decisions, determined by context, about how much evidence is appropriate to collect, what level of scrutiny to subject it to, and so on. When we are conscious of these decisions, we may be willing to assert belief, but not knowledge. This is again a matter of judgement. For McDowell, we exhibit our intellectual freedom precisely when we administer our conception of the world with sensitivity to such considerations. This is as true when reason is in the service of high theory as when it is exploring such mundane matters as the trustworthiness of an acquaintance.

Owens draws a sharp contrast between the role of reflection in theoretical and in practical reasoning. He argues that action, unlike belief, *is* under reflective control. In practical deliberation we are often aware that our reasons for action are inconclusive. After reflecting upon our grounds for action, and upon relevant pragmatic constraints (e.g., the urgency of acting soon), we make a practical judgement about what to do. Such a judgement is an executive decision that has intrinsic authority: once the agent has decided to ϕ, and formed the intention to ϕ, the agent cannot be rational unless he ϕs (Owens, 2000, p. 111). Thus, such practical judgements allow us to control what it is rational for us to do. This is the source of practical freedom, the kind of freedom that Owens thinks really matters, but there is, he argues, no parallel for theoretical reason.

But a parallel can be discerned. In active empirical thinking I can come to a view about what I ought to believe, despite my inclination not to. Admittedly, I do not make an 'executive decision' about what to believe; rather, I resolve to believe what I recognise I must believe. Matters are similar in practical reasoning where we see that action is required by moral considerations. In such cases, practical judgement is not an executive decision, but a resolution to do what we must. In these cases, part of reflection's role is to ensure that we remain vigilant for the possibility of error. But here there enters another dimension to reflection, merely noted above. By reflecting on our reasons, we ensure that they move us *because* we endorse them as the grounds of our thoughts or deeds. Through reflection, our responsiveness to reasons is mediated by our appreciation of those reasons for what they are, and the reasons compel us rationally in virtue of that recognition. Once again, reflection is an aspect of our responsiveness to reasons, not a supplement to it.

This brings us to the fourth dimension of intellectual freedom that we discerned in the quotation from McDowell considered at the outset of this chapter: the Kantian idea of the coincidence of freedom and rational necessitation. Owens takes Korsgaard to be denying 'that our beliefs need be dominated by evidence any more than our actions are dominated by desire' (2000, p. 10). But a proponent of intellectual freedom need not hold that such freedom requires escape from the domination of evidence. The crucial thing is that it should be *evidence* that dominates our beliefs—that is, considerations that provide reasons for belief, that influence us rationally—and not something else. What is it, then, to have one's thoughts and actions guided or compelled by reasons? For McDowell, it is constitutive of rational necessitation that it either does, or could, proceed via the mediation of reflective endorsement. We can understand our thoughts and actions as guided by reasons only in so far as those reasons are something we can, and would, acknowledge.

Reflective endorsement is an important constituent of self-consciousness; by endorsing our reasons, we make them our own, and we recognise the beliefs and actions that issue from them as aspects of our lives for which we must take responsibility.[12]

In this Kantian framework, if reflection is portrayed as liberating us from something, it is not from domination by reasons, but from the domination of thought and action by non-rational determination. Here we are returned to an important theme in our socio-historical account of human development. As McDowell puts it, human beings are born mere animals; at birth their mode of life consists in responding to a succession of biological needs. But through *Bildung*, human beings become thinkers and agents, as they are initiated into language and acquire powers of conceptual thought. These powers enable them to judge and act in light of reasons, thereby controlling their lives rather than living as playthings of non-rational causal forces. Thus we become persons, whose lives are lived in the world, with its infinite horizons, rather than played out in a local environment, as the lives of non-human animals are.

Given the stark contrast between the causal and the rational that marks so much Kantian and post-Kantian philosophy, it is important to recall that McDowell does not think of enculturation as somehow lifting us out of nature. What we acquire through *Bildung* is a second nature, and its acquisition is part of normal human maturation.[13] As McDowell puts it, we are animals whose natural being is 'permeated with rationality' (1994, p. 85). It is true, as we saw in chapter 3, that second nature cannot be understood using explanatory tools designed to render intelligible 'first nature'—the nomological framework of the natural sciences. The lives of rational animals must be understood 'from within'; this is a hermeneutical project rather than a causal-explanatory one. But second nature is no less natural for all that.[14]

FREEDOM AND THE SOURCES OF NORMATIVITY

Let us take stock. In response to Owens's arguments, I noted that McDowell expressly repudiates the image of the epistemically self-sufficient subject, whose reason occupies 'a province within which it has absolute control over the acceptability of positions achievable by its exercise, without laying itself open to risk from an unkind world' (McDowell, 1993/1998b, p. 442). Rejecting this view, however, is compatible with embracing a more modest, and more realistic, picture of the respects in which rational agents are in control of their mental lives. I tried to bring out how reflection, conceived as openness to criticism, enables us to exercise control over our beliefs, and how active empirical thinking can involve something appropriately described as 'deciding what to think'. In this way I sought to give content to the second and third ideas found in the quotation from McDowell with which this chapter began. Towards the end of the last section I turned to another idea in the quoted passage—the Kantian theme of the coincidence of freedom and rational necessitation. I argued that reflective endorsement is an essential component of responsiveness to reasons: an agent thinks or acts *for a reason* only if she does or could endorse the grounds of her thoughts or actions.[15] Thus in so far as reflective endorsement is itself a mode of intellectual freedom, responsiveness to reasons presupposes intellectual freedom. Furthermore, our responsiveness to reasons in turn manifests our freedom because the thoughts and actions of a being guided, or compelled, by rational considerations cannot be seen as the outcome of non-rational causal processes, and transcending the nomological order of natural science is, of course, traditionally seen as a mark of freedom.[16] Finally, I tied this view of responsiveness to reasons into the socio-historical framework, representing it as an achievement made possible by *Bildung*.

Someone might complain that my strategy so far has been insufficiently ambitious. I have spoken of the Kantian idea of the coincidence of freedom and rational necessitation. 'Coincidence' here is a weasel word. Strictly speaking, the Kantian thesis, as McDowell endorses it, is that 'rational necessitation is not just compatible with freedom but constitutive of it' (McDowell, 1994, p. 5). On this view, which is a staple of the rationalist tradition after Kant, our freedom is manifest in our subordination to rational requirements: when we think what we must think because we must think it and do what we must do because we must do it.[17] It might be argued that the way to refute Owens is not to pussyfoot around the concepts of reflection and deciding what to think, which a sceptic about intellectual freedom will never find adequate, but to make proper sense of this bold rationalist thesis.

The idea that rational necessitation is *constitutive* of freedom suggests that we are free just to the extent that we respond appropriately to rational requirements, that the finer our appreciation of what we must think and do, the greater is our freedom. This is a difficult thought to capture. Consider the example of a concert pianist who produces a brilliant interpretation of a Beethoven sonata. Her achievement consists in her ability to act on her perception of how the work ought to be played, a perception that may leave little or no room for choice once she has established a particular interpretative context.[18] We are impressed by her authority, by the fact that she is in control of her performance, and that the performance is, as it were, her utterance. If her performance represents an exhilarating manifestation of freedom, this is not because it is open to her to perform the piece differently, or to perform it less well, but because she succeeds in playing it as the context requires it must be played. Thus her freedom is expressed precisely through subordination to a kind of necessity. It is an expression of the powers of a being that can conform its behaviour to ideals.

Similar remarks might be made about a scholar who, in debate, succeeds in perfectly capturing the essence of the matter, in saying exactly what the subject under discussion demands be said. The thinker is able to bring the facts of the matter into view; to show how there is nothing else to think.[19] As a manifestation of freedom, it is possible only in virtue of conformity to rational necessity. We might say that the pianist and the scholar are free in so far as they are able to discern the topography of the space of reasons and, therefore, to move effortlessly across it.[20]

A natural suggestion is that we can make the constitutive thesis palatable by introducing a further Kantian idea: that the normative constraints to which we subordinate ourselves are in fact constituted *by us*. In Kant's moral philosophy the idea that we must conform to the moral law is coupled with the claim that the moral law is one we give ourselves and is thus the supreme expression of our autonomy. Though the normativity of reasons often takes the form of constraint, we are nonetheless free when we subordinate ourselves to such constraints if we are the source of normativity itself. A similar theme can be discerned in Kant's epistemology, which, under one interpretation, holds that transcendental enquiry into the necessary preconditions of experience reveals that the fundamental structure of the empirical world is a product of our subjectivity. Hence, although theoretical judgement is compelled to seek conformity to how things are, this is a matter of the intellect subordinating itself to that which is, in some sense, the outcome of its own spontaneity. 'Freedom in thinking', Kant writes, 'means the subjection of reason under no other laws than those it gives itself' (Kant, 1786/1949, p. 303). Where Kant speaks abstractly of 'reason' giving itself laws, modern Kantians tend to embrace a more anthropocentric view of the source of normativity: for *reason* read *us*.

These themes are developed and extended by many in the post-Kantian tradition. Hegel, for example, shares the view that to be free is, as Charles Taylor puts it, 'to be governed by a law that emanates from ourselves' (Taylor, 1975, p. 374). For Hegel, the core of freedom is the idea of self-determination, and self-determining beings are the source of their own determinations. In post-Kantian philosophy, the origins of normativity are typically seen as profoundly social in character. Robert Pippin argues that Hegel advances 'a radical anti-realism or constructivism about norms' according to which 'there is just nothing left to "counting as a norm" other than being taken to be one, effectively circulating as one in a society' (Pippin, 2000, p. 163; discussed in McDowell, 2008/2009a). Indeed, the very status of *free individual* is constructively determined in the same manner: 'being a free agent consists in being recognized as one' (ibid.). Thus, in the moral and social domains, the norms to which we submit ourselves are not other to us: they are constructed through processes of mutual recognition. The idea of the transcendence of otherness manifests itself throughout Hegel's philosophy. For instance, it is present in his conception of activity: when we act upon, and thereby change, the world, the world as we have changed it confronts us not as something alien but as something in which we can recognise ourselves. And it informs Hegel's view of absolute knowledge as Spirit's attaining a conception of the world as identical with itself. An overarching theme is that we are free in so far as the world is not other to us but is experienced as a home.[21]

Elements of Hegel's thought clearly inspire McDowell, who picks up from Gadamer the image of rational beings 'at home in the world' (McDowell, 1994, p. 118).[22] But for now, I want to set aside Hegelian variations on Kant's theme and consider the more straightforward and accessible account of the sources of normativity by an influential contemporary Kantian, Christine Korsgaard.

SOURCES OF NORMATIVITY I: PRACTICAL REASONING

In *The Sources of Normativity* (1996), Korsgaard examines what she calls the 'normative question': how are reasons (or 'oughts') possible? Since there are many different kinds of reason, the normative question is best asked in some particular domain. Korsgaard's focus is practical. She primarily discusses moral obligation, where the question becomes: what justifies the claims that morality makes on us? However, Korsgaard takes her position to have implications beyond the moral.

Korsgaard argues that normativity is possible because of the reflective structure of our minds. Here she invokes considerations familiar from the discussion above. We have the capacity to attend to our own mental activities, stand apart from them and interrogate them. Perception may give me a strong inclination to believe that p, but I can make that inclination the object of critical attention and ask: Should I believe that p? I find myself with a desire to act, but I can step back and ask whether I ought to so act. Reflection demands reasons for belief and action, and responding to reasons involves (at least in principle) endorsing or acknowledging them as grounds for belief or action.

But how is reflection to decide what our reasons are? In the case of morality, Korsgaard's explanation is as follows. I find myself desiring to ϕ. But should I ϕ? I must ask myself whether I can will that the maxim on which I would be acting if I ϕ-ed could be adopted as a law. So far, so Kantian. But now Korsgaard adds a less Kantian ingredient. For her, the question of whether the maxim can be willed as law is not simply a matter of whether it can be consistently universalised. Rather, the question is whether the law is consistent with what she calls the agent's 'practical identity'. Each person has a practical identity composed of certain roles and self-conceptions:

> a description under which you value yourself, a description under which you find your life to be worth living and your actions to be worth undertaking. ... [F]or the average person there will be a jumble of such conceptions. You are a human being, a woman or a man, an adherent of a certain religion, a member of an ethnic group, a member of a certain profession, someone's lover or friend, and so on. (Korsgaard, 1996, p. 101)

Suppose I find myself wanting to strike my egregiously misbehaving child. I reflect and ask myself whether this kind of action is consistent with my practical identity. Is this the sort of thing that I, as a parent, should do? (More strictly: is there a principle that permits such acts?) If I conclude that it is not, I recognise that I have an obligation not to do it. If I strike my child regardless, I violate my identity as a parent. But to violate an identity that is crucial to my conception of myself as valuable is to be 'for all practical purposes dead or worse than dead'. 'An obligation', Korsgaard concludes, 'always takes the form of a reaction against the threat of a loss of identity' (p. 102).

But if obligation is relative to practical identity, what ensures that the practical identities in question are morally acceptable? As G. A. Cohen points out, Mafiosi have practical identities too (Cohen, 1996, pp. 183–4). For Korsgaard, behind our particular practical identities stands our identity as human beings. The reflective structure of consciousness makes the normative question possible, since it demands of us that we act for reasons. But it also makes possible its solution, since it is in virtue of this reflective structure that we are self-conscious and can form a conception of our identity and act in its light. Once we recognise this, we see that the fact that we have normative identities is crucial to our identities as human beings. Since we cannot act without reasons, and our humanity is ultimately the source of all our reasons, we must value our humanity if we are to value anything. Rational action is possible only if human beings find their humanity to be of value. 'It does not make sense', Korsgaard concludes, 'to identify oneself in ways that are inconsistent with the value of humanity' (1996, p. 126). Thus our practical identities will be consistent only if we treat others, in Kant's words, as ends-in-themselves.

So here we have an account that reconciles rational necessitation and freedom by representing the law to which we must conform as an expression of our own autonomy. Hence, in subjecting ourselves to that law, we affirm our freedom.

SOURCES OF NORMATIVITY II: THEORETICAL REASONING

As Korsgaard acknowledges, we can devise a parallel account of the structure of theoretical reason. Just as reflection assesses our desires, so it asks of the deliverances of perception whether they are genuine reasons for belief. In this, we might portray reflection as asking whether some candidate for belief is consistent with the subject's 'epistemic identity'; i.e., the subject's lived conception of the world, informed by principles of inference, ideas of rationality, standards of evidence and cognitive sensibilities (here we might invoke Owens's epistemic virtues). And behind our epistemic identity we might see a more general identity: our identity as rational agents.

In what way might such a picture represent the source of normativity as residing in us? The matter is complex because the normative question has many dimensions in the theoretical domain. First, there is the issue of the nature and authority of reasons for belief and epistemic norms—i.e., principles of inference, justification and of the collection and assessment of evidence. Second, there are questions of the normative authority of rules: questions of the kind discussed by the later Wittgenstein concerning the nature of rationality, the 'hardness of the logical must' and the nature and possibility of meaning. Nonetheless there are influential responses to each of these issues that locate the source of normative authority in us, either because what counts as a good reason for belief is identified with what members of a certain culture or community would accept as a good reason, or because epistemic norms are presented as our creations, or because correctness in a rule-governed practice is taken to be determined by the assent of the community, or because our theoretical identity in some sense constitutes the world it theorises. These are all themes that emerge in the social constructionist tradition examined in chapter 2, though that is by no means the only place they are to be found. Indeed, we shall encounter other, more subtle variations in the next chapter. But for now we shall consider merely the general shape of such a position.

One significant disanalogy with Korsgaard's account of moral reasons is that, in the latter, the process in which reasons are constructed can be transparent to the agent, and the thought that *this is what my humanity requires* is a reason I can acknowledge and cite in support of my actions. In contrast, anthropocentric accounts of theoretical normativity tend to represent agreement or convention as the ultimate source of normative authority, but the agreement or convention in question is tacit and cannot be overtly cited. Views that hold that epistemic justification rests ultimately in the agreement of the community do not usually hold that conformity to what the community believes can be invoked as a reason for believing those propositions that have the community's assent. Nonetheless, whether they seek to do so or not, such anthropocentric views do express the idea that *we* are the source of the constraints to which thought must conform and hence that the subordination of theoretical reason is to requirements of our own making.

This is why the ethos of such views is often a curious combination of anti-rationalism and the celebration of agency. Rorty's well-known proposal to substitute solidarity for objectivity, for example, aspires both to diminish the individual by attacking the pretensions of individual reason while affirming our agency and creativity (see Rorty, 1989).

A McDOWELLIAN RESPONSE

A Korsgaardian strategy yields a modern, suitably anthropocentrised version of Kant's vision of the relation between freedom and rational necessitation. We can embrace it, however, only by forsaking a fundamental tenet of McDowell's philosophy. McDowell is firmly committed, in both practical and theoretical domains, to the idea that rational requirements can be genuine constituents of reality (a view he calls 'modest', 'benign' or 'naturalised' platonism). Even though such requirements can be discerned only by beings with the appropriate second nature, their presence is simply fact; they are not constructed by us. It is thus a mistake to think that normative requirements somehow originate in us, and hence we cannot redeem the constitutive thesis by arguing that the norms to which reason must conform are ultimately of our own construction.[23]

A detailed response to Korsgaard will take the following form. Korsgaard holds that my desire to ϕ becomes a reason to ϕ if it withstands reflective scrutiny. Reflection constitutes the desire as a reason.[24] But surely my desire to ϕ withstands reflective scrutiny because reflection reveals that there are reasons to ϕ. Suppose I am deliberating about whether to help a friend. What I look for are considerations in light of which it would be appropriate for me to help (e.g., my friend's need, the fact that I am well placed to offer sound advice) and weigh these against considerations that speak against acting (e.g., possible damage to my friend's self-esteem, risk of exaggerating the significance of the problem in my friend's eyes).

Such considerations are my reasons, but my desire is not. The considerations show my desire to be appropriate, but they do not turn it into a reason.[25]

In my view, enquiry goes in search of reasons and the reasons we encounter have a normative force independently of the process of enquiry itself. For Korsgaard, the legitimacy of a proposed action depends on whether it is consistent with the agent's practical identity. However, it is not as if that identity simply defines what actions accord with it. The matter is contestable. Many contemporary parents feel that to strike their children (or even to want to strike them) would be against values definitive of good parenting, but this is not a view that has been long held. Our practical identities as parents are as equally open to scrutiny as our desires. By appeal to what are they to be assessed?[26] By appeal to considerations that speak in favour of certain ways of parenting and against others. Such considerations must have an authority independent of the particular identities they aspire to vindicate. And it is by no means certain that that authority can be derived from their compatibility with our higher, and thinner, identity 'as human beings'. So, unless there are considerations that have a normative authority independently of the procedures of reflection, reflection will be impotent to vindicate or undermine its objects. It follows that we cannot think of ourselves as the source of normativity. As McDowell puts it, following Aristotle, although moral demands will be perceptible only to a creature who has had the appropriate upbringing, 'the fact that the demands bear on us is just, irreducibly, itself' (1994, p. 83).

For Korsgaard, such a view represents a form of normative realism that holds that some features of the world possess intrinsic normativity as a matter of plain fact. To assert the reality of such facts is, she maintains, just to announce the normative question solved. Korsgaard's suspicion of normative realism derives principally from two sources: one epistemological, one metaphysical. First, she sees the realist as a foundationalist who thinks she can respond to moral scepticism by appealing to reasons that, in virtue of their intrinsic normativity, are ultimate and can stand alone (Korsgaard dismissively refers to the realist's commitment to 'eternal normative verities' (2009, p. 64; see also Korsgaard, 2003/2008)). But the realist need not be a foundationalist, nor need she think that such reasons cannot be explicated and supported. That the suffering I would cause him is a reason not to embarrass him does not need a further reason, standing behind or beneath it, from which to derive its authority, but that does not mean nothing can be said—or shown—about why his suffering matters.

Second, behind Korsgaard's response to the question of moral normativity lurks the normative question in its most general form: how are 'oughts' possible? The general question derives its urgency from the idea that we are beholden to explain how, in a natural world operating according to causal laws that exhaustively determine everything that goes on within it, there can be reasons that influence us rationally and not (or not just) causally. The solution is to show how we are in fact the source of normativity and that the reasons, values, obligations, etc. that present themselves to us as normatively loaded features of reality that guide or command us are projected onto reality by human beings, the powers of which we suppose we can fully explain in terms consistent with our best scientific accounts of the natural order.

McDowell would argue—and I think he is right—that this style of philosophising is misconceived. Although various epistemological and metaphysical anxieties about the status of the normative prompt us to think that we owe an account of how normativity 'gets into the world', the trick is to calm those anxieties rather than to attempt such an account. The source of those anxieties is the scientism that insists that all that is authentically real is that which can be explained by natural-scientific means. But that is precisely the conception of reality that we reject when we adopt a robust view of second nature. Once the grip of scientism is loosened, the normative question loses it urgency.[27] The notion of self-legislation, so fundamental in the German philosophical tradition after Kant, must be treated as consisting in our subjecting ourselves to norms by our freely acknowledging them, but the authority of those norms is prior to and independent of that acknowledgement, rather than constituted by it (McDowell, 2002, pp. 276–7; see also 2007b/2009a, pp. 199–203, and 2008/2009a).

This is not a surprising conclusion. The idea that we somehow institute the norms by which we are bound is paradoxical. If I am to act out of respect for a norm, I must acknowledge its authority. But that authority cannot issue from my acknowledgement; it must precede it, otherwise my acknowledgement is groundless and arbitrary.[28] Introducing a social context complicates the issue, but does not resolve it. We cannot do without a basic notion of normative authority. Of course, some norms can be invented, and have no authority independently of the practices that sustain them—the rules of soccer, for example. But this is a poor model of normative authority as such.

These strictures against a constructivist account of the sources of normativity apply equally to the domain of theoretical reason. McDowell is adamant that if we reject the view that thought is rationally constrained by reality, we will have no plausible account of empirical content, and hence no workable conception of knowledge or belief. Indeed, if we transpose a Korsgaardian model into the theoretical domain, the result will recall one of McDowell's targets in *Mind and World*: the idea that perceptual experience exercises a causal, but not rational, influence on belief. On such a view, perception is the causal origin of inclinations to believe, but such inclinations are pre-rational; they are not reasons to believe. The result is the form of coherentism about justification, advanced by Davidson and admired by Rorty, according to which there are no rational constraints upon belief from outside: in Davidson's slogan, 'nothing can count as a reason for holding a belief except another belief' (1983/2001, p. 141). It may appear that, on such an approach, the prospect of intellectual freedom is substantial because reason is ultimately accountable only to itself. But what mitigates this freedom is that the rational domain is beleaguered by causal impingements from beyond its frontiers. McDowell objects to such coherentism on the grounds that it risks turning thought into 'frictionless spinning in a void' (McDowell, 1994, p. 11). In a sense, things are worse still because the impetus that keeps thought spinning is non-rational influences that the intellect must accommodate. In so far as the world is seen as the source of those influences, it is presented as something profoundly alien to thought.

Things look very different if we represent experience itself as having a rational bearing on judgement. The content of experience is conceptual in character and, as such, it brings the world into view for us. No story needs to be told about how causal impacts become such that they stand in rational relations to belief. The world is not something alien to reason, but such that 'experience enables the layout of reality itself to exert a rational influence on what a subject thinks' (McDowell, 1994, p. 26). Thus McDowell represents thought and reality, mind and world, as at one with one another, and their unity is exemplified when rational agents think and act as they should in light of reasons that the world presents to them. Here freedom is manifest.

CONCLUSION

I have been exploring the idea that rational necessitation is constitutive of freedom: that we are free because we are, and in so far as we are, responsive to reasons, even where those reasons necessitate what we must think or do. We can come at this idea by considering the explanation of thought and action. When an action is done in recognition of reasons that are compelling, then appeal to those reasons serves fully to explain the action. Such an explanation represents the agent as the source of her actions.[29] Indeed, to see an action as issuing from the agent's appreciation of compelling reasons is precisely what it is to see her as originating the action—as self-determining—even if the balance of reasons leaves her no option as to what to do. In this chapter, I have tried to defend the view that we can say something similar in the case of belief. Now, in a recent article, McDowell has made clear that it does not suffice that the agent should merely *take* herself to be guided by reasons: what the agent takes to be reasons should genuinely *be* reasons. If they are not, then 'the weight of explanation falls through the supposed reasons, and comes to rest on whatever accounts for the subject's taking them to be reasons—say social subservience or the hold of dogma' (McDowell, 2008/2009a, pp. 169–70). In such a case the agent's freedom is compromised. We cannot see her as self-determining.

This seems uncontentious. If rational necessitation is constitutive of freedom, then it had better be responsiveness to *reasons*, rather than something else, that is the source of the agent's thoughts and deeds. We need to be clear, however, about exactly what McDowell means when he says that freedom 'can be more or less fully realized, and its degree depends on the extent to which the supposed reasons in the light of which someone acts are genuinely reasons' (p. 169). Clearly, ignorance of what one has reason to think or do does not in itself compromise one's freedom. There are plenty of innocuous cases where one takes oneself to have reasons that one does not in fact have. I can think I have a reason to apologise when in fact no offence has been caused, or that the smoke in the kitchen is a reason to raise the alarm when in fact nothing is amiss. If I act on such non-reasons, my doing so in no way compromises my freedom. Such cases do not suggest that something is awry with my ability to respond to reasons: if my error is pointed out to me, I revise my view. What McDowell has in mind are cases where an agent's understanding of what she has reason to think or do is so egregiously in error that appeal to the reasons as she sees them fails to provide explanation of her beliefs and actions. We need to understand how she could have come to see things that way. An extreme example might be the thoughts and actions of someone who has been brainwashed by a cult, or who is in the grip of an extreme political ideology. In such cases, the person's erroneous conception is deeply entrenched and will resist attempts made to correct or revise it by rational means. Here, one might say, it is not just that the agent is wrong about what she has reason to think or do, but that, at least in the relevant domain, her responsiveness to reasons is impaired, and with this her freedom is compromised.

Of course, this is not an area where it is easy to draw sharp lines. There will be a wide range of cases between the egregious and the innocuous, where an agent's perception of what she has reason to think or do may be warped or obscured by prejudice, ignorance, insensitivity, self-deception, fear, anxiety, phobia, etc., and where mention of such factors and their causes will need to enter a complete explanation of her beliefs and actions. The extent to which appeal to such factors serves to diminish our sense of the agent as free or autonomous will depend on the details of the case.[30] But the guiding idea of what McDowell calls '"the rational agency" conception of freedom' is that we are free to the degree that we are attuned to and guided by what are genuine reasons, and, we might add, though more controversially, that our freedom finds its fullest expression where we think and act in attunement to rational necessity and know our reasons for what they are, thereby securing for ourselves smooth passage through the space of reasons. This expresses a link between the idea of freedom and knowledge—knowledge of what is a reason for what—and brings out the intimate relation between the rational agency conception of freedom and McDowell's anti-constructivist view of normative authority. McDowell maintains that to make good this view, we need to 'make sense of the force of reasons as something we can be right or wrong about' and this we cannot do, he thinks, if we represent normative authority as somehow instituted by us (p. 170).

What then of the image, so prominent in German idealism, that one is autonomous in so far as one is subject to laws that are 'one's own'? On the one hand, McDowell seems to approve of the idea that subjection to norms does not undermine our freedom because 'we are authentically subject only to norms whose authority we acknowledge' and hence that 'the norms that bind us are our own dictates to ourselves, not alien impositions'. On the other, he is adamant that 'any intelligible case of agency, legislative or any other, whether on the part of an individual or a group, must be responsive to reasons. It makes no sense to picture an act that brings norms into existence out of a normative void. So the insistence on freedom must cohere with the fact that we always find ourselves already subject to norms' (McDowell, 2002, p. 276). Is there a way of reconciling these claims? Sebastian Rödl offers one. We can take 'one's own' to refer not to the *origin* of the law, but to its *form*. These are norms that govern beings like us, beings with a rational nature. As Rödl puts it, when a being, N, acts autonomously, 'the N's own nature, and in this sense the N itself, as opposed to something other than it, subjects it to the causality of the cause that acts on it ... A law of autonomy explains acts that exemplify it by the nature of the subject of this act and by it alone' (2007, pp. 118–19). I take Rödl's position here to be in harmony with the view that when an action issues from an agent's perception of compelling reasons, appeal to those reasons alone suffices to explain her action and her responsiveness to reasons is taken to be the sole source of her action. The action is seen as an expression of her rational nature determined by nothing other than an appreciation of the norms that govern beings of our kind.[31]

Rödl's account might appeal to considerations of *form*, but it invites a natural segue into substantive issues. He maintains, as I do, that beings of our kind are *persons*, human beings in whom a rational nature has developed. To understand the rational requirements that govern persons requires us to ask what it is for beings of this kind to live well. In his treatment of Aristotle on the virtues, McDowell stresses that activity in accordance with virtue is constitutive of living well. If we take Owens's recommendation and adopt a virtue-centred approach to epistemology, we can say that living according to epistemic virtues is also constitutive of flourishing.[32] If we embrace the view that truth and knowledge are genuine goods, then we can affirm that the oneness with reality to which the virtuous person aspires—a harmony that is achieved through conformity to genuine reasons—is the highest expression of our rational nature, and fully expressive of our freedom.[33]

Alasdair MacIntyre has suggested that a life lived in accord with virtue should be seen as a quest, a quest to discover the true and the good.[34] To succeed in this we have to be able to see things anew, to produce novel understandings of the world. This is because, as MacIntyre stresses, the quest is not a search for something 'already adequately characterised'. Thus we need the liberation of creative thought to get from our present limited conceptions to a deeper understanding. The world does not wring that deeper understanding from us; it is something we must achieve. But creative thought does not escape subordination to norms. On the contrary, it requires conformity to norms of language, logic and enquiry, for example.[35] And its object is the conformity of thought to the truth.

As MacIntyre affirms, the quest is not just an education 'as to the character of that which is sought'. It is also an education 'in self-knowledge' (1981, p. 219). It strives for an understanding of what kind of beings we are and how it is fitting for us to live. This position presupposes that we are capable of self-determination. And this means, *contra* Owens, that the virtues must be understood as qualities of character that we can control, at least to a degree. We cannot create them or modify them in ourselves by acts of will or reflection, but we can seek to hone them and cultivate them. It is important that this is not to be conceived as principally a project for the individual; it is a collective matter, just as the process of reflection is. This brings out further the significance of *Bildung* or enculturation. *Bildung* is a process of self-making. And it involves instilling in the child not just concepts and propositional knowledge, but virtues, moral and epistemic. One of the dictates of virtue is that one must cultivate virtue in one's children; moreover, that one should aspire to cultivate in them genuine qualities of character that one may have tried, and failed, to cultivate in oneself. Of course, success in this project is limited by all kinds of factors over which we have no control. But though that shows the project to be an ideal, it does not diminish it. Again, the ideal makes no sense unless we see the dependent others whom we bring up as capable of eventually taking control of their lives and continuing the search for knowledge, and this reinforces the idea that intellectual freedom is precisely what *Bildung* must seek to foster.

The position at which we have arrived makes freedom a legitimate educational ideal. As I noted at the outset of this chapter, there are venerable traditions in educational thinking that extol autonomy and self-determination as the ends of education. In some respects, the position I have defended here is less ambitious than recent liberal philosophy of education, because my view gives freedom such broad application: it is manifest in all rational human thought and action. It follows that in so far as education aspires to the acquisition and exercise of the capacities that enable self-conscious responsiveness to genuine reasons, education makes freedom its end. In other respects, however, my view is more ambitious than the liberal's precisely because it treats issues of self-determination as pervasive: every act of deliberation requires that we make up our minds, that we make our judgements our own, that we take responsibility. This suggests that educators are beholden to equip children to think for themselves, and this is a duty not easily discharged. The ability to think for oneself is not a default position, maintained just so long as one is not subjected to domineering, subversive or illiberal influences. It is an achievement that requires help to acquire and sustain. Admittedly, we cannot lack or lose this power and remain rational agents, but we can possess it and exercise it poorly, and in such cases we compromise our freedom.

We shall return to such themes in chapters 6 and 7. For now, let us attend in more detail to a notion that figures prominently in McDowell's thought, and to which we have already had recourse in this and previous chapters: the space of reasons.

NOTES

1 This is the notion of freedom favoured by the empiricists Locke and Hume (see, e.g., Locke, 1689/1975, II.21.15; Hume, 1748/1975, §VIII, Part I, p. 95).
2 Such a view is sometimes portrayed as part of the legacy of the London School (e.g., Dearden, 1972; see also White, 1982).
   Since the advocates of rational autonomy usually hold that agents must subordinate judgement and choice to norms recognised to be rationally compelling, their views are sometimes contrasted with positions that affirm the value of authenticity and self-creation (see Bonnett and Cuypers, 2003). If the argument of this chapter is correct, however, it is a mistake to suppose that the ideals of autonomy and authenticity are necessarily in conflict.
3 Such a being may of course be unfree in another perfectly ordinary sense; for example, by being incarcerated or physically restrained.
4 The classic article on 'deciding to believe' is Williams (1970b/1973). Some contend that since freedom essentially involves choice, there is no hope for the notion of intellectual freedom. Gaskin, for example, argues against McDowell that since freedom 'involves the subject's having a genuine choice between alternatives', freedom must be located 'between the formation of judgement and action' rather than in the formation of judgement itself (see Gaskin, 2006, pp. 72–5). Gaskin would be sympathetic to much of Owens's critique discussed in the next section.

5 As we have seen, McDowell argues that our intellectual freedom is still operative even where beliefs are passively acquired because (i) the beliefs actualise conceptual capacities that have a home in active thinking, and (ii) believers are under a standing obligation to subject beliefs, including those passively acquired, to critical scrutiny. McDowell discusses sense perception, but sense perception is only one case in which we come by beliefs passively. In many educational contexts, for instance, beliefs do not result from decisions about what to think, but are simply 'taken on' or absorbed by a kind of osmosis (see Claxton, 1997, ch. 2). McDowell's argument carries over to such cases (although where the passively acquired beliefs are not consciously articulated we cannot say that their acquisition 'actualises' conceptual capacities, only that the beliefs are states *of a kind* that bring into play capacities of a kind that have a home in active thinking). It is less obvious, however, how McDowell's analysis is to apply to beliefs acquired in the course of enculturation into traditions of thought. If *Bildung* involves the acquisition of a world-view, then many of the beliefs that comprise it are not acquired in acts of judgement. As Wittgenstein writes in *On Certainty*: 'But I did not get my picture of the world by satisfying myself of its correctness; nor do I have it because I am satisfied of its correctness. No: it is the inherited background against which I distinguish between true and false' (1969, §94). Now it is an important part of Wittgenstein's view that beliefs fundamental to our world-view are not open to critical assessment in the way that ordinary empirical beliefs are. One might say that the acceptance of such fundamental beliefs is a precondition of the possibility of critical reflection. This is why general sceptical concerns about the cogency of such beliefs are misplaced. Should we concede, then, that the fact that we must simply accept such fundamental 'background' beliefs represents a limit on our intellectual freedom? We can concede this, so long as we also recognise the sense in which this background also makes intellectual freedom possible: *something* must be taken for granted if active thinking is to get off the ground. Moreover, it would be a mistake to think that background beliefs are simply exempt from critical assessment, for any part of the background *can* be brought under scrutiny if circumstances bring it into question. Of course, critical assessment is only appropriate in light of doubts motivated by genuine reasons (not the concoctions of philosophical scepticism). It will therefore be meaningful to question background beliefs only in very special circumstances, but no belief is in its nature immune from critical reflection.

6 Rather than motivating scepticism, Owens thinks his position helps explain it (Owens, 2000, p. 54). The quest for certainty, he suggests, issues precisely from an insistence that epistemic responsibility is possible only if belief is under reflective control. For the latter to be true, we must exclude all pragmatic influences on belief formation. This is possible, however, only if the question of how much evidence is sufficient does not arise, and we can rule out that question only by demanding certainty. But if we reject the demand for reflective control, the sceptic's project loses its seeming inevitability.

7 For example, Owens thinks that the idea of epistemic self-reliance makes it impossible to understand the epistemology of testimony, since beliefs we acquire by testimony are not themselves pieces of evidence nor do they bring the evidence that supports them along with them. If I come to believe that it has been raining in Reading because John tells me this on the phone, the evidence that justifies my belief is not John's telling me, but the evidence John himself had when he formed the belief that it was raining there, but this evidence need not be conveyed to me for my belief to be justified. When I acquire a belief through testimony, the probative force of the reasons that support it is somehow preserved in the transaction, even though the reasons themselves are not, and for my belief to be justified, I just need to know that there are reasons that support it; I do not need a transparent grasp on what those reasons are. Owens makes a similar argument for memory. He maintains that his position is psychologically realistic, but its plausibility cannot be recognised so long as we hold that epistemic responsibility requires that we be fully in control of our beliefs.

It is surprising that educational theory does not pay more attention to the epistemology of testimony (there is a brief discussion of relevant matters in Davis, 1999, pp. 38–41).

Freedom, Reflection and the Sources of Normativity 95

8 What is at issue here is *epistemic* externalism: namely, the view that factors relevant to the justification of belief can include considerations to which the believer may have no cognitive access (such as the causal history of the belief in question). This view is distinct from externalism about meaning or mental content, to which McDowell is more sympathetic.
9 Suppose that, in light of exposure to evidence, *e*, I form the belief that *p*. In such a case, various questions can be raised in reflection. Is *e* really good grounds to believe that *p*? Is there further evidence that should be taken into account? Are considerations of the kind that *e* is, in this context, the sort that ought to warrant the belief that *p*? Are considerations of this kind *ever* the sort that ought warrant the belief that *p*? Are we right in thinking that there even exist considerations of the kind we take here to warrant the belief that *p*? Some of these questions are of a 'higher order' than others, but nothing of significance hangs on this. It is not that some higher-order judgements have a special role in securing the justification of first-order beliefs.
10 Scientific reasoning provides many apposite examples of the role of reflection in deciding questions of method, experimental design, collection and interpretation of evidence, etc.
11 Owens argues that when I claim to have a rational belief that *p*, without claiming to know that *p*, there is in fact a related knowledge claim that I am willing to make. In the case in question, I am able to claim to have conclusive grounds to believe that my acquaintance is *probably* trustworthy. But there is a difference between a knowledge claim about the probability of *p* and a claim to believe, but not to know, that *p*.
12 There is an excellent discussion of this theme in Moran, 2001, ch. 4.
13 Some thinkers contrast maturation, conceived principally as a purely biological process, with enculturation and learning (e.g., Hamlyn, 1978, p. 26). McDowell, however, takes initiation into culture to be part of normal human maturation.
14 Our right to think of second nature as natural was discussed at the conclusion of chapter 3. To that we might add the following. In harmony with the view of conceptual development outlined in the first chapter, we should not think of the child's transition to freedom as a sudden, abrupt transformation. We should follow Hegel when he writes of children that they are 'potentially free and their life directly embodies nothing save potential freedom' and describes them as possessing 'a freedom still in the toils of nature' (Hegel, 1821/1967, §174; see Schacht, 1972, p. 311). Their potential is actualised in so far as they become capable of self-conscious, rational self-determination, but the exercise of this capacity can be partial and limited, still subject to the 'toils of nature'. And even when fully actualised, our freedom is still wholly *within* nature, just not subject to its toils.

It is also important not to overemphasise the contrast between human beings and other animals. McDowell has been criticised by MacIntyre (1999, pp. 60–1) and, following him, Lovibond (2006) for speaking of 'the brutes' and of 'mere animals' as if non-human animals were an undifferentiated group. MacIntyre and Lovibond rightly attest that we must do justice to the continuity between human beings and non-human animals, as well as to the differences between them, if we are to take seriously the view that human beings are rational *animals* and products of evolution, and this requires us to appreciate the distinctive modes of life of higher animals. The point is well made, but I doubt McDowell would deny it. There is a touch of tongue-in-cheek in his talk of 'the brutes' and so on. (See, e.g., McDowell, 2002a/2009b, pp. 286–7; 2006/2009a, pp. 132–4; cf. above, chapter 3, note 24).
15 This thesis needs careful handling to be consistent with the claim made in chapter 1 that there are cases of responsiveness to reasons where agents cannot express verbally the grounds for their actions or judgements. A jazz musician may not be able to articulate the reasons why a phrase should be played *just so* in the form of an argument (as argument is normally conceived), but she may be able to demonstrate what *this* way of playing it has over the alternatives. We need a suitably flexible notion of reflexive endorsement that does not treat every case as a matter of endorsing a conclusion inferred from articulate premises.
16 I say '*non-rational* causal processes' to leave open the possibility that rational determination might itself be seen as a species of causation. McDowell, and other like-minded

thinkers such as Sebastian Rödl, no more want to gift the concept of causation to the scientific naturalist than they do the concept of nature. Note also that to say that human beings *transcend* the nomonological order of natural science is not to say that our lives are somehow outside nature, only that our rationality cannot be captured by scientific modes of explanation.

17 See Schacht, 1972 (especially §§I–IV), on the concept of freedom in Spinoza, Kant and Hegel.
18 But isn't the interpretative context a matter of *choice*? I do not think that the notion of choice has any more purchase here than it does on episodes within the performance itself. Of course, there is no one right way to play a Beethoven sonata: interpretative possibilities are numerous. My point is just that a performer manifests her freedom no less when she responds to what she perceives to be an aesthetic necessity than when she consciously makes interpretative 'choices'. What is critical is that the performance should be an expression of her decision about how the work can or should be played, even if that decision is dictated by reasons.
19 David Wiggins has made use of the idea of there being 'nothing else to think' (see, e.g., Wiggins, 1991, p. 348; 1996, pp. 272–4; Moore, 1996).
20 Should we speak of *the* space of reasons or of *a* space of reasons, recognising the possibility of a plurality of such spaces? The idea of contrasting spaces of reasons is benign if it is just the idea that different traditions of thought can embody profoundly different conceptions of the world and different styles of reasoning. However, McDowell, drawing on Davidson (1974/1984), resists a stronger relativistic reading of the plurality that would make the idea of a world relative to a conceptual system, so that inhabitants of different spaces of reasons are taken to live in different worlds. However different conceptual systems may be, they all engage with the one and only world there is. Thus if we can recognise someone as a thinking subject, then their world-view, however remote it may seem from our own, will be intelligible as a conception of the world that we too have in view. There is therefore no in principle barrier to mutual understanding—to what Gadamer called a fusion of horizons. In this sense, all world-views are in principle open to one another and the idea of a plurality of spaces of reasons is not a concession to relativism (see McDowell, 2002b/2009b, pp. 140–1). Another sense in which we might speak of a plurality of spaces of reasons concerns relations between different domains of enquiry *within* a world-view. There are many different kinds of reason—epistemic, moral, prudential, aesthetic, etc.—that require different sensibilities to detect and that make demands on agents that can be hard to reconcile with one another, and there are different modes of intelligibility, the rational on the one hand, the natural-scientific on the other. Recognising this might lead us to speak of different spaces of reasons (e.g., the space of moral reasons ...) or at least of different 'tracts' or areas within the space of reasons. The main thing is not to get carried away by the metaphor, which we will explore in more detail in the next two chapters.
21 See the excellent discussion in Neuhouser, 2000, especially ch. 1.
22 McDowell's papers on Hegel are collected in McDowell, 2009a.
23 It is important that McDowell describes his position as *naturalised* platonism to distinguish it from traditional other-worldly varieties that conceive 'the space of reasons as a peculiar tract of reality, constituted independently of anything human, into whose layout we are capable of insight by virtue of a more or less mysterious faculty that we naturally, or perhaps supernaturally, have' (McDowell, 2008/2009a, p. 170). When McDowell says that the space of reasons is not 'constituted independently of anything human', he means that it cannot be rendered intelligible independently of the sort of life that a human being leads, not that it is a construction, a product of human activity. (This is a reason why he prefers to use the term 'second nature' to describe the rational capacities of human agents, but not the rational requirements those capacities enable us to discern; see above, chapter 3, note 28).
24 Korsgaard writes: 'I believe that all values and reasons are human creations, and that the materials from which they are created are things like our desires' (2009, p. 209).
25 There may be circumstances in which my desiring to ϕ is among my reasons to ϕ, and then we might speak of my desire as a reason, but in such cases it is really *the fact that I desire to ϕ* that

is the reason rather than the desire itself. My account of reasons is much influenced by Jonathan Dancy's *Moral Reasons* (1993) and *Practical Reality* (2000), of which more in later chapters.

26 Raymond Geuss (1996) raises important issues about Korsgaard's view of practical identities. Korsgaard's reply is instructive, but fails to be wholly reassuring (Korsgaard, 1996, pp. 238–41).

27 McDowell writes: 'If someone asks how claims about reasons can be simply true, our first response should be to ask why it should seem that they cannot. If the question of how claims about reasons can be simply true is to be pressing, there needs to be a determinate difficulty about how it can be so. If the supposed difficulty results from a scientistic conception of reality, it lapses when we see that scientism is a superstition, not a stance required by a proper respect for the achievements of the natural sciences' (2002, p. 295). Korsgaard would no doubt resist the idea that her position is motivated by scientism. Her work certainly does not look unduly deferential to the natural-scientific world-view—her recent writing on the metaphysics of normativity is much inspired by Aristotle. For her, the issue is to understand the nature of practical reasoning and how its results can be 'normative' for us; that is, how they can have an authority that binds us and necessitates our acting. The aim is to answer moral scepticism, rather than to reconcile morality with scientific naturalism. But this in turn raises the question of whether metaphysical worries about reconciling the moral and the natural are really behind the conviction that moral scepticism deserves a response. Surely *nothing* will answer the moral sceptic, who needs to be brought to see moral reasons for what they are, rather than to be given a reason to be moral.

28 Rödl makes this point well (2007, p. 116).

29 There is a parallel here with Dearden's claim that a person is autonomous 'to the degree that what he thinks and does cannot be explained without reference to his own activity of mind' (1972, p. 453).

30 This is a matter of some subtlety and one that raises some difficult issues. For example, McDowell suggests that if the 'ultimate explanation' of a person's action makes reference to such factors as 'social subservience or the hold of dogma', then the action is 'not a full expression of the subject's self' (p. 170). However, while we may want to say this of the person in the grip of a cult, it does not ring true, say, in the case of someone who has internalised the profoundly racist views of the society in which he has been brought up. Here we may wish to say that his prejudice is fully expressive of the kind of person he is. We should be careful not to work with an ideal of the 'true self' whose thoughts and actions are free so far as they are entirely unencumbered by anything but rational determination. The distinction between rational and non-rational influences on thought and action needs careful treatment. Non-rational influences do not always act to distort our perception of what we have reason to think or do; on the contrary, they can sometimes help bring reasons into view. We will consider such matters further in chapter 6. Moreover, in a case such as the racist, even if we grant that his freedom is compromised to the degree to which his conception of what he has reason to think and do is error-ridden, it does not follow that we should absolve him of responsibility for his noxious opinions. So long as we see him as rational (or rational enough), we accord him the responsibility to ensure that his thoughts and deeds are guided by compelling reasons. Only where the agent has been severely damaged by upbringing or circumstance do we absolve him of that responsibility.

31 For simplicity's sake, here I follow Rödl following Kant and speak of rational necessitation in terms of conformity to law. It is a substantive issue, however, whether all rational or normative requirements are ultimately to be understood in terms of laws, rules, or principles. In his influential writings on moral philosophy, McDowell maintains that the capacities that enable us to respond to moral requirements are often non-codifiable in kind, and hence that the capacity to inhabit that area of the space of reasons is not to be understood in terms of a grasp of rules (McDowell, 1979/1998a). This position inspired Jonathan Dancy (2004) to develop a particularist account of moral reasons, an approach I have defended in a number of papers (see, e.g., Bakhurst, 2000, 2005d), and to which I will return briefly in chapter 7.

32 Interestingly, Owens seems committed to such a view since he holds that when someone is praised and blamed for her epistemic virtues and vices, it is her quality *as a person* that is the object of assessment.
33 To see Rödl as leading us to ask what is required of us if we are to do well as human beings—beings of a kind who determine themselves through self-conscious deliberation about what to think and do—suggests something of a rapprochement with Korsgaard, whose philosophy also arrives at this question (see, e.g., Korsgaard, 2009, especially ch. 10), though the routes to it, and the methods involved in answering it, remain importantly different.
34 My graduate students complain that the notion of a quest has been fatally comprised by *Monty Python and the Holy Grail*. They are right, of course, that talk of 'quests' is a bit portentous. But a suitable alternative is hard to find: 'journey' is too hokey, 'endeavour' or 'enterprise' too corporate.
35 Of course, creative insight may demand the transformation of our norms, but that does not represent an escape from the demands of reasons, merely a reconsideration of what those demands are.

5
Exploring the Space of Reasons

We have been developing a socio-historical account of mind according to which the responsiveness to reasons constitutive of our distinctively human mental powers emerges through our induction into traditions of thinking. I have followed John McDowell in describing this process of formation, or *Bildung*, as 'initiation into the space of reasons' (McDowell, 1994, p. 125). It is now time to take a hard look at the idea of 'the space of reasons'. The notion is attractive, but elusive. Are we to treat it merely as a helpful image? Or should we expect the concept to pull real explanatory weight in elucidating the nature of rationality and its socio-cultural preconditions?

In what follows, I examine three contrasting pictures of the space of reasons: McDowell's, Robert Brandom's and one elicited from the work of Russian philosopher Evald Ilyenkov. The discussion may seem more abstract than previous chapters, but with a clearer understanding of what it means to be an inhabitant of the space of reasons we will be well placed to ask whether and how the idea might inform our thinking about education.

McDOWELL ON THE SPACE OF REASONS

Although the idea of the space of reasons has come to prominence recently through the work of McDowell and his Pittsburgh colleague Robert Brandom, it was first introduced by Wilfrid Sellars in his influential article 'Empiricism and the Philosophy of Mind'. Sellars writes:

> In characterizing an episode or a state as that of *knowing*, we are not giving an empirical description of that episode or state; we are placing it in the logical space of reasons, of justifying and being able to justify what one says. (1956/1963, §36)

Sellars aims to demarcate a certain style of explanation or, in McDowell's terms, a 'mode of intelligibility'. If I say of Sarah that she knows that p, then I can substantiate this claim only by showing that she believes that p, and that, given her situation, she is entitled to believe that p and, finally, that p is in fact the case. To put it another way, I have to show that she has cognitive purchase of the right kind on the fact that p. This sort of explanation essentially invokes normative notions: I aim to show how her belief is one she has a right to hold in virtue of her access to the right kind of reasons for belief. To ascribe knowledge to someone is to accord her a certain 'normative standing'.

Sellars's point is not restricted to knowledge, but bears on all content-involving states. In the attribution of (mere) belief, for example, the ascriber must consider what is, or would be, reasonable for the subject to think in light of her situation, her other beliefs, and so on. And when we describe a subject as desiring such-and-such, or intending to do so-and-so, we render those states intelligible by integrating them into normative structures of judgement, theoretical and practical. One natural way to generalise Sellars's position is by appeal to a Davidsonian view of interpretation on which the attribution of mental states to a person proceeds holistically as part of an explanation of the person's behaviour.[1] Such interpretation, governed by what Davidson calls 'the constitutive ideal of rationality', aspires to make best overall sense of persons by appeal to their reasons for belief and action, on the assumption that they are rational (Davidson, 1970/1980, p. 223).

Sellars contrasts locating an episode or state in the space of reasons with giving an empirical description. Suppose James breaks a vase by picking it up and throwing it to the floor. We can imagine an empirical description of this event, cast perhaps in exhaustive physical and physiological detail (perceptual stimuli, brain events, muscular movements, the trajectory of the vase's flight, its impact with the floor, etc.), as part of a causal-scientific explanation of what occurred. But when we attribute psychological states to James, or explain his action of breaking the vase, we aspire to a different kind of understanding—one cast in terms of reasons. In the belief that the vase was his late aunt's favourite object, and in light of his learning that his aunt was a Nazi sympathiser, James smashed it as an affront to her memory. The latter explanation renders James's actions intelligible—it 'rationalises' them, as Davidson would say—by showing the favourable light in which James saw his action, thereby displaying the reasons for which he acted.

I have focused on contexts of third-person psychological ascription and explanation. Taking the first-person perspective, we can say that when I claim to know that p, I am attesting to the truth of p and thereby undertaking a commitment to justify my claim. Similarly, when someone describes herself as believing that p, wanting A, intending to φ, or hoping that p, she is neither merely describing her states of mind, nor causally predicting her behaviour. Nor is she (normally) trying to render her behaviour intelligible to herself. Rather, she is making herself intelligible to others, by expressing or avowing her states of mind. She thereby incurs obligations of various kinds (e.g., if she says she wants to eat dinner within the next half hour, then, other things being equal, she is committed to acting in a way consistent with that event's being possible; if she goes off and takes a lengthy bath, then either she does not want to eat when she said she did, or her desire to bathe turned out to be stronger, or her actions bespeak a failure of rationality.) The point is that when one makes an assertion, one immediately places oneself, as Sellars says, in a normative context 'of justifying and being able to justify what one has said'.

McDowell accepts the spirit of Sellars's position, but not quite the letter. As we saw, Sellars contrasts locating something in the space of reasons with giving an empirical description of it. McDowell, however, denies there is a tension between space-of-reasons characterisations and empirical description: That James believes his aunt was a Nazi sympathiser, and knows he broke her favourite vase as an affront to her memory, are features of the world there to be described. In addition, McDowell does not operate with a sharp contrast between reasons and causes, rational and causal explanation. On the contrary, he holds that reasons can be causes.[2] McDowell prefers to draw the central contrast as one between the space of reasons and 'the realm of law', where the latter is the realm of nomological explanation characteristic of natural science.[3] Space-of-reasons explanations are not nomological, but that does not mean that they are neither empirical nor causal.

McDowell speaks of the space of reasons in the course of arguing for a number of distinctive theses that should be familiar from earlier chapters. It first figures in his argument that experience has a rational, rather than purely causal, bearing on judgement. As we have seen, he maintains that the content of experience is conceptual in character: the deliverances of experience are not 'bare presences' or preconceptual episodes. They possess conceptual content that bears rational relations to judgement. The space of reasons is also invoked in developing the thesis that rationality is a natural phenomenon even though it cannot be understood in natural-scientific terms. The structure of the space of reasons is said to be *sui generis*, in that it cannot be reduced to, or otherwise integrated into, the realm of law. As we noted, McDowell holds that this appears mysterious only if we are in the grip of the conception of reality as disenchanted, characteristic of natural science. It is open to us, however, to work with a broader conception of nature that includes the rational capacities that human beings acquire through *Bildung*.[4] To acquire these capacities is to acquire a 'second nature', but second nature is nature nonetheless.

It is significant that, although McDowell writes that 'the theme of placing things in the space of reasons is of central importance' for him (1994, p. 5, n. 4), he does not introduce the concept as an object of constructive philosophical theorising. He thinks that the 'bare idea of *Bildung*' should suffice to convince us that there is no longer any 'need for constructive philosophy, directed at the very idea of norms of reason, or the structure within which meaning comes into view, from the standpoint of the naturalism that threatens to disenchant nature' (p. 95). As we saw when considering a McDowellian response to Korsgaard's view of the sources of normativity, he holds that if we make the mistake of identifying nature with the realm of law, it will seem as if we need an account of how the space of reasons is possible. But once we foreswear that identification, the need evaporates. Indeed, McDowell makes so bold as to assert that there are 'no genuine questions about norms, apart from those that we address in reflective thinking about specific norms, an activity that is not particularly philosophical' (ibid.).

102   *The Formation of Reason*

But of course there is considerable middle ground between constructive philosophy designed to explain the very possibility of the space of reasons, on the one hand, and first-order normative thinking, on the other. It is an abiding theme of McDowell's philosophy that our conceptual capacities cannot be understood 'sideways-on', but must be grasped from within the perspective from which they are exercised. We cannot, for example, aspire to characterise ethical reasoning in terms that do not presuppose an understanding of the concepts, mastery of which constitutes the moral point of view. And in the philosophy of language, although McDowell follows Davidson in thinking that we can adapt Tarski's theory of truth to give the meaning of each sentence of an object language by pairing it with its truth conditions, he denies that such a theory is informative in the sense that a person could learn the meaning of object language expressions from it (McDowell, 1987/1998b). To put it simply, someone will only understand the theory if she has learnt the object language. The *idée fixe* is that the topography of the space of reasons must be appreciated from within, and not theorised from some philosophical vantage point. Yet accepting all this does not preclude sustained speculative reflection on our practices from within, reflection aimed to deepen our appreciation of their nature. Such reflection might yield an array of concepts that enable us to attain critical distance from our subject matter without casting it from sideways-on. A good deal of McDowell's writing—on ethics and value, on Wittgenstein, on the theory of meaning, on knowledge—occupies just such middle ground. Admittedly, much of it is concerned with what *not* to think. But it would be wrong to deny that a positive vision emerges in this work, and if one had to say what that vision is of, 'reason's place in nature', 'the nature of normativity' or 'the character of the space of reasons' would be appropriate answers.

Thus, even if we eschew a constructive account of how the space of reasons is possible, there remain many good questions to press about exactly how we should understand that space. One is: what kinds of entities are in it? It would be natural to suppose that the answer is *reasons*, or perhaps better, states and episodes that stand in rational relations—those for which reasons can be given or which can be cited as reasons. On such a view, intentional states, experiences, actions and even facts (in so far as they have a rational bearing on judgement) are, or can be, in the space of reasons.[5]

So construed, 'the space of reasons' does not seem to demarcate a homogeneous realm. Sometimes, however, McDowell endorses what looks like a narrower view. This is when he identifies the space of reasons with the space of concepts, or the realm of the conceptual.[6] He writes: 'The space of reasons is the space within which thought moves, and its topography is that of the rational interconnections between conceptual contents; we might equally speak of the space of concepts' (1995/1998b, p. 408). McDowell in turn identifies the conceptual realm with the realm of thought, and, since the constituents of thoughts are senses, he argues that 'conceptual' should be understood as 'belonging to the realm of Fregean sense' (1994, p. 107). Thus, for McDowell, it is more accurate to say that it is 'thinkable contents' that occupy the space of reasons, or the mental states or utterances that bear such content. So when I say that my reason for opening the door was that someone knocked, the relevant rational relations hold between content-bearing states, such as certain mental states of mine (beliefs, desires) and my movements conceived in a certain way (or 'under a description'), or between the fact that someone knocked and my seeing this as a reason to open the door, and opening it in light of that reason.

There might appear to be a tension between the idea that the space of reasons demarcates a specific mode of intelligibility and the idea of the space of reasons as the realm of the conceptual. On the first view, to place something in the space of reasons is to explain or justify it in a certain way. But on the second, it might seem natural to suppose that to place something in the space of reasons is just to think about it. Yet to think about something is not necessarily to subject it to any particular mode of intelligibility, for the realm of the conceptual is the vehicle of *all* modes of intelligibility.[7] It is therefore preferable to say that, on the second view, what can be placed in the space of reasons are content-bearing states or episodes—the sorts of things that are what they are in virtue of their rational relations to other such states and episodes, and that can be explained only by the specific mode of intelligibility McDowell calls 'space-of-reasons intelligibility'.

It might be thought that by identifying the space of reasons with the realm of concepts, McDowell intends us to view its 'topography' as essentially *general* in character. To be at home in the space of reasons is to possess a general knowledge of concepts and their relations, rules of inference, epistemic norms, and so on, so that to place something in the space of reasons is to bring that general knowledge to bear on a particular case. On such a view, the topography of the space of reasons would include the relation between the concept *dog* and the concept *animal*, but not particular reasons, such as the reason someone might now have to think there is a dog in her yard. But this is not McDowell's position. In 'Knowledge and the Internal', he writes:

> If we rescue the idea of the space of reasons from the distortions of fantasy, we can say that the particular facts that the world does us the favour of vouchsafing to us, in the various relevant modes of cognition, actually shape the space of reasons as we find it. (McDowell, 1995/1998b, p. 406)

The idea of 'the space of reasons as we find it' suggests that navigating the space of reasons is a matter of sensitivity to particular reasons in the here and now. He continues: 'The effect is a sort of coalescence between the idea of the space of reasons as we find it and the idea of the world as we encounter it' (p. 407). So on this view, finding one's way in the space of reasons is finding one's way in the world.

This talk of 'a sort of coalescence' between the space of reasons and the world suggests that McDowell is committed to idealism. He is adamant, however, in his rejection of any form of idealism that slights the independence of reality by portraying the world as a reflection or construction of, or as a projection from, 'self-standing subjectivity'. On McDowell's view, the world is 'everything that can be truly thought or said' ('everything that is the case', as Wittgenstein famously wrote in the *Tractatus*), and a being with the appropriate conceptual capacities can think what is in fact the case (McDowell, 2006/2009a, p. 143; 1994, p. 27). We can judge *that the cat is on the mat* and it can be the case *that the cat is on the mat*. What is the case is independent of particular acts of thinking (except in special cases, such as certain thoughts about the contents of our own minds), but transactions in the conceptual realm enable us to frame thoughts about what is the case, and when we do so successfully, our minds are open to reality.[8] Indeed, McDowell speaks of experience enabling 'the layout of reality itself to exert a rational influence on what a subject thinks' (McDowell, 1994, p. 26). It is true, however, that he writes of an identity between the *form* of thought and the *form* of the world (see McDowell, 2006/2009a, pp. 142–4). As such, he holds that the world is 'conceptually structured' (p. 144, n. 18). And over the years, as McDowell's respect for Hegel has grown, he is ever more willing to allow that his position can be called a form of idealism, though one, he maintains, that insists that how things are is independent of how any act of thinking represents them as being. If this is idealism, then it is a form that coincides with common-sense realism.[9]

McDowell also speaks of *persons* as 'inhabitants' of the space of reasons. Persons, after all, have content-bearing states and persons are themselves subject to normative assessment in light of their being in those states. We can be praised for fineness of judgement or criticised for ill-founded beliefs or ill-considered desires. As we saw in the previous chapter, McDowell links our status as rational agents to our standing obligation to reflect critically on the credentials of our beliefs, desires, intentions, and so on. It is not just episodes and states that have a standing in the space of reasons; persons do too. Hence McDowell's talk of our 'initiation into the space of reasons', of 'being at home in the space of reasons', and so on (1994, p. 125).

To unify the various ways McDowell uses the notion, we can say the following. Human beings' responsiveness to reasons consists in their possessing conceptual capacities that enable them to experience and think what is the case and to act in light of what they take to be the case. The exercise of these conceptual capacities yields content-bearing states that stand in rational relations and as such require a distinctive mode of intelligibility. Human beings are 'at home in the space of reasons', in the sense of being responsive to reasons, when they possess such states and when they can understand themselves and others as possessing them. One could equally say that persons are at home in the space of reasons when they have the ability to move within the realm of the conceptual. This ability enables them to bring the world into view.[10] Thus the ideas of (a) space-of-reasons intelligibility, (b) the coincidence of the space of reasons and the space of concepts, (c) the coalescence of the space of reasons and the world as we find it, and (d) persons as the inhabitants of the space of reasons, all come together as aspects of the same picture.[11]

BRANDOM'S INFERENTIALISM

Brandom concurs with McDowell that what is significant about human beings is our responsiveness to reasons, and he invokes the space of reasons to make his point. 'We are the ones', he writes, 'who live and move and have our being in the space of reasons' (Brandom, 1994, p. 5). Brandom chides McDowell, however, for failing to appreciate the social character of the space of reasons. For McDowell, the space of reasons is the space in which thought moves, and he considers thinking to be an activity of individual minds. Admittedly, McDowell does maintain that we should not 'interiorise' the space of reasons in the sense of withdrawing it from the external world (McDowell, 1995/1998b, p. 395). He wants to say that the content of certain thoughts is 'world-involving': the content of singular thoughts depends upon the real existence of their objects. And, as we saw in the last chapter, he also holds that a person's standing in the space of reasons may be something that she cannot achieve by her own unaided resources without suitable cooperation from the world (1993/1998b; 1995/1998b). But there is nothing distinctively social in this. McDowell does of course hold that initiation into the space of reasons has a social dimension. And he thinks that concepts, even those we use to describe subjective states, are public in character. But what he fails to understand, according to Brandom, is that the space of reasons has an 'essentially *social* articulation' (see Brandom, 1995a, p. 895; 1995b, pp. 256, 258).

Brandom supplements the idea of the space of reasons with a famous metaphor from Wittgenstein: *the language game*. Rather than the space in which thought moves, the space of reasons is cast as the arena where 'the game of giving and asking for reasons' is played. In this game, norms determine which moves can be made. It is tempting to portray norms as rules, but Brandom invokes Wittgensteinian reasons why it cannot be rules 'all the way down'. At the basis of the game must lie norms that are simply implicit in our practices. Brandom's principal project, then, is to make 'explicit the implicit structure characteristic of discursive practice as such' (1994, p. 649).[12]

Brandom argues that the fundamental move in the game of reasons is *assertion*.[13] Someone who asserts that *p* undertakes certain discursive commitments. She is committed to showing her *entitlement* to the assertion, if called upon to do so. And since one assertion authorises others in virtue of its inferential consequences, she is also committed to whatever follows from her assertion. Thus players in the game of reasons must keep track of each other's commitments and their entitlement thereto. Brandom calls this activity 'deontic scorekeeping'. He argues that the game of reasons is 'inherently perspectival'; that is, a person's standing in the space of reasons can only be elucidated by appeal to more than one perspective. So for me to count as knowing that *p*, it is not just that I must be willing to assert that *p* and incur the resulting commitments. *Others* must be willing to attribute to me the belief that *p*, acknowledge my entitlement to it, and undertake commitment to *p* themselves. This is one thing Brandom means by the essentially social articulation of the space of reasons. The structure is 'I–Thou' rather than 'I–We'; that is, at issue are discursive transactions between a speaker's undertaking commitments and an audience of individuals attributing them, rather than an individual's relation to a super-individual community (1994, p. 508).

Another thing Brandom means is that social practice is the *source* of norms: normative statuses are *instituted* by our practical activities and attitudes.[14] Brandom advances what he calls a 'phenomenalist' account of norms according to which he first offers 'an account of the practical attitude of *taking* something to be correct-according-to-a-practice', and then explains 'the status of *being* correct-according-to-a-practice by appeal to those attitudes' (1994, p. 25).[15] In turn, meaning or content is represented as 'conferred on' states, attitudes and performances by the way in which they are 'caught up in the game of giving and asking for reasons' (p. 117). Brandom argues that linguistic expressions and intentional states have the content they do in virtue of their position in a network of doings, possible and actual, and he identifies their content with their inferential articulation: 'Utterances and states are propositionally contentful just insofar as they stand in inferential relations to one another: insofar as they can both serve as and stand in need of reasons' (2002, p. 6). This notion of content then figures in an account of intentional states. Thus, although Brandom's account of normativity is avowedly non-reductive—he does not think that normativity can be explained in naturalistic terms without reference to normative notions—he does move from an account of the origin of norms in practice, through a theory of content, to a substantive account of intentionality. His view of the social articulation of the space of reasons therefore issues in a strongly social theory of mind.

Brandom's philosophy is impressive in its breadth and detail.[16] I have reservations, however, about whether so ambitious an approach can bear the explanatory burdens it assumes. My first concern echoes one raised by McDowell himself (1997). Brandom's inferentialist theory of content is designed to challenge the representationalist tradition that, according to Brandom, has dominated philosophy of mind and language since Descartes. Representationalists hold that the content of some utterance or state is to be understood by appeal to what it represents; that is, what would be the case if it were true. Brandom, in contrast, reverses the order of explanation. Instead of invoking such representational notions as truth and reference to explain conceptual content, he explains content by appeal to inferential relations, understood in light of the game of reasons, and then explains representational idioms by their role in discursive practice.

We might agree with Brandom that the representational dimension of content cannot be understood prior to the inferential relations that obtain between content-bearers, but complain that reversing the direction of explanation makes the equal and opposite mistake. Surely, the notion of content needs to draw equally on representational and inferential notions: there is no prospect of conjuring the one out of the other. Even if the inferential articulation of an assertion is partly constitutive of what it says, we can only understand its inferential role if we have in play some idea of its representational content. Only consider the primacy of the notion of *assertion* on Brandom's view, which surely imports the idea of saying how things stand. Better to drop the idea that there is explanatory priority one way or the other.[17]

Among the reasons Brandom is wedded to reversing the order of explanation is that he shares Rorty's view that the representationalist tradition deploys the notions of truth and reference in a way that is philosophically malignant. By subordinating these notions to the concept of inference, we can cast them in the more modest role of intralinguistic expressive devices rather than concepts that bear the metaphysical burden of bridging the gap between mind and external reality.[18] But this is an overreaction, born of the assumption that the primary philosophical use for the ideas of truth and reference is to capture relations between thought and world in the context of a metaphysical realism that views the relation of mind and world sideways-on: *here* mind, *there* world, with truth and reference tracing lines between them. McDowell has argued, in contrast, that a Tarksi-style theory for a language captures truths—mundane truths, without metaphysical pretension—about the conformity of content-bearing states to reality and about word–world relations.[19] These are not truths intelligible independently of considerations about language use, inference, interpretation, and so on, but neither are they truths reducible to such considerations.

His hostility to representationalism notwithstanding, Brandom recognises that his inferentialism must provide a suitably robust account of representation. Moreover, unlike the constructionists considered in chapter 2, he appreciates that this involves nothing less than an account of objective truth conditions and objectively correct inference, according to which truth and correctness are not collapsed into what we *take* to be true or correct (see, e.g., Brandom, 1994, pp. 63, 280, 593, 594). Thought and talk ultimately answer, not to what people believe to be the case, but to 'attitude-transcendent facts' (1994, p. 137). Brandom therefore sets out to show how the content of representational idioms is defined by their inferential articulation in such a way that their content 'answers to how things are with the things represented' (p. 607).

Brandom argues that *de re* propositional attitude ascription is 'the primary representational locution in ordinary language' (p. 519). His argument turns on the technical distinction between *de re* and *de dicto* attitude ascription. Suppose that Godfrey is Bartholomew Professor of Philosophy and the vainest fellow of Dinsdale College. Suppose further that someone claims that, in January 1965, Godfrey's paternal grandmother believed that the future Bartholomew Professor deserved a good hiding. The claim is ambiguous. We might think of it as identifying a proposition believed by Godfrey's grandmother; namely *that the future Bartholomew Professor deserves a good hiding*. This is the so-called *de dicto* interpretation. This interpretation is almost certainly false, since we may assume that Godfrey's grandmother entertained no thoughts whatsoever about the Batholomew Chair and its occupants. But there is another possible interpretation, namely that Godfrey's grandmother believed, *of* the future Bartholomew Professor (i.e., of Godfrey), that he deserved a good hiding. On this '*de re*' interpretation, the object of the belief, the person the belief is about, is identified using an expression that the believer may not recognise as referring to the object in question. Read *de re*, the ascription may very well be true. *De re* and *de dicto* ascriptions can be distinguished from one another by their respective inferential articulations: the *de re* reading licenses the inference that Godfrey's grandmother believed that the vainest fellow of Dinsdale deserved a good hiding, but the *de dicto* reading does not.

Thus Brandom argues that 'the required notion of objective correctness is just what is expressed by *de re* specifications of the conceptual contents of ascribed commitments' (1994, p. 595). The fact that the content of the *de re* ascription is specified from the ascriber's standpoint, not the believer's, brings with it the idea that what the believer takes to be the case may depart from what is the case, since the believer may not know the inferential consequences to which she is committed. Objectivity is thus 'a structural feature of each scorekeeping perspective' (ibid.), a feature of perspectival form, rather than non-perspectival content: 'What is shared by all discursive perspectives is *that* there is a difference between what is objectively correct in the way of concept application and what is merely taken to be so, not *what* it is' (p. 600). With this appeal to perspective, the social articulation of the space of reasons is again up front and centre.

One might wonder, however, whether a crucial question has gone missing. Just what must be the case for a *de re* ascription to be warranted? What is it for Godfrey's grandmother to have had a thought that had Godfrey as its object? What it is to *take* her to have had such a thought can be expressed in terms of inferential commitments and entitlements, but to presume that that is the whole story is just to assume the truth of Brandom's phenomenalism. We need an account of how our minds can be *en rapport* with objects (or, as Brandom himself puts it, how 'thought and talk give us a perspectival grip on a nonperspectival world' (1994, p. 594)), but it is hard to see how this might go without recourse to representational notions Brandom disparages.

Brandom would no doubt deny there is a case to answer. We are 'in touch' with objects in perception, and through the use of expressions such as indexicals, demonstratives and proper names. There is no deep philosophical issue about how thought or words are anchored to reality: rather, there is a variety of stories to tell about how different species of *de re* ascription operate. But for Brandom these are all stories about structures of inference. Those who see some truth in representationalism will feel there is a further tale to be told about how the contents figuring in those inferences are possible at all.

Behind these questions lies a more general concern over Brandom's view of normativity. How could a *phenomenalist* account of norms ever be reconciled with a robust view of objective correctness? The term 'phenomenalism' suggests that there is nothing more to normative authority than the attitudes of those who implement the norms in question. It is hard to see how objectivity could 'precipitate out of' such norms (1994, p. 54). As Gideon Rosen points out (1997), Brandom's view has to be, not that some ascription is correct if and only if it is taken to be correct, but that it is correct if and only if it *merits* being taken as correct. Leaving aside the issue of whether the idea of meriting introduces intentional notions, it suggests a conception of normative authority that is in tension with phenomenalism.

Brandom might reply that we are able to *delegate* normative authority to attitude-transcendent facts. Consider the rule that a goal is scored only if the whole of the ball crosses the goal-line. The norm is our creation, a function of our attitudes, but whether some event should be counted as the scoring of a goal depends on facts that obtain independently of us and about which we can all be mistaken. However, the example is not strong enough. A better case is the norms of assessment for philosophy texts. Here too there is a sense in which we invent the standards, but we invent them to be responsive to qualities that obtain independently of them; namely, insightfulness, creativity, truth, and so on. These standards recognise a normative authority that is not delegated to anything by us. But once that kind of normative authority is in the picture, phenomenalism is undermined.[20]

It might be complained that, in view of the concerns of this book, I should be more conciliatory to Brandom's philosophy. After all, his is a strongly social theory of mind, and one open to a developmental perspective that could have application in psychology or education. Might it not be better to overlook Brandom's grander explanatory ambitions and concentrate instead on his detailed analysis of our discursive practices? The difficulty, however, is that the significance of the detail depends on the wider theoretical framework of which it is part.[21] The inferentialist analysis of singular terms, ascriptions of truth and knowledge, and so on, is philosophically exhilarating just in case it fully captures the content of the expressions in question. If it does not, it largely amounts to a complex redescription of our practices. As such it can be insightful, but hardly the basis of a new and radical social vision of mind.

ILYENKOV ON THE IDEAL

In the early 1960s, Evald Ilyenkov published a remarkable article on 'the ideal', a category he takes to include thoughts (broadly conceived), concepts, ideas, experiences and meaning—the very phenomena that McDowell portrays as items in the space of reasons.[22] What Ilyenkov calls 'the problem of the ideal' is the issue of how to integrate such phenomena into nature. His primary concern, as a Soviet Marxist, is to give an account of the ideal consistent with some form of materialism. He argues passionately, however, against those who would reduce the ideal to the mental and then reduce mind to brain activity. In contrast, he maintains that we cannot explain the nature of the mental unless we grant that some ideal phenomena exist objectively, prior to and independently of individual consciousness. Like McDowell and Brandom, Ilyenkov holds that our mindedness consists in our responsiveness to reasons (or, to use a more Ilyenkovian formulation, in our ability to commune with the ideal), and this, he maintains, we can understand only if we credit the ideal with objective existence. We might say that, for Ilyenkov, we should think of the space of reasons as a real presence in the world.

Ilyenkov's position, like McDowell's, can look like a form of platonism, and, also like McDowell, he is anxious to mitigate the appearance of metaphysical extravagance. Ilyenkov invokes the idea, derived from the German idealist tradition of which he was much enamoured, that 'social consciousness' is the vehicle of the normative constraints constitutive of the ideal. Social consciousness:

represents an historically formed and historically developing system of 'objective representations' (independent of the particularities of individual consciousness and will), of forms and schemes of the 'objective spirit', the 'collective reason' of humanity (or more directly of 'a people' with their distinctive spiritual culture). This system comprises the general moral and religious norms regulating people's daily life, legal structures, forms of governmental and political organisation, ritually established patterns of activity of all kinds, rules of life that must be obeyed by everyone ... up to and including the grammatical and syntactical structures of speech and language and the logical norms of reasoning. (Ilyenkov, 1979/1991, p. 247 [1977a, p. 77])[23]

Ilyenkov develops this idea—which recalls McDowell's appeal to tradition—in a number of ways. He invites us to think of social consciousness, and the ideal forms it embodies, as a cultural formation. Culture, in turn, is understood to exist only in and through human activity. Ideality thus represents:

forms of human social culture embodied (objectified, substantialised, reified) in matter, that is, [a quality] of the historically formed modes of the life activity of social beings, modes of activity which confront individual consciousness and will as a special nonnatural objective reality, as a special object, on a par with material reality, and situated in one and the same space as it (and hence often confused with it). (1979/1991, p. 249 [1977a, p. 79])

It is important that, for Ilyenkov, culture is materially embodied not only in the form of practice. We need to appreciate how activity transforms the material world itself, so that human beings live their lives in a world laden with significance and value. He writes:

'Ideality' is like a peculiar stamp impressed on the substance of nature by social human life activity; it is the form of the functioning of physical things in the process of social human life activity (1979/1991, p. 256 [1977a, p. 86]).

Ideality is a characteristic of things, but not as they are defined by nature, but by labour, the transforming, form-creating activity of social beings, their aim-mediated, sensuously objective activity (1979/1991, p. 268 [1977a, p. 97]).[24]

Now, Ilyenkov's position is not just that our ontology needs to encompass the reality of what might be called 'social objects', such as artefacts and institutions, which we are to understand as embodiments of human activity. Ilyenkov holds that 'in human beings, all of nature is idealised, and not only that part that they directly produce or reproduce or that they use in utilitarian fashion' (1974, p. 202 [1977b, p. 276]): that is, all objects brought into the sphere of 'human spiritual culture', incorporated in whatever way into human ends and purposes, acquire "a new form of existence" that is not included in their physical nature and differs from it completely: an ideal form' (1979/1991, p. 256 [1977a, p. 86]). This 'new form' is inexplicable by natural-scientific means, but real.[25]

Thus, for Ilyenkov, we inhabit a world made significant by its relation to human activity and its objects speak to us as they are incorporated into this domain of meaning:

> Outside the individual and independently of his consciousness and will exists not only *nature*, but also the socio-historical environment, the world of things, created by human labour, and the system of human relations, formed in the process of labour. In other words, outside the individual lies not only nature as such ('in itself'), but also *humanised* nature, nature re-made by human labour. From the point of view of the individual, 'nature' and 'humanised nature' merge together into the surrounding world.
>
> To this we must add one more consideration: nature 'as such' is given to the individual only in so far as it is transformed into an object, into the material or means of production of material life. Even the starry heavens, where human labour directly changes nothing, became an object of attention (and contemplation) only when transformed into a natural 'clock', 'calendar' and 'compass'; that is, a means and 'instrument' of our orientation in time and space. (1964, pp. 41–2 [1997, p. 22])

Thus we have a vision of the space of reasons as a realm of phenomena that have a normative bearing on thought and action. This is part of the reality individuals confront in experience. It is objective in that it confronts each individual as an external reality, both in the form of its embodiment in culture and in the meaning the world takes on through our interaction with it.[26]

Two parallels with McDowell suggest themselves. We can see Ilyenkov as arguing for what McDowell calls a 'coalescence between the idea of the space of reasons as we find it and the idea of the world as we encounter it' as part of a vision designed to overcome the appearance of a metaphysical gap between thought and reality. Ilyenkov affirms the 'identity of thinking and being'; that is, in McDowell's terms, the identity of what we can think and what can be the case. Second, Ilyenkov also gives pride of place to *Bildung*, or enculturation.[27] Our status as minded beings is constituted by our ability to engage with the ideal. But the activities constitutive of thought are not innate in us. Rather we assimilate them 'as [we] are assimilated into culture' (Ilyenkov, 1974, p. 208 [1977b, p. 285]). The human child becomes a thinking being in so far as she learns to orientate herself in the realm of the ideal:

> [T]he subject of thought becomes the individual in the nexus of social relations, the socially-defined individual, whose every form of life activity is given not by nature, but by history, by the process of the formation of human culture. (1974, pp. 207–8 [1977b, p. 284])

Ilyenkov wrote relatively little about the details of the *Bildungsprozess*, but he did ally his philosophy with the psychology of what is sometimes called the socio-historical (or cultural-historical) school of Vygotsky and his followers, which, he felt, promised to give empirical content to his philosophical framework.[28]

It might be countered that such supposed parallels between Ilyenkov and McDowell are far less significant than those between Ilyenkov and Brandom. Ilyenkov's talk of the objectification of activity is, after all, an unabashed account of the sources of normativity, of how meaning 'gets into' the world. Is it not exactly the kind of account McDowell finds wanting? Moreover, Ilyenkov appears to be beset with the problem of how normative authority can reside in anything over and above patterns of activity to which individuals are trained to conform. Indeed, he is also stuck with a problem about how thought can bear on an independent world. His frequent appeals to activity figure in an argument that the world becomes a possible object of thought only in virtue of our active engagement with it. But if nature is given to us only in so far as it is transformed by activity, we lose a sense of thought's accountability to an independent world. Ilyenkov looks to be in a similar game to Brandom—though he lacks the latter's theoretical sophistication—and he is saddled with similar problems.

This is no superficial objection.[29] Nonetheless, I believe that bringing the ideas of McDowell and Ilyenkov into dialogue is the most fruitful avenue to pursue. This can be achieved if the Ilyenkovian is prepared to make a concession, in return, perhaps, for one from McDowell. One of Ilyenkov's primary concerns is to reject scientism—which he thought had infected Soviet ideology—and this was his rationale for the defence of the objectivity of the ideal. Like McDowell, Ilyenkov disdains the disenchanted conception of reality. Ilyenkov's affection for the German idealist tradition, however, manifests itself in a commitment to what Paul Franks calls 'derivation monism': i.e., 'the view that, in an adequate philosophical system, the *a priori* conditions of experience must somehow be derived from a single, absolute first principle' (Franks, 2005, p. 17). It is this that leads Ilyenkov to accord transcendental significance to *activity*, casting it as the principle from which emerges both the thinking subject and the world as a possible object of thought. The resulting picture is profoundly anthropocentric, but Ilyenkov plugged his ears against the unpalatable consequences of this, preferring instead to embrace anthropocentrism as part of his defence of a humanistic form of Marxism against a scientistic and technocratic one.[30] The concession the Ilyenkovian must make is to reject derivation monism while preserving anti-scientism. We must keep Ilyenkov's view of the objectivity of the space of reasons, while abandoning the idea that it is constructed by human activity. For Ilyenkov, this means upholding the idea that reality itself is a normative space, that the world we confront presents us with reasons for belief and action, understood as genuine features of reality, and that as we act in response to these reasons we influence the space of reasons as we find it: what we have reason to think and do is in part a function of what we make of ourselves in active dialogue with the world.[31]

The concession the Ilyenkovian demands of McDowell is to take even more seriously the idea of the normative character of reality. To pick up the discussion of chapter 3, we can hear Ilyenkov as agreeing with McDowell that we must work with a richer conception of reality than that countenanced by natural science, but adding that that requires a richer conception of second nature than McDowell allows. McDowell maintains that our conception of nature must be extended to include some phenomena that cannot be explained in natural-scientific terms. This includes the rational capacities we acquire through *Bildung*, so that responsiveness to reasons becomes 'second nature' to us. As we observed earlier, McDowell writes as if it is enough to understand second nature in terms of the capacities of human beings. What Ilyenkov perceives is that we need more than the idea that the world contains rational beings; we also need the idea that the world contains ideal phenomena to which those beings respond. I think he would therefore recommend that we take second nature to include not just our responsiveness to reasons, but the reasons and other ideal phenomena that we respond to.

Only in this way can we give credence to the unity of subject and object, a unity Marx sought to recognise with his image—admired by McDowell (1994, p. 118) and Ilyenkov (1974, p. 209 [1977b, p. 286])—of 'the whole of nature' as 'the inorganic body of man'. To make this point good, it is not necessary to cast activity in a transcendental role. The point is that we do not live in a static world of facts—of all that is the case—with the activity of reason reduced to apprehending them. Our active engagement with reality is our being: reality is the site of activity, and persons are active principles standing in dynamic relations to each other and the world. But to get this right, we must think of reality as a normative space. Indeed, we must acknowledge, as John Haugeland puts it, that 'intelligence abides in a meaningful *world*: not just in books and records, but roads and plows, offices, laboratories and communities' (Haugeland, 1995/1998, p. 236). Ilyenkov helps us appreciate this.

How significant is the concession we are asking the Ilyenkovian to make? Ilyenkov's idea of the world-constituting role of activity sought to naturalise the platonistic dimensions of his position: the space of reasons is real, but it is natural in that it issues ultimately from our activity. If the Ilyenkovian drops that idea, in favour of McDowell's view that a genealogy of the normative is neither necessary nor possible, he has to come to terms with the fact that the normative character of reality *just is*. It remains open to Ilyenkov to say, with McDowell himself, that 'the structure of the space of reasons is not constituted in splendid isolation from anything merely human' (McDowell, 1994, p. 92), but this will come to the claim that the space of reasons cannot be understood without recourse to considerations about the kind of beings that we are, the kind of beings that can have their eyes opened to its topography by *Bildung*. This looks like a significant retreat from Ilyenkov's philosophical ambitions, but perhaps the appearance is deceptive. For although part of Ilyenkov's philosophical personality is in thrall of Hegel, another part is allied to the early Marx and the desire to naturalise German idealism by substituting for the odyssey of spirit a story about human natural history. One can see McDowell's appeal to *Bildung* and second nature as one way of fulfilling that desire, a way that appreciates, as perhaps Ilyenkov did not, that its fulfilment involves not just a philosophical inversion, but a rethinking of the very aspirations of philosophical enquiry and philosophical explanation.

How large a concession would it be for McDowell to heed the Ilyenkovian's call to locate the space of reasons in the world? No great one, I think. McDowell's identification of the space of reasons with the realm of concepts should be no obstacle, because the identification is made in the course of arguing that we should not think of reality as lying beyond 'an outer boundary that encloses the conceptual sphere' (1994, p. 26). The conceptual sphere is itself part of the world. What the Ilyenkovian should demand is recognition of objective reasons as constituents of the world we inhabit, so we think of our form of life as a matter of engagement with a world that is alive with reasons for thought and action. In McDowell's writings on moral philosophy, the idea of moral requirements as aspects of reality is prominent, as is the idea that there can be 'external' reasons, i.e., objective reasons that a person might have that are not to be understood as a function of her desires (e.g., McDowell, 1978/1998a; 1979/1998a; 1995/1998a). Such ideas are central to McDowell's hostility to scientism. And, as we have seen, McDowell writes of experience allowing 'reality itself to exert a rational influence on what a subject thinks' (1994, p. 26). The concession demands that we return to the idea that the space of reasons is populated by reasons (among other things), and that we abandon a psychologistic conception of reasons. Not all reasons are mental contents: reasons can be worldly states of affairs. For example, *its hurting him* is a reason to stop twisting his arm; *its being likely to make her happy* is a reason to give her the vase; *the Sun's coming out* is a reason to believe that the rain will stop shortly. The effect is to deny that the space of reasons is *purely* a logical space. But so long as we maintain that states of affairs influence us rationally via mental contents—via our experiencing them or thinking about them—the concession seems benign.

There are many ways in which one might seek to develop the picture that issues from the alliance between McDowell and Ilyenkov. I shall mention only one avenue here, and only briefly. One philosopher who has advanced a conception of reasons congenial to this picture is Jonathan Dancy, who in turn is much indebted to McDowell.[32] Dancy holds that reasons are features of situations (such as those illustrated in the previous paragraph), and he offers a holistic view of reasons, according to which such features have the specific normative significance they do only in relation to other features of the situation (so *its being likely to make her happy* is no reason to give her the vase if the vase is in fact stolen). On Dancy's account, the features that constitute reasons are in themselves metaphysically unremarkable: they are natural features of situations. What is critical to their status as reasons is their interplay with other factors. Thus becoming an inhabitant of the space of reasons is a matter of our upbringing equipping us with conceptual capacities and other sensibilities necessary to discern the normative significance of features case by case. This demands the exercise of judgement. Dancy famously argues that in many cases, epistemic, moral and aesthetic judgement cannot be exhaustively anticipated by rules or principles.[33] Learning to discern normative significance is a matter of catching on to patterns of similarity and difference that cannot be instructively codified. When we add to this the Wittgensteinian claim, of which McDowell is enamoured, that even in cases where we follow explicit rules, the judgement involved in understanding and applying those rules cannot itself be codified on pain of a regress, we arrive at a further reason why our rational capacities could only be acquired through enculturation. For the best model we have for such learning is initiation into practices through apprenticeship.

CONCLUSION

We have considered the notion of the space of reasons as it figures in the work of McDowell and Brandom, and as it might be read into the work of Ilyenkov. In Brandom's case, the space of reasons has an essentially social articulation, and hence, for him, initiation into social practices is constitutive of our mindedness. I complained, however, that Brandom's view leaves us without an adequate account of normative authority or of thought's bearing on an independent world. Ilyenkov's position unreconstructed, is beset by similar difficulties. I suggested how Ilyenkov's view might be modified to bring it into line with McDowell's, and so modified it suggests a picture of the space of reasons as the world as we find it. This is, of course, an image familiar from McDowell, though in Ilyenkov's philosophy it has a somewhat different emphasis. We are to think of reality as a normative space, with which we engage in a dialectic of recognition and transformation. I think this is an attractive picture.

What, then, of the potential significance of the idea of the space of reasons for educational theory and practice?[34] In this chapter, we have seen the image deployed in three ways: (1) to demarcate a specific mode of intelligibility; (2) to describe the site of the game of giving and asking for reasons; (3) to express the idea of reality as a normative space. In my view, it is the second, Brandomian, use of the space of reasons that is most likely to be viewed as a fertile notion among educational theorists and practitioners because it suggests a framework for modelling educational interaction and its settings. Consider, for example, the potential of the idea of the game of giving and asking for reasons for modelling classroom interaction, or the concept of deontic scorekeeping for representing children's emerging conceptual competence. And if such models proved useful, it might even be proposed that we develop metrics and quotients to quantify students' facility in the space of reasons. I have to confess I am sceptical of such proposals. I think there would be a serious risk of the superficial appropriation of Brandom's ideas if they were not anchored to the intense theoretical framework from which they derive their sense, and if they were so anchored, then they would be hostage to the cogency of that framework, which I have tried to bring into question (though given the complexity and detail of Brandom's epic contribution, and the relatively cursory nature of my treatment of it, the latter amounts to little more than a statement that Brandom's approach is not to my philosophical taste).

I am far more optimistic about the first and third uses, though neither has much potential for describing educational practice. Their contribution lies in illuminating what we can call the circumstances of reason—the nature of our rational powers and the context of their acquisition and exercise. In addition, the first use has some far reaching implications for educational policy. It bears, not just on how we understand the educational process, but on questions of what that process should be like. If we must distinguish the modes of explanation deployed by the natural sciences from those forms of sense-making appropriate to content-bearing states, then this has an obvious relevance to the rationale for the humanities and for non-reductionist methods in the social sciences. Indeed, to understand what it is for human beings

116   *The Formation of Reason*

to be inhabitants of the space of reasons is to understand why the humanities have an essential place in any credible education system and why qualitative methods are indispensable in any of the human sciences. Such issues bear on the conceptual foundations of educational theory and policy. This is where the idea of the space of reasons belongs, rather than in characterising pedagogical activity.[35]

Some have said that our lives are lived on the seas of language. But it might be better to say that our lives consist in navigating the space of reasons. In the next chapter, I pursue this line of thought further by confronting an objection that my discussion may have provoked in many readers; namely, that all this talk of human beings as inhabitants of the space of reasons suggests an ideal of personhood that is over-intellectualised and unduly rationalistic. In what follows, I do my best to counter this objection and offer a realistic phenomenology of life at home in the space of reasons, one consistent with a conception of persons fit to inspire a compelling vision of education.

NOTES

1 The appeal to Davidson would be the better for incorporating Wiggins's insights on interpretation discussed in chapter 3, and the reservations about psychological ascription as an exercise in theory building presented in chapter 2.
2 McDowell credits Davidson (1963/1980) for showing that reasons can be causes (though arguably Sellars himself took that view before Davidson (see deVries, 2005, p. 251)). McDowell's view of the relation of the causal and the rational is, however, rather different from Davidson's. McDowell, for instance, rejects Davidson's famous anomalous monism. Davidson holds that all events are physical events. But events are particulars that are open to different modes of description, and some physical events can be given true descriptions in mentalistic terms. Causal relations between events, however, are perspicuous only when the events are under appropriate physical descriptions: all causal relations are nomological, and only physical explanations exhibit the relevant nomologicality. Thus events are causally linked only *qua* occupants of the realm of law, and not *qua* events that warrant description in space-of-reasons terms. Thus a reason (which Davidson thinks of as a belief–desire pair) can be a cause (since a reason is a physical event), but not in virtue of its rational or mental character. McDowell, in contrast, rejects the nomological character of causality, allowing him to argue that reasons may indeed be causes in virtue of their rational character and that there is no bar to space-of-reasons intelligibility involving genuinely causal notions. McDowell is committed to this by his view that perception is a causal process the deliverances of which have a rational bearing on judgement (see McDowell, 1985/1998a; 1994, pp. 72–6; cf. Hornsby, 1997).
3 Or so he did in *Mind and World*. More recently, he has recast the distinction as one between space-of-reasons intelligibility and the more general category of 'the kind of intelligibility revealed by explanations in natural science' in order to recognise that 'natural-scientific intelligibility has more to it than subsumability under natural law' (McDowell, 2006b, p. 236).
4 In this McDowell departs from Sellars, who denies that space-of-reasons characterisations describe 'natural facts' (in keeping with the contrast Sellars draws between locating something in the space of reasons and giving an empirical description of it).
5 I should immediately address a potential confusion. It can be tempting to argue that *all* facts must be in the space of reasons, since facts are open to rational scrutiny—we give reasons why facts obtain, construct arguments and theories to explain them, and so on. And some who are so tempted proceed to argue that if all facts are in the space of reasons, then we should declare that

science is too. After all, science is a 'mode of intelligibility' and any mode of intelligibility is surely in the space of reasons. It is crucial, however, not to lose sight of the fundamental distinction between rational and non-rational modes of explanation which gives the notion of the space of reasons its sense. Science aims to explain facts by appeal to processes in which reason is not operative. That is the sense in which the facts with which it deals are not in the space of reasons. Of course, the *doing* of science is in the space of reasons, since scientific enquiry is a matter of the formation of belief, but that does not compel us to grant the same status to the objects of scientific enquiry.

6 McDowell writes that 'the space of concepts is at least part of what Wilfrid Sellars called "the space of reasons"' (1994, p. 5), but in a note (p. 5, n. 4) he explains that the qualification 'at least' is designed only to leave open the possibility, which he later rejects, that the space of reasons extends more widely than the space of concepts.

7 This style of thinking can lead to a similar confusion to the one addressed above in note 5.

8 It is important not to be spooked by McDowell's reference to the *Tractatus*. As we have seen, McDowell works with a rich conception of reality that includes many facts that would not obtain if thinking beings did not exist, such as facts about moral and aesthetic properties, and 'social facts', such as *this player is offside* or *that note is worth $20*. Such facts are not independent of thinking as such, in that they would obtain independently of intelligent activity. The point, however, is that whether such facts obtain does not depend on any particular act of thinking (a player can be offside regardless of whether anyone thinks she is offside).

9 An important question naturally prompted by McDowell's view is this: if the development of our conceptual capacities is a fact of human natural history, why should we be confident that our concepts genuinely put us in touch with reality? If their development is contingent, what excludes the possibility that our concepts radically misrepresent how things are? Someone gripped by this concern will not be reassured by the claim that thought and world share the same form, for the recognition of the contingency of our conceptual development will seem to undermine the plausibility of any straightforward philosophical strategy for underwriting the claim. It is important to recognise that a McDowellian response to this concern involves a number of considerations of different kinds. First, and obviously, McDowell moves to undermine various philosophical misconceptions that exacerbate the worry that thought might be out of touch with reality. For example, he attacks the dualism of scheme and content, which invites the concern that our modes of organising experience may not be faithful to reality in itself. Second, McDowell offers a conception of singular thought (i.e., *de re* thought about particulars—*that* man, *this* cat, the Leaning Tower of Pisa, etc.) according to which some propositional attitudes are irreducibly *de re*; that is, they would not be thinkable at all if the relevant object did not exist. This ensures that if such singular thoughts are to have content, their objects must exist and hence that thought cannot be wholly out of step with reality (see McDowell, 1984/1998b; 1991/1998b). Such a position requires a special account of the content of thoughts about non-existent entities (e.g., the Leaning Tower of Bishops Stortford), fictional characters, etc. Similarly, in perception, 'for a conceptual episode to possess intuitional content just is for it to stand in a certain relation to an object' (1998c, p. 477 [2009a, p. 50]). The result is a relational theory of intentionality in which the very idea of mental content depends upon our relatedness to an independent reality. Third, McDowell argues that we should not think of the subject's standing in the space of reasons as consisting entirely in relations between their mental states (1993/1998b; 1995/1998b; see chapter 4 above). If a person knows or sees or remembers that p, then her knowing or seeing or remembering is a standing in the space of reasons that incorporates cognitive purchase on the fact that p (it is not that the contribution of the fact that p is an extra component over and above her standing in the space of reasons, as in standard externalist accounts of knowledge). Thus McDowell brings the world into the very constitution of cognitive states. These considerations taken together, and complemented by other cognate themes in McDowell's work, combine to make plausible

a vision of thought's harmony with reality. Nothing, of course, guarantees that any particular belief is true. McDowell's picture is thoroughly fallibilist.

10 This simple characterisation is not meant to preclude recognition of the fact that human beings are prone to irrationality. (Indeed, only inhabitants of the space of reasons can be irrational), and where the irrationality is extreme or enduring we might say that the person in question has lost her grip on the world. We must also countenance transitional states (e.g., the infant entering the space of reasons), and marginal or twilight states (such as that of the victim of a severe stroke or of dementia.) The next chapter takes steps towards introducing some of the needed complexity.

11 It might be objected that the idea of coalescence between the space of reasons and the world goes far beyond anything Sellars says and is at odds not only with the scientific elements of his thought (which McDowell happily rejects) but with the original image of *placing* a state or episode in the space of reasons. For what sense are we to make of 'placing' a state or episode in 'the world'? If we say, following McDowell's understanding of 'the world', that to place a state or episode in the space of reasons is to understand it in relation to what may be truly thought or said, we fail to capture the key idea of a distinctive mode of rational intelligibility. Nevertheless, I believe the image of coalescence between the space of reasons and the world is well worth pursuing: it suggests, rightly in my view, that our understanding of rationality should look beyond transactions between content-bearing states and encompass our engagement with the world understood, at least in part, as a normative space. We return to this theme later in the chapter when we consider Ilyenkov.

12 Brandom's reading of Wittgenstein is questionable. The centrepiece of the latter's famous 'rule-following considerations' is a regress argument. We cannot resolve the question of whether a rule should be followed *this* way rather than *that* by citing a further rule since the same question of interpretation can be asked of the second rule, and so on. This shows, Brandom concludes, that it cannot be rules all the way down. One might wonder, however, how appeal to implicit norms could stop the regress, since once the norms are made explicit, as Brandom intends, the regress will get going again. As McDowell points out, the moral Wittgenstein would have us draw from the regress argument is that 'there is a way of grasping a rule which is *not* an *interpretation*, but which is exhibited in what we call "obeying the rule" and "going against it" in actual cases' (Wittgenstein, 1953, §201). The point is that following a rule involves 'the ability to act immediately on an understanding' (McDowell, 2002c/2009b, p. 103; see also McDowell's papers on Wittgenstein collected in his 1998a). *Contra* Brandom, there is nothing 'implicit' about this understanding: it is plainly exhibited in action. Nor does it imply a level of normativity somehow more fundamental than that governing rule-following, as if conformity to a rule rests upon conformity to something other than the rule itself.

The understanding of rules of which Wittgenstein and McDowell speak must be acquired, and the process of its acquisition is a large part of what McDowell means by *Bildung*. But what is acquired is simply the ability to understand and follow rules, not an ability to participate in some more fundamental practices that ground rule-following.

13 In this again he differs from Wittgenstein, who was concerned to emphasise the diversity of our language practices rather than to grant primacy to any particular kind of speech-act.

14 Brandom's philosophy is heir to the Enlightenment problematic of explaining how normativity is possible in a world of 'meaningless objects and meaning-generating subjects' (Brandom, 1994, p. 49). He writes, in a sympathetic paraphrase of Pufendorf: 'Our activity *institutes* norms, *imposes* normative significances on a natural world that is intrinsically without significance for the guidance or assessment of action. A normative significance is imposed on a nonnormative world, like a cloak thrown over its nakedness, by agents forming preferences, issuing orders, entering into agreements, praising or blaming, esteeming and assessing' (p. 48). McDowell expresses concern about Brandom's view of the 'instituting' of norms in McDowell, 2002 p. 303, n. 10 (which he qualifies at McDowell, 2007b/2009a, p. 201, n. 14).

15 By using the term 'phenomenalism', Brandom draws an analogy between his view of normativity and theories of perception that portray physical objects as constructions out of sensory experience. Just as Brandom wants to explain what it is to *be* correct in some practice by appeal to the attitude of taking-to-be-correct, so the phenomenalist about perception wants to explain what it is for an object to *be* such-and-such by appeal to a range of actual and possible appearances.

16 Brandom's magnum opus, *Making It Explicit* (1994), was followed by a shorter and more accessible presentation of his philosophy, *Articulating Reasons* (2000) (the latter being a kind of *Enquiry* to the former's *Treatise*), and a rich account of the historical tradition in which Brandom locates his work, *Tales of the Mighty Dead* (2002). His most recent works to date are *Beyond Saying and Doing* (2008), which advances a form of analytic pragmatism incorporating a systematic practice-based theory of meaning and intentionality, and *Reason in Philosophy* (2009), which skillfully weaves together themes from many of his earlier writings.

17 McDowell writes: 'What I urge against Brandom is that we cannot make sense of discourse-governing social norms prior to and independently of objective purport. Answerability to each other in discourse is not a self-standing foundation on which we could construct a derivative account of how talk and thought are directed at reality. That is not to propose ... that we should simply reverse the order. In my picture answerability to the world and answerability to each other have to be understood together' (2002, p. 275; see also de Gaynesford, 2004, p. 25).

18 To this end, Brandom advances an anaphoric theory of truth which models truth on pronominal relations. Just as the pronoun 'he' derives its content from the antecedent use of some prior expression (e.g., 'David Bakhurst is struggling to expound Brandom's philosophy. He [i.e., the one struggling to understand ...] should have quit while the going was good'), so '... is true' is construed as a 'prosentence-forming operator'. It applies to a sentence nominalisation (e.g., 'Goldberg's conjecture') or to a term that picks out a sentence tokening (e.g., 'Everything she said'), yielding a prosentence that derives its content from the prior tokening as its anaphoric antecedent. The anaphoric theory is superior to redundancy and disquotational theories, with which it shares a good deal, because it gives a more accurate representation of the use of truth idioms. It can also be extended to the concept of reference. But it is not clear that it exhausts the concepts of truth and reference. To assume that it does is to beg the question in favour of the use-based theory of content.

19 McDowell gives the following example. In the context of such a theory, we can assert sentences such as: ' "Snow" and snow are related thus: concatenating the former with, e.g. "is white" yields a sentence usable to assert a truth just in case the latter is white' (see McDowell, 1997, p. 159).

20 Brandom might respond that in this context such reflection on the institution of norms is unnecessary. All that is required to make sense of the objectivity of propositional content 'is that the commitments and entitlements they [i.e., linguistic practitioners] associate with ordinary empirical claims such as "The swatch is red" generate incompatibilities for these claims that differ suitably from those associated with any claims about who is committed to, entitled to, or in a position to, assert anything' (Brandom, 2000, p. 203). (For example, the claim (a) 'The swatch is red' is incompatible with the claim (b) 'The swatch is not red', but the claim (c) 'We believe the swatch is red' is not incompatible with (b).) Yet this sounds to me closer to a restatement of the problem rather than the solution. *Of course* our practices of assertion distinguish between what is the case and what people think is the case—that is, they embody a robust conception of objectivity. The question is whether Brandom can explain that robust conception or can only explain it away.

21 And there are also many bones to pick with the details of Brandom's position. For example, he portrays perception and action as, respectively, input and output to the game of giving and asking for reasons. Neither are themselves wholly inferential in character: perception is a matter of reliable differential responses to stimuli; action is a matter of non-inferential realisation of certain commitments. But both are inferentially situated, because perception provides input to inference,

and can be challenged and vindicated inferentially, and action is the outcome of (more or less explicit) practical reasoning and requires justification by appeal to reasons. Nevertheless, there is a sense in which Brandom places both perception and action outside the space of reasons proper, the latter being treated purely as the site of transactions between conceptual contents. The result is the intellectualisation of the space of reasons, a withdrawal of that space from the messy, material, embodied character of perception and action. This is visible in Brandom's claim that we can understand the notion of conceptual contents in terms of inferential articulation prior to an account of the kind of content involved in observation or action. His account of empirical and 'practical' content is presented as supplementing and enriching a pure inferentialism that has already brought conceptual content into view (1994, pp. 233–4). It is as if, when it comes to content, pure mathematics is explanatorily prior to what we might call real, situated discourse. There is also a potential dislocation between Brandom's view of action and practice. How does the view of action as output of the space of reasons relate to the view of practice as its very life blood? Inference, as Brandom often tells us, is a form of doing. Of course, Brandom might say that he means to distinguish particular intentional actions as the outcome of practical reasoning from the ongoing activity constitutive of practice. But too sharp a distinction between action and practice risks obscuring interesting phenomena. For example, Brandom claims that there is no correlate of testimony in the case of action. In the case of belief, he writes, 'a doxastic commitment to which an interlocutor is entitled licenses further commitments with the same content, by other interlocutors. This is its authority as *testimony*. It is invoked to vindicate the commitments it authorizes, by *deferral* to the one whose testimony is relied upon' (Brandom, 1994, p. 239). Anything I see as a good reason for belief for me, I must take to be a good reason for belief for you. But, Brandom argues, this is not true of reasons for action, for whether a consideration that is a reason for me to act is a reason for you to do the same action will depend on our respective ends. As a result, we cannot in general show that we are entitled to do some action by pointing to the fact that someone else is doing it. Clearly, there is something in the contrast Brandom wants to draw, but the denial of a parallel to testimony in the practical realm strikes me as wrong. How are we to understand apprenticeship, let alone the kind of initiation into practice constitutive of *Bildung*, unless we try to develop just such a parallel?

22 Ilyenkov worked on 'the problem of the ideal' throughout his career. He incorporated his 1962 article into chapter 8 of his 1974 book *Dialekticheskaya logika* (translated as *Dialectical Logic* (1977b) and included in Ilyenkov, 2009a, pp. 1–214). One of his last writings was a long article on the subject published posthumously in *Voprosy filosofii* in 1979 (Ilyenkov, 1979/1991; this article has been republished several times in various versions, most recently as Ilyenkov, 2009b, which restores material excised from the original manuscript). An extract from the manuscript had been published earlier in English translation (Ilyenkov, 1977a, reprinted in Ilyenkov, 2009a). I have expounded Ilyenkov's account of the ideal a number of times in different presentations of his philosophy (e.g., Bakhurst, 1991, ch. 6; 1995c; 1997; 2005a). Note that McDowell uses the terminology of 'the ideal' in McDowell, 1995, p. 291.

Ilyenkov wrote a number of papers on education, which I discuss in Bakhurst, 2005b. Some of these writings are collected in Ilyenkov, 2002a, and are translated into English in the *Journal of Russian and East European Philosophy*, 45.4, 2007. An English version of his 'Activity and Knowledge', which explores educational issues, appears in Ilyenkov, 2009a, pp. 215–24.

23 The first citation is to the Russian text, followed by a reference in square brackets to a published English translation.

24 The metaphor of ideality as 'a stamp impressed on the substance of nature' serves to emphasise the objectivity of the ideal, its real presence in the world, but it is somewhat crude. Ilyenkov's position is perhaps best expressed in more dialectical voice, locating the reality of the ideal in the interplay of practice and world. For example: 'The ideal form is the form of a thing, but outside this thing, in human beings as a form of their dynamic life activity, as aims and desires. Or conversely, it is the form of the dynamic life activity of human beings, but outside them, in

Exploring the Space of Reasons 121

the form of a created thing. "Ideality" in itself only exists in the constant succession and replacement of these two forms of its "external embodiment" and does not coincide with either of them taken separately. It exists only through the unceasing transformation of a form of activity into the form of a thing and back—the form of a thing into a form of activity (of social beings, of course)' (1979/1991, p. 269 [1977a, p. 98]).

25 Ilyenkov's emphasis on *form* is important. It is not that the ideal represents any kind of substance alongside the material.

26 There might appear to be similarities between Ilyenkov's conception of 'the ideal' and Karl Popper's famous notion of 'World 3' (see Niiniluoto, 2000, p. 8; cf. Maidanskii, 2009, pp. 4–5). In his 1972 book, *Objective Knowledge*, and his 1978 Tanner Lecture, Popper argues for an ontological pluralism that acknowledges the existence of three worlds: (1) the world of physical things; (2) the world of mental states; (3) the world of products of the human mind. In his initial formulation, the third world 'is the world of intelligibles, or *ideas in the objective sense*; it is the world of possible objects of thought: the world of theories in themselves, and their logical relations; of arguments in themselves; and of problem situations in themselves' (1972, p. 154). In the Tanner Lecture, World 3 is said to include such things as 'languages; tales and stories and religious myths; scientific conjectures or theories, and mathematical constructions; songs and symphonies; paintings and sculptures. But also aeroplanes and airports and other feats of engineering' (1978, p. 144). With the inclusion of artefacts, Popper's vision of the third world seems to incorporate everything Ilyenkov would include in his conception of the ideal, and Ilyenkov and Popper are certainly of one mind in stressing the importance of acknowledging the objective character of ideal phenomena. There is, however, a crucial difference in their approaches. Where Popper embraces ontological pluralism, Ilyenkov is a monist. Although both would agree that much philosophy works with a dualism of two worlds—the physical world and the individual mind conceived as a kind of self-contained subjective world of thoughts and experiences—Ilyenkov's response is not to supplement two-worlds dualism with another world, but to argue that a proper understanding of the status of ideal phenomena enables us to replace dualism with a satisfying monism in which mind, matter and ideality are aspects of a single world, the only world there is (see Bakhurst, 1991, ch. 6; Ilyenkov briefly discusses Popper's World 3 in Ilyenkov, 1984, pp. 61–2 (the relevant passages are reprinted in Ilyenkov, 2009b, pp. 50–1, but do not appear in Ilyenkov 1979/1991)).

27 Ilyenkov, however, sees the acquisition of language as less crucial to the child's inauguration into culture than McDowell does. For Ilyenkov, language is just one—albeit sublime—example of the idealisation of the material. Words and signs are not the only meaningful entities in the child's environment and their mastery is premised upon the child's more general ability to manipulate socially meaningful objects in joint activity. Thus Ilyenkov urges us to understand the nature and possibility of linguistic meaning in the wider context of the idealisation of nature. Ilyenkov can therefore be seen as supplementing the Wittgensteinian maxim that the life of the sign is its use with a further claim: namely, that the systematic character of language reflects (in an oblique way) the structure of human practice. This leads him to speculate that the deep structure of language lies not in an innate universal grammar, but in the form of the fundamental human activities at the root of the idealisation of nature. (See Ilyenkov, 1977c; 1974, pp. 199–200 [1977b, pp. 273–4].)

28 Ilyenkov does not mention Vygotsky himself in his writings, though he does discuss the work of a number of prominent psychologists influenced by Vygotsky, such as V. V. Davydov (Ilyenkov's close friend), D. B. Elkonin, and A. N. Leontiev, and he sometimes makes use of Vygotskian concepts (e.g., 'internalisation', 'higher mental functions') (e.g., Ilyenkov, 1970). Ilyenkov was also much involved in Meshcheryakov's work on the education of the blind-deaf, which was influenced by Vygotsky (see Ilyenkov, 2002c; Bakhurst 1991, ch. 7; Bakhurst and Padden, 1990). Levitin, 1982, is an engaging introduction to the psychologists of the Vygotsky school.

29 A full response would take us into terrain very difficult to navigate. In my view, Ilyenkov's appeal to such concepts as activity and practice is markedly different from Brandom's. Ilyenkov would have no use for Brandom's project of making discursively explicit the norms somehow implicitly embodied in our practices. Ilyenkov's point is, or ought to be, that normativity is explicit (indeed it is embodied in the form our world takes on through our interaction with it), if one is suitably equipped by *Bildung* to respond to it. (This is to say that an Ilyenkovian ought to favour McDowell's reading of Wittgenstein over Brandom's (see note 12 above).)

30 It is important to remember that Ilyenkov's story of the idealisation of nature is not meant merely as an abstract philosophical solution to the problem of mind and world, but a form of speculative anthropology charting the process of humanity's self-creation, a process that will eventually issue in humanity's fulfilment through communism.

31 It might be thought that for the Ilyenkovian to forsake derivation monism would be a concession to Popper's ontological pluralism (see note 26 above). This is not so. The Ilyenkovian can maintain, as McDowell does, that there is but one world, and yet hold that what the world contains demands a plurality of modes of intelligibility.

32 See Dancy, 1993; 2000. Whether Dancy's view is in fact a suitable complement to McDowell's depends upon the details of how both positions are developed. In my brief remarks here, I speak of Dancy's view of reasons, not even distinguishing between reasons for action and reasons for belief. It might be argued that Dancy's view applies far better to the former than the latter (see, e.g., McDowell, 2006a, in reply to Dancy, 2006). McDowell, for example, grants that the fact that there are carpenter ants in my roof can be a reason for action, because it is a consideration that can be cited to explain my action (e.g., calling the exterminator). He denies, however, that a parallel account can be run for belief, as Dancy wants. The fact that there are carpenter ants in my roof cannot be my reason for believing that there are. If someone asks for my reason for believing that there are ants in the roof, I cannot cite the fact that they are there ('Why do you believe there are ants in your roof?'; 'There are!'): I need to appeal to my experience ('I saw ants up there', etc.). However, it is open to Dancy to say that it remains the case that my reasons for belief are factual considerations. These do not include the fact believed itself, but facts about how things look (i.e., facts about the deliverances of experience), or facts that constitute grounds for inference (e.g., there's sawdust on the attic floor). Holism is equally true of the status of such considerations as reasons as it is for reasons for action (i.e., the fact that things look this way might lose its standing as a reason to believe that *p* if I have been taking hallucinogenic drugs). Thus I think it possible to reconcile a Dancyesque approach to reasons with a McDowellian view of experience that allows reality to bear rationally on our thoughts.

33 This is Dancy's primary rationale for embracing ethical particularism, the view for which he is best known.

34 One thinker who has invoked the notion in writings on education is Jan Derry (2008a, 2008b). Though I am sure there is much in this chapter she would contest, I suspect she would agree with what I have to say about the potential of the notion to inform educational thinking.

35 I fear that were the language of the space of reasons to get into pedagogical discourse, the result would be ripe for parody—*Exasperated teacher to class:* 'Really Form 1B, I wish you would spend more time in the space of reasons!'

6
Reason and Its Limits: Music, Mood and Education

The socio-historical conception of mind I have expounded in this book has implications for many areas of philosophy, not least of all philosophy of education. If human beings acquire their status as rational agents only through the acquisition of second nature, and if this occurs only by initiation into social practices, then education, broadly conceived, does not just make a contribution to the formation of minds; it is a precondition of their very possibility. Indeed, the socio-historical conception answers the age-old question, 'What makes human beings special?', with an appeal to our capacity to educate and be educated. It is hard to entertain such a view and hold that questions about education can be shunted, as they so often are, into a siding of philosophical enquiry. On the contrary, such questions become philosophically unavoidable.[1]

The relevance of the socio-historical conception to philosophy of education does not consist only in its bringing questions of education to the centre of philosophical attention. It also advances a substantive view of *Bildung* as embodying a specific end: namely, the creation of rational agents, autonomous, reflective, critical. This is what persons are or ought to be. So the picture furnishes us with an ideal of the end of education.

This last claim might be thought to commit a kind of naturalistic fallacy, moving blithely from considerations about the sorts of things human beings are to claims about what the ends of education ought to be. But the concern is misplaced. As I have argued in previous chapters, the very idea of a rational being brings with it the idea of autonomy. A rational being is one that makes up its mind what to think and do. As Richard Moran has shown (2001), this is critical to the idea of a first-person perspective. A rational agent knows her own mind by deciding what to think and do in light of reasons; she does not work out what she thinks by a kind of inner observation, she determines what to think. In this sense, a person is in control of her thoughts because she has rational authority over them as the subject of a self-conscious mental life. These are not trivial observations. They speak to the nature

The Formation of Reason, First Edition. David Bakhurst.
© 2011 David Bakhurst. Published 2011 by Blackwell Publishing Ltd.

of beings like us: human beings. It is a thesis of this book that our rationality is not just given, but develops in us as we acquire conceptual capacities through initiation into language and traditions of thought. Our rational capacities emerge through *Bildung*. Thus, whether we identify education with *Bildung* or think of education as merely part of what *Bildung* entails, such a view invites us to think of education as a matter of cultivating in children the ability to determine what to think and do. This invites us to give new life to a familiar idea in the philosophy of education: that the end of education is autonomy.

It would be wrong to object that the kind of autonomy implied by the idea of a rational being is too thin a notion to inform educational theory. Autonomy is a *power*: the power to determine what to think and do in light of what there is reason to think and do. The exercise of this power is essential to personhood, but it is a power that develops and grows, that can be cultivated and honed, impeded or damaged. Anything that lacks this power altogether is not a thinking thing, but a thinking thing can possess the power to a greater or lesser extent and exercise it more or less well.[2] Autonomy is thus a legitimate object of pedagogical attention. When I think about what to write here, I must be guided by considerations about what there is most reason to believe, not about what to write in order to bring my book to a speedy conclusion. And when I think about how to act in light of what I perceive to be an injustice, I must strive to have my actions determined by the balance of reasons of the right kind. These cases involve the exercise of the same fundamental power, a power we must learn to exercise well.

This says nothing, of course, about how to organise an education system to educate for autonomy. The emphasis on 'making up one's mind' might suggest a focus on reasoning, theoretical and practical. But reasoning cannot be treated formally and schematically. Reasoning demands knowledge, the ability to engage in enquiry, and sensibilities conducive to good judgement. The latter takes us into the domain of virtues of character, intellectual and moral. So there is a sense in which the appeal to autonomy takes us everywhere and nowhere: it poses for us the question of what education should be and it demands a certain kind of answer—to equip us to live lives determined by reason, where we can make up our minds what to think and do in light of what we know to be true and good. *How* to equip people for such lives is a question this book leaves open. Indeed, this could be said to be the great open question of educational theory. All I can pretend to have achieved here is to have shown why the question is inevitable, how it is properly posed and which fundamental ideas should inform our answers to it.

I want to turn now to a potential objection to the position I have endorsed. It might be argued that, although I have stressed that rational agents are persons and that persons are human beings, McDowell's emphasis on persons as 'inhabitants of the space of reasons' paints an unduly *intellectualistic* or *rationalistic* portrait of the kind of beings we are. There is a kind of purity about the idea that we are autonomous in so far as we are moved only by reasons, and this seems to ignore the messy, material dimension to embodied being. Moreover, the idea that the space of reasons is *sui generis* reveals that the position is infected with a kind of *dualism*, embodying a stark contrast between the movement of reason, spontaneous and free, and mere happenings subsumable under scientific law. It is one thing to stress the value of autonomy as an educational ideal—who among my readers would disagree?—another to foster an image of the subject as free in so far as she moves across the ethereal terrain of the space of reasons, attuned to reasons and to reasons alone.

In this chapter, I defend the socio-historical approach from these objections. I believe they are wide of the mark, but the errors on which they rest are easily made. By confronting them, I hope to counter a natural misreading of McDowell's philosophy, or of the use I make of it. If I am successful, my socio-historical conception should emerge the stronger, and better able to inform our thinking about education.

AN INITIAL RESPONSE

It is tempting to make short work of the objection. Nothing in the socio-historical approach as I have so far developed it suggests that it is wedded to a conception of rationality that warrants the epithet 'rationalistic'. The position does not confine rationality to formal, abstract, situation-independent modes of reasoning, or restrict its province to rule-following or inference.[3] On the contrary, responsiveness to reasons is taken to include sensitivity to considerations that are constitutive of reasons for belief and action, and to their relative significance in particular cases. Such sensitivity is best understood on the model of perception, rather than inference.

McDowell's moral philosophy provides a precedent for such a view. There he describes sensitivity to moral reasons as 'a sort of perceptual capacity' (McDowell, 1979/1998a, p. 51). The virtuous person *sees* what moral situations require of her, she does not infer, or otherwise calculate, what to do (indeed, the need to proceed by inference would in many instances bespeak failure of the relevant sensibility). Her ability to perceive what is a reason for what puts her in touch with how things stand morally.

This account of moral judgement must be understood in light of McDowell's view of sense perception as such. McDowell holds that, in normal cases, the deliverances of experience—how things are, say, visually presented as being—provides reason to believe that that is how things are. In favourable cases (e.g., where we are not subject to illusion, etc.), experience puts us in touch with the facts. Reason enables this because our conceptual capacities are drawn into play in perceptual experience, and it is only in virtue of its conceptual content that experience can bear directly and rationally on judgement. This is a view of the workings of reason securing openness to empirical reality, sensitivity to the world. There is no implication that the work of reason must be formal, abstract, situation-independent, rule-bound or otherwise 'rationalistic'.

McDowell's critics sometimes fail to appreciate this. Consider Hubert Dreyfus's attack on McDowell's view that perception and action are permeated with conceptual rationality (Dreyfus, 2005). Dreyfus argues that 'embodied coping', practical wisdom (what Aristotle called *phronesis*) and the manifestation of expertise all proceed independently of conceptual thought and are thus forms of non-conceptual interaction with the world. Dreyfus makes this criticism because he thinks of reasons as articulable, general, rule-like considerations, with reference to which the agent determines what to think and do. Acting for reasons thus lacks the kind of fluidity and immediacy of so much of our engagement with the world. But this is a view of reasons and rationality that McDowell disavows (2007b/2009b). For him, embodied coping, *phronesis* and expertise are all forms of responsiveness to reasons.[4] As such, they are permeated with the conceptual (how could *expertise* not be?), but the responsiveness in question involves sensitivity to relevant factors rather than explicit rule-following.[5]

One thing that provokes Dreyfus is McDowell's view that perceptual receptivity issues in *judgement*. Although McDowell appreciates that creatures capable of judgement are embodied beings actively engaged with an independent world, and that judgement may be expressed in action, the centre of gravity of McDowell's philosophy is thought and its bearing on the world. This strikes some critics, particularly those of a phenomenological persuasion, as too intellectualistic. Unlike Dreyfus, Joseph Rouse is willing to grant McDowell that our engagement with reality is always 'permeated by mindedness', but he complains that McDowell does not appreciate how this is true of our *bodily* interaction with the world. Drawing on the work of Samuel Todes, he enjoins McDowell to

> replace the notion of 'receptivity' with that of responsive bodily interaction with the (verbally articulated) world. The meaningful accord of bodily intentionality and worldly significance would then not be 'already there' in the natures of objects or commitments of subjects, but would only arise and be sustained through ongoing interaction within a conceptually articulated tradition. (Rouse, 2005, p. 56)[6]

It is not difficult, however, for a McDowellian to accommodate Rouse's point. Admittedly, McDowell portrays the space of reasons as 'the realm in which thought moves', but he does not think of this as a self-contained realm, set apart from reality. On the contrary, as we have seen, he speaks of 'a sort of coalescence' between 'the idea of the space of reasons as we find it and the idea of the world as we encounter it' (1995/1998b, p. 407). In the last chapter, I argued that there is an intriguing parallel between McDowell's talk of this 'coalescence' and Ilyenkov's idea of the world as a normative space, permeated with the ideal. The point of bringing McDowell's position into contact with Ilyenkov's is precisely to make clear that to describe someone as an inhabitant of the space of reasons is not to represent her as occupying some rarefied conceptual domain, but to ascribe to her a certain mode of living in the world. This mode of living is marked by exactly the characteristics Rouse finds wanting in McDowell's philosophy—namely, an accord between the bodily activity expressive of our mindedness and the significance of the world in which we live. We do not need to oust the notion of 'receptivity' to see this. On the contrary, we can say that perception *is* a form of 'bodily responsive interaction' with a meaningful world and that this is made possible by the perceiver's relation to 'a conceptually articulated tradition'.

Let us turn now to the charge of dualism. Just what form is the dualism supposed to take? Not, surely, a dualism of reason and nature. The point of the appeal to second nature is to overcome that dualism by representing responsiveness to reasons as an aspect of our natural development. Nor can it be a dualism between the rational and the animal in our nature, for again the discussion of second nature is designed to illustrate their connectedness. Indeed, as I argued in chapter 3, a proper appreciation of *Bildung* reveals the intimate relation between our rationality and our animality. Nor can it be a dualism of reasons and causes, for we can follow McDowell and insist that reasons can be causes. So the charge of dualism fares no better than the accusation that the position is rationalistic.

THE CHALLENGE RECONFIGURED

I suspect, however, that many will find this swift rebuttal unsatisfying, believing that something in the objection remains unaddressed. One way to capture the source of unease is to return to the pivotal distinction between two modes of intelligibility—explanation by appeal to scientific law ('natural-scientific intelligibility') and explanation by appeal to reasons ('space-of-reasons intelligibility')—and correlatively, as McDowell puts it, between 'two kinds of happenings in nature: those that are subsumable under natural law, and those that are not subsumable under natural law, because freedom is operative in them' (2006b, p. 238).[7] The distinction between modes of explanation is fundamental to McDowell's philosophy, and to many of the arguments in this book. Some events, such as actions or judgements, are explained by appeal to reasons; others by recourse to scientific means. This is supposed to be a commonplace. We operate with this contrast all the time, when we differentiate between doings undertaken in light of reasons and open to rational assessment—such as my predicting that it will rain tomorrow—and those that are not—such as my tripping over the carpet or spilling my wine. The contrast is central to our understanding of ourselves as responsible for our thoughts and actions.

The distinction has its roots in Kant, who writes, in the third section of the *Groundwork*, that we must conceive 'man in one sense and relationship when we call him free and in another when we consider him, as part of nature, to be subject to nature's laws' (Kant, 1785/1948, p. 116). He continues:

> In thus regarding himself as intelligence man puts himself into another order of things, and into relation with determining causes of quite another sort, when he conceives of himself as intelligence endowed with a will and consequently with causality, than he does when he perceives himself as a phenomenon in the sensible world (which he actually is as well) and subjects his causality to external determination in accordance with the laws of nature ... That he must represent and conceive of himself in this double way rests as regards the first side, on consciousness of himself as an object affected by the senses; as concerns the second side, on consciousness of himself as intelligence—that is, as independent of sensuous impressions in his use of reason (and so as belonging to the intelligible world). (p. 117)

McDowell improves Kant's picture, correcting the impression that rational beings are outside the natural order, thereby ostensibly affirming the unity of our rational and animal being. For all that, however, the position preserves what might be called a 'double-aspect', or 'two-standpoints', view of persons. We can see ourselves under the aspect of rationality—as inhabitants of the space of reasons, subject to normative constraints. Or we can see ourselves as material things influenced by physical forces, explicable in scientific terms. We insist, of course, that these are views of the *same* thing: persons, who are both rational and animal. But the idea is that some episodes in the lives of rational animals require space-of-reasons intelligibility, some natural-scientific explanation.

The problem is not so much the distinction itself, as what it might be thought to imply. It suggests that episodes in a person's life can be factored into two kinds: those open to rational explanation, in which 'freedom is operative', and those not. So my judging, or deciding, or intentionally doing are occurrences 'in the space of reasons', as are some things that just happen to me, such as my perceiving such-and-such. In contrast, my bumping my head or digesting my supper are outside the space of reasons, as are many things that just happen to me (e.g., getting wet in the rain), as well as things that happen inside me, such as my heart's beating, which, in contrast to digestion, is not thought of as something I do. Now one might suspect that a kind of dualism lurks in the assumption that events can be neatly factored into the two 'realms', and, moreover, that the assumption is faulty in a way that reflects something deep about the human condition.[8]

The distinction applies nicely to specific events, isolated from the flow of activity. We can ask, with perfect sense: is this event best explained by appeal to reasons or causal law? Of course, the answer may not be neatly either/or. We might have to draw on factors of both kinds (consider someone asking, e.g., 'Why did I hit him?'). There is, after all, such a thing as being partly responsible for one's action, and things are complicated by the fact that what happens to us can be perceived by us and factored into our reasoning as we navigate the world. Nonetheless, the basic distinction seems sound. But when we examine more extended passages of activity, such as interacting with one's partner or children, or working on a paper, or having a meal with friends, the distinction loses some of its definition. Now everything involves matters of degree. We may be more or less autonomous in what we are doing; reason may be more or less operative in it; and our agency will involve both active and passive elements. This is not just because an activity is composed of many events, some of which lend themselves to rational, some to scientific, explanation. There is rather a *commingling* of the active and passive, and of the rational and non-rational, in the flow of activity. If we fail to keep this in view, we risk promulgating an idea worthy of the insult 'rationalistic': namely, that navigating the space of reasons is, at least at the ideal, a matter of thinking unencumbered by all but rational determination, and that this image of thought moved only by rational causes—of thought as pure activity—yields an ideal of authentic personhood.[9]

We need a more realistic picture. Once again, I do not think there is a serious obstacle to providing one. But it will not do simply to emphasise that we are animals or to affirm that *Bildung* does not transport us out of nature. We need to discredit the myth of unencumbered reason. This work was already begun in chapter 4 when we considered McDowell's view that we should reject 'the thought that reason must be credited with a province within which it has absolute control over the acceptability of positions achievable by its exercise' (McDowell, 1993/1998b, p. 442). But the issue concerns not just reason's role in the constitution of a person's standings in the space of reasons. We need to consider also reason's contribution to our *movement* within the space of reasons, focusing on process rather than position. In this, it will be important not simply to replace the idea of unencumbered spontaneity with one of encumbered spontaneity, in which the pure flow of pure thought is pictured as bumped and battered by non-rational influences, such as passions or urges. We need to appreciate how the non-rational does not always detract from our status as rational animals, but can enable and facilitate rationality. We need a phenomenology of life in the space of reasons that does justice to the commingling of the rational and non-rational. This should silence the suspicion that the distinction between modes of intelligibility serves to cast human lives as curiously split between rational and animal elements, and thereby complement the view of persons affirmed in chapter 3.

To this end, I shall explore two phenomena that resist characterisation in terms of a neat division between the rational and the non-rational: moods and music. But first I want to present some reflections on the phenomenology of thinking.

PASSIVITY WITHIN SPONTANEITY

One thing that tells against the idea of unencumbered spontaneity is the fact that so much in the life of the mind *just happens*.[10] But it is easy to lose sight of this and to fall into a way of speaking that suggests that all movement in the space of reasons is the outcome of activity. Robert Brandom, for example, takes inference as our primary mode of travel through the space of reasons, and his use of the metaphor of 'the game of giving and asking for reasons' suggests that all transactions in the space of reasons are, or issue from, actions. For him, perception provides inputs to the game, offering materials for reasoners to work with, but perception is not itself wholly in the space of reasons. Transactions involve inference, inference involves judgement and (following Kant) judgement 'is assimilated to action' (Brandom, 2000, p. 80).[11]

As we have seen, McDowell's view is rather different. He represents some transactions in the space of reasons—namely perceptual experiences—as passive in nature. Experiences come to us unbidden, but they are nonetheless conceptual in character and hence impose a rational constraint on judgement. So McDowell clearly acknowledges that not all movement in the space of reasons issues from moves deliberately made. Where experience compels judgement non-inferentially (e.g., when we find ourselves believing that there is a mouse in the kitchen because we see one there), reason is active only retroactively; it monitors the plausibility of judgements issuing from experience, but does not actively elicit them.

McDowell's view, however, implies that transactions in the space of reasons are either a matter of action (thinking, reasoning) or passive reception from without (perception). But there is something missing here, for there is an element of passivity in the internal operations of reason itself. Consider, for example, the phenomenon of something's occurring to one. Suddenly it strikes me that I have left the stove on; or that I might have offended Hugh; or that Rosemary would enjoy *The Mikado*. These occurrences are not the outcome of deliberation or inference. They just happen. Sometimes their happening can be accounted for (I was musing about the film *Topsy Turvy*, and suddenly it occurred to me that Rosemary would enjoy *The Mikado* ...), and sometimes they come out of the blue. We are passive in the reception of such thoughts, but the context is unlike perception, in which independently existing objects impinge upon our senses. There is also an element of passivity in understanding something. Indeed, we only think of understanding as an action when *trying* is required; otherwise it is something that just occurs. We may do things to enable understanding (e.g., attend, concentrate, reflect), and we may recognise that we understand, but the understanding itself just happens.

Consider now some examples of intellectual creativity. We are inclined to construe such creativity as a paradigm of free activity, but there is often a strikingly passive element in play.[12] Suppose you are struggling with a philosophical problem. Frustrated, you decide to sleep on it. In the morning, you awake and the solution comes to you. In such cases, we cannot say the answer comes unbidden, since one certainly has bid (even begged) it come. Yet the reception of the answer is passive. It is just there for you. Its coming to you is no less an episode in the space of reasons, but, as in the perceptual case, reason's role is primarily retrospective—to make sense of what has come to mind, to integrate it into the appropriate context, to justify it, and so on.

Sleeping on a problem, and other forms of 'incubation', provide graphic examples of passivity in creativity, but passive elements are present in many other cases. When one responds to a question in a seminar, one sometimes waits for the answer to come to one. First one does not know what to say, and then one does. Sometimes one starts a response without knowing how it will turn out: what one ought to say arrives as one speaks. In some cases, when one is in full flow, one stands to one's words almost as a spectator, and can surprise oneself with what one says. Musical improvisation provides similar examples. In such cases, although the subject is actively speaking or playing, there is a significant element of passivity, both in the manner in which ideas arrive and in the manner in which their significance is perceived.[13]

We represent this passive side of creativity in a number of ways. The ideas of a muse or of divine inspiration are familiar images that acknowledge the passivity of the subject, who is seen as a vehicle for the activity of someone or something else. Another familiar thought is that the creative process is primarily subconscious or sub-personal. So when you sleep on a problem, you stop consciously deliberating and delegate the problem to sub-personal mechanisms that, as it were, do the thinking for you, and you wake up to reap the results. Finally, the idea of dialectic locates the source of creativity in the play of ideas themselves: once again the subject is a vehicle, but this time for dialogue rather than dictation. The subject does not exactly conduct the dialogue, but neither does she simply observe it. She is somehow party to its speaking through her and the beneficiary of its outcome.

None of these figures is of much explanatory use. The first and last are merely colourful ways of describing the phenomenon. The second appears to have theoretical potential, but is deeply problematic, especially from a McDowellian perspective.[14] I introduce them first because they acknowledge phenomena that counter a naive view of the spontaneity of mind. But second, they reveal how wedded we are to that view, since they insist on preserving the image of creative insight as issuing from agency—they just locate the agency either outside the self-conscious subject, or deep inside her. Better to recognise that reason cannot plausibly be portrayed as a purely active principle, fully unencumbered and self-determining. Not only is it the passive recipient of content from without, it is often surprised by its own operations. Much of its control is retroactive: it can vindicate and extol, censure and revise, but the extent to which its activities are transparent to itself is limited, as, accordingly, are its powers of self-control.

MOOD

Let us now turn to the commingling of the rational and the non-rational. Moods provide a good example. Consider depression. ('Depression' is, of course, a term that covers a spectrum from utterly debilitating cases of 'clinical' depression to mild cases of the blues. We shall take a case from the middle.) Harry is an academic, in mid-career, and prone to depression. He considers himself unfulfilled, not exactly a failure, but less successful than he could have been, than he ought to have been. He deems himself underappreciated by his colleagues and students. He sometimes gees himself up by reflecting on his accomplishments, which are in fact many, but soon dismisses these efforts as self-deceiving, and chastises himself for his weakness. In his heart, he knows what might have been. Sometimes his depression lifts and he feels satisfied by what he has achieved, but then he sees that his earlier depression issued from his own vanity and he becomes disgusted with himself. This makes him depressed again.

One evening, Harry attends a dinner party. He has been suffering a bout of depression, but he expects that the dinner will distract him. As it turns out, his mood affects his behaviour for the worse. He seems indifferent to the conversation, tuning in and out, except when he becomes preoccupied with something another guest has said. His sustained rebuttal offends her and embarrasses the others. As the evening wears on he makes a number of distasteful remarks. He is first to leave, and when he does he is insufficiently appreciative to his hosts. The remaining guests wonder what is up with him. The hosts apologise on his behalf, explaining that Harry is susceptible to depression and this makes him 'difficult'.

The hosts invoke Harry's depression to explain his behaviour. How does this work? Peter Goldie, in one of the few discussions of mood in the literature, argues that moods are insufficiently specific to explain particular actions. He claims that while we have an idea of action 'out of' an emotion, we lack a 'clear idea of action *out of* a mood' (Goldie, 2000, p. 147). Moods shape *how* one acts, and they manifest themselves in action, but they are too general to explain specific deeds. This does not seem quite right, however, since we do invoke Harry's depression to explain specific actions. It explains *why* he insulted the other guests, not just *how* he insulted them. Admittedly, it may not explain why he insulted them by saying *this* rather than *that*, but such specificity is not typically the kind of thing we demand when we explain an agent's actions by appeal to her emotions.

The key question is whether invoking his depression yields 'space-of-reasons explanations' or not. This is a delicate issue. Depression is the kind of factor, recognition of which might lead us to suspend what Strawson (1962/1974) calls 'reactive attitudes', such as resentment, anger or indignation. Learning of Harry's depression can mitigate blame: we might no longer feel indignant at his callous remarks; perhaps we feel pity or compassion instead. Does this show that depression is operating as a non-rational factor? Depression does not, except in extreme cases, influence our actions as a force entirely beyond rational control. Moreover, some explanations in which depression figures are clearly rationalising ones. We seek to understand what Harry did by appeal to the favourable light in which he saw his actions. That he is depressed explains why he took a special interest in the guest's remarks and why he set out to refute them as he did. It might be claimed that his depression is simply part of the causal background invoked in these rationalising explanations. It may be a reason *why* he behaved as he did, but it was not a reason *in light of which* he acted. Yet his depression does not operate as a mere cause independently of matters rational. Its effect is somehow to modulate the reasons for which Harry acts (this is perhaps Goldie's point).

We should also ask of Harry's depression whether it is reasonable and whether it is responsive to reasons. One way in which a mood can be 'within the space of reasons' is if it is rationally motivated; that is, if the reasons why it set in can be thought of as justifying it. If someone is cheerful as the result of hearing good news, then what they have heard is not just the cause of their cheerfulness. It provides reasons to be cheerful. Similarly with Harry's depression. Perhaps he is right that he has not fulfilled his potential and that he is vain and self-deceiving. If so, we might think his depression warranted by his situation. This is not to justify his bad behaviour. The point is that his mood is not a merely causal phenomenon, like measles.

A mood that is rationally motivated may be responsive to reasons in the further sense that it can be influenced by the presentation of reasons. If I am elated because I have come to believe that Spurs are to acquire the services of Wayne Rooney, my euphoria ought to dissipate when I learn that the deal has fallen through. Likewise, Harry's depression might be open to rational critique. If he can be shown that he *is* genuinely accomplished, valued by his colleagues, etc., his depression might lift. I say 'might' because sometimes talking cures work and sometimes not. It depends. Harry's depression might be a fully rational state, motivated by reasons and fully responsive to rational considerations. Or it might be non-rational in kind, neither motivated by rational considerations, nor responsive to them. Or it might be irrational; it might grip Harry even though he knows he has no reason to be depressed. Or it might partake of some mixture of rational, non-rational and irrational elements. The proper diagnosis depends on the particular case. And since moods endure, the mix can change over time. What is critical is that we do not commit ourselves to some simple typology of moods that places them either inside or outside the domain of the rational. Things are not so straightforward, as any decent psychotherapist will attest.[15]

MOOD, SALIENCE AND SHAPE

How should we conceptualise the influence of moods? I suggest we draw on an idea Jonathan Dancy has developed, after Wiggins (1975–6/1991) and McDowell (1979/1998a). As we saw at the end of the last chapter, Dancy advances a broadly cognitivist conception of reasons, according to which reasons are constituted by features of the world (Dancy, 1993; 2000; 2004). On such a view, *her becoming embarrassed* is a reason to change the subject; *its starting to rain* is a reason to think the streets will be wet; *its hurting him* is a reason to stop slapping him on the back, and so on. Such reason-constituting considerations do not operate in isolation. Dancy is a holist about reasons, so some feature's being the reason it is depends on the presence or absence of other factors, some of which may themselves be reasons, while others may be factors that, although not reasons themselves, enable, disable, intensify or attenuate reasons. Thus we can understand the way that factual considerations are operative as reasons by thinking of situations as exhibiting a structure that determines their rational bearing upon us. We can think of the facts as having a profile or 'shape'—certain features have a significance or 'salience' in virtue of which they are, or contribute to, reasons for belief or action (Dancy, 1993, pp. 111–16). Dancy intends the metaphor of shape to have both objective and phenomenological resonance. That is, we are to picture the subject's view of the circumstances in which she finds herself as exhibiting a shape in which certain considerations will be prominent as reason-giving and others backgrounded. At the same time, judgements about shape have objective purport; that is, some considerations do actually constitute reasons, while others may be less important or lack significance altogether. So we can ask if the considerations a subject takes to be salient really are so. What shape she takes the facts to have may not be the shape they really have.

In chapter 5, I recommended Dancy's way of thinking about reasons as a suitable complement to the idea, central to the alliance between McDowell and Ilyenkov, that the space of reasons coincides with the world as we encounter it. I want now to suggest that Dancy's notion of shape can illuminate one of the ways in which moods operate. Moods are sometimes motivated by an appreciation of the significance of some salient consideration—sadness at a friend's disloyalty, for example. But once motivated, we can think of the mood as influencing the subject's perception of the shape of the facts before her. So depression throws into relief some features of a situation and obscures others; it makes certain considerations appear important, while others are taken to have little weight, or it robs features that we formally recognise as salient of motivational or cognitive significance. We normally think of depression as having a distorting influence, though in some cases it might simply reflect just how bad things really are. Parallel accounts can be given for the influence of anxiety or melancholia, and 'positive' moods such as cheerfulness and optimism, though in each case the factors they highlight or shadow will be different. These moods may make the subject more open to the real shape of things, but they can also distort in familiar ways.[16]

This style of thinking can be incorporated into a general way of treating such standing states as virtues, character traits and other dispositions, some of which will be viewed as sensibilities that enable accurate perception of reasons, and others as factors that are, or can be, a distorting influence. It might even be extended to such conditions as Asperger's Syndrome, which is often marked by what might be seen as unusual perceptions of salience. Those who have the syndrome often find it difficult to attend to considerations others see as significant, while being preoccupied with matters in which others see no import. Setting such speculations aside, the point is that our ability to navigate the space of reasons is influenced by certain standing states: virtues, sensibilities, character traits, moods, and so on, which enable our responsiveness to reasons and in which we see the commingling of the rational and non-rational. To coin a slogan, receptivity and spontaneity are not the only factors in play: there is a third, which we might call 'personality', that is critical to the way in which we apprehend the world and find our way through it.

MUSIC

Music is another phenomenon that resists tidy factoring into rational and non-rational components. As we have seen, McDowell holds that the content of perceptual experience is conceptual in nature and hence within the space of reasons. 'In experience', he writes, 'one takes in, for instance sees, *that things are thus and so*. That is the sort of thing that one can also, for instance, judge' (1994, p. 9). He would therefore seem to be committed to the view that the content of musical experience is conceptual.[17]

This might provoke scepticism. What kind of conceptual content is a phrase of, say, Beethoven's 4th Symphony supposed to have? In the case of visual experience, we can understand what its conceptual content amounts to: it is what, in virtue of the experience, we are entitled to think or say that the environment is like. But when it comes to sound, thinking about the content of the auditory environment is not much like entertaining a linguistic thought of the form *things are thus and so*. Of course, forms of musical notation express conceptual structures, but facility with those structures is not a necessary condition of musical experience.

In response, the conceptualist can reply that our experience of music is permeated by the conceptual in the following sense. Any musical experience draws into play at least a range of basic concepts of pitch, rhythm, harmony, discord, location, intensity, and so on. Some of these concepts are sortals that can be used with demonstratives—*that* tone, *this* beat, etc.—others are adjectival notions—loud, quiet, fast, slow, high, low, concordant, discordant, etc., and their corresponding comparatives, and so on. These basic building blocks can then be refined into musical concepts that sustain systems of notation, languages of interpretation and criticism, and so on. These concepts are drawn into play in experience and in acts of musical imagination, as when we hear something 'in our mind's ear'. Not that the subject must have words for all these concepts. The conceptualist's point is that, for a human being, experience is conceptually unified, so that anything entering the field of experience can be integrated into it. It follows that all experience must have a conceptual *form*—it must be the sort of thing that *can be* entertained in thought and encompassed by language. It does not follow that the subject must already be able to put it into words (see McDowell, 2007b/2009b).[18] The scepticism expressed in the previous paragraph rests on a bogus contrast. The auditory environment often discloses to us that things are thus and so. Just as I can see that the cat is on the mat, I can hear that someone has opened the door. Moreover, I can hear that she thinks it will rain on the picnic by listening to what she says. Of course, complex auditory events, such as a performance of Beethoven's 4th, cannot usually be construed as asserting something of the form, *this is how things are*; but then the same is true of a visual experience of an abstract painting. But in both cases concepts are drawn into play in the experience—indeed, in both cases the respective experiences owe their unity as experiences of, on the one hand, a work of music, on the other, a work of art, to the work of concepts.

There is an important distinction, however, between musical concepts and ordinary empirical concepts, like *horse*. As we saw in chapter 1, anyone who has the concept *horse* must have certain abilities: she must be able to recognise and re-identify horses, to entertain thoughts about horses, to draw certain inferences, and to be equipped to acquire certain theoretical knowledge about the sorts of things horses are. Not everyone who has the concept has the whole spectrum of abilities, but the abilities lie on a developmental path we have all trodden to a greater or lesser extent. Musical concepts are no different, but in their case the developmental path has less to do with facility with content in propositional form and more with the emergence of abilities exemplified in musical practice of one kind or another. It is not just that many musical concepts, like colour concepts, can be acquired only through acquaintance with their objects. Properly to grasp the concept 'from within' requires the exercise of certain musical abilities, and for many people these do not come easily. This presupposes initiation into a musical culture—by which I mean being enculturated into certain kinds of music. Having a well-developed language for discussing music is not a necessary condition for possessing even sophisticated musical concepts, because facility with the concepts can be exemplified in performance, or in response to the music, including attentive listening. So, for example, a musician might have the concept of a certain interval in that she can recognise it, produce it, appreciate its relations to other intervals, its bearing on melody and harmony, yet be unable to describe or notate it.

The outcome of this discussion is that musical experience does bear conceptual content that can stand in relation to judgement. The judgements in question may be descriptive in character (e.g., 'That's a major 6th'), or they may pertain to questions of aesthetics (e.g., 'That's cacophonous') or interpretation (e.g., 'This should be resolved *just so*'). The latter judgements might be exemplified in practice rather than words—they might be concepts of what to *do* (see McDowell, 2007c/2009b). Judgements might also be made about the overall character of the music or its 'message', if such it has. A strength of the conceptualist approach is that it makes this easy to appreciate. At the same time, however, the conceptualist must acknowledge the obvious truth that the effect of music upon us does not reside exclusively in yielding judgement or its analogues. Music exhilarates, inspires, placates, appals, and so on. In musical performance, composition or appreciation, we cannot clearly distinguish what music gives us reason to think and feel from what it *makes* us think and feel. Music does not move us by anything akin to argument. It grabs our feelings; it evokes attitudes. But for all that, those feelings and attitudes are prompted in ways that are open to normative assessment. Music's influence on us is not *merely* causal. If it were, it would be senseless to hold that certain ways of responding to the music find in it aesthetic elements that are genuinely aspects of the work, while other responses fall short. Appreciating music, either as performer or listener, is a matter of making a certain sort of sense and, as such, it involves navigating the space of reasons, even if one can justify the path one has taken only retroactively, inarticulately and demonstratively.

It is no surprise that in this regard music shares an affinity with mood, for music is a wonderful means of the expression of mood, and is so because it has power to work on mood. It is a truism that this kind of influence is not confined to music. Similar things might be said about the visual arts and about some instances of spoken or written language, especially poetry. Many song lyrics, for example, work to create a certain sort of mood or atmosphere. In some cases, this is a by-product of a more conventional message. But sometimes this is the lyric's very point.[19] A line may have the form of an assertion *that things are thus and so*, but its object is not a description of states of affairs, as that would normally be understood, but something that might be called the evocation of image in the service of mood. We cannot understand such phenomena if we work with a naive contrast between rational and non-rational modes of influence.

EDUCATION

I want now to return the discussion to the theme with which this chapter opened: autonomy as the end of education. The position I have defended in this book invites the following view of the process of education. Learning is a matter of acquiring the conceptual capacities and qualities of character that enable responsiveness to reasons, and teaching is a matter of facilitating their acquisition and development. Learning is successful to the degree that the learner gains command of the subject-matter or practice, where to have such command is to be able to make up one's mind about what to think or do in the relevant domain in light of what there is most reason to think or do.[20] This involves the development and cultivation of theoretical and practical reasoning, understood not as formal or abstract techniques of thought, but as powers to engage intelligently with concrete subject-matter in all its presentness and particularity.[21] As I have tried to bring out in this chapter, these are not powers of pure intellects, but of human beings, finite and embodied, whose manner of responding to reasons cannot be understood without appreciating the way their lives are informed by sensibility and emotion, personality and mood. Such phenomena do not merely constrain or inhibit rationality and autonomy. On the contrary, human rationality and autonomy would be unrecognisable without them.

It is important that the notion of autonomy does not stand alone, but must be understood in light of the internal relations it bears to other key concepts, including the concept of *knowledge*. In the discussion of the rational agency conception of freedom in chapter 4, I followed McDowell in holding that, where an agent thinks and acts freely, her thoughts and actions are determined by reasons. Here, McDowell insists, it does not suffice that she *takes* the considerations that guide her to be reasons, they must genuinely *be* reasons. This establishes a relation between the idea of freedom and the idea of knowledge of what is a reason for what. We can complement this with a corresponding view of the nature of autonomy. If we treat autonomy as the power to make up one's mind about what to think or do in light of what there is reason to think or do, then we can say that the exercise of that power finds its fullest expression when our making up our mind expresses knowledge of what to think or do. So, the idea that autonomy is the end of education coincides with the idea that learning aims at knowledge of what to think and do, not just because knowledge is necessary for making informed judgements and choices, but because the power to make up one's mind in light of reasons *aims at* knowledge. Knowledge is, as it were, its ideal.[22]

Throughout this book, I have followed McDowell in speaking of human beings acquiring conceptual capacities through *Bildung*, understood, at least in part, as induction into traditions of thought and reasoning. What conception of learning does such a view imply? Central to the idea of *Bildung*, thus understood, is a process we can call 'learning through initiation'. On this view, if a learner initially lacks the conceptual resources to find her way in the domain at issue, the first step is for her to be brought to behave in ways that conform to correct practice in the domain. For an infant entering the space of reasons, the first vehicles of such learning are imitation and habituation. The learner must then gradually move from simply acting in accord with correct practice to acting in the knowledge that this practice is correct.[23] In this process, she is beholden to others in various ways—first, to exemplify correct practice; second, to hold her to the relevant standards of correctness; and third, to assist her in meeting those standards. But merely knowing that one is acting in a way that counts as correct is not enough. The proper end of the learning process is when the learner not only thinks and acts in accord with correct practice in the domain, but does so out of an understanding of the grounds for so acting and thinking. In such a situation, her thought and action are controlled by reasons that she understands and endorses. She moves from reproducing *what* is required of her, to knowing *that* it is required of her, to acting out of an understanding of *why* it is required; that is, an understanding of the normative demands constitutive of the domain in question.[24] With such an understanding, the learner is in a position self-consciously to allow her thought and action to issue from her appreciation of the logic of the subject alone. As such, she is no longer beholden to others in the way she was before. In view of her mastery of the subject, she has independence of mind and can take responsibility for her thoughts and actions in the domain.

This account represents learning as a movement from a non-rationally secured conformity with correct practice, through increasing knowledge of correct practice, to a state of rational command of the grounds of correct practice.[25] The distinction between acting in conformity with a practice and acting out of a self-conscious appreciation of the grounds for so thinking and acting is a familiar one. It is important, however, that when applied to learning, the distinction yields only a schema. The critical transition to understanding can be abrupt and dramatic (such as the 'ah-ha' moment when one suddenly sees how to do a certain kind of mathematical question, or grasps a difficult grammatical form in a foreign language), or gradual (where, in Wittgenstein's famous phrase, 'light dawns gradually over the whole'). Moreover, in many cases understanding is not an all-or-nothing condition, and learners may occupy various transitional states of partial or fragmented understanding before attaining command of the subject-matter, if they ever do so. The end may not be attained, because of shortcomings of the learner or in the conditions of learning. Or it may be thwarted by the elusive nature of the subject-matter itself. In my view, a good deal of learning in philosophy proceeds according to the schema, but our mastery of the subject-matter is always provisional: a grip on even the most basic philosophical concepts is always at risk of being loosened by new insights.

One account in the philosophical literature of learning through initiation is Aristotle's picture of moral development in the *Nicomachean Ethics*, which, as we noted, McDowell cites to illustrate what he means by *Bildung*. Following Myles Burnyeat, we can reconstruct Aristotle's view of the learning process as follows: the learner first acquires by habituation knowledge of 'the *that*'; that is, knowledge of what virtuous conduct consists in. This is attained by acquiring good habits of action. The knowledge must be internalised—the learner must know not just what virtuous people think is appropriate conduct and act accordingly, she must herself see the conduct as appropriate. Action in accord with virtue must become second nature to her.[26] Finally, the learner is helped to reach a conception of 'the *because*'—an understanding, case by case, of the ground of virtuous action, that which explains and justifies 'the *that*'. Such a person possesses *phronesis* or practical wisdom.

Burnyeat makes the following perceptive comment on Aristotle's account:

> From all this it follows not only that for a long time moral development must be a less than fully rational process but also, what is less often acknowledged, that a mature morality must in large part continue to be what it originally was, a matter of responses deriving from sources other than reflective reason. These being the fabric of moral character, in the fully developed man of virtue and practical wisdom they have become integrated with, indeed they are now infused and corrected by, his reasoned scheme of values. (Burnyeat, 1980, p. 80)

I want to suggest that what Burnyeat says in this passage has wider application than the domain of moral development. There are lessons here for our understanding of the infant's entrance into the space of reasons as such. For a precondition of the child's acquiring conceptual capacities that open up the world to her is that she shares with those around her what Stanley Cavell, expounding Wittgenstein, calls:

routes of interest and feeling, modes of response, senses of humour and of significance and of fulfilment, of what is outrageous, of what is similar to what else, what a rebuke, what forgiveness, of when an utterance is an assertion, when an appeal, when an explanation—all the whirl of organism Wittgenstein calls 'forms of life'. (Cavell, 1969, p. 52)[27]

Throughout this book, I have stressed the social character of *Bildung*, but *Bildung* can occur only if the child is in tune with those around her, and, for that, child and adult must have enjoy the kind of fundamental agreement that Wittgenstein marks with the expression 'form of life'. Reason can grow in the child only on the basis of a commonality of being, shared by the child with those around her, and agreement that is not itself secured by reason. In harmony with Burnyeat's observation, and with the overarching theme of this chapter, we should not think of the non-rational foundations of reason as transcended in the lives of mature rational animals. Our shared form of life is the ever-present background of our activity, and the shared sensibilities Cavell captures so beautifully continue to be operative even though 'now infused and corrected by reason'. We are no less creatures of mood, even though moods have a different place in the lives of mature, rational agents than they do in the lives of infants. Something similar can be said for music, and for so much else in our lives.[28]

We need to reflect further on the end point of the learning process. How are we to understand the state of being in rational command of some subject-matter? We have cast this in terms of the learner acting out of an appreciation of what there is most reason to think or do. It is easy to assume, therefore, that anyone with such an appreciation must be able explicitly to formulate her reasons and explain how they justify her beliefs or actions. This is certainly an appropriate aspiration for learning in some domains. But not all. Where the outcome of learning is mastery of a skill, the successful learner may command the skill without being able verbally to articulate the grounds of her actions (think of the case of Sissy Jupe discussed back in chapter 1). The learner's command can be manifest in the manner of her acting, and in her ability to exercise the skill from case to case. We say 'she knows what she is doing' when she can allow her activity to be fluidly controlled by the normative context—where she lets herself follow the topography of the space of reasons. She does not have to put that knowledge into words, she just has to exemplify the relevant concepts in action.[29] Often, of course, we expect of rational agents practical knowledge, manifest in activity, *in consort with* the power verbally to articulate and endorse reasons for belief and action. This is so in morality, where we typically demand that agents act not just in accord with the right reasons, but that they endorse those reasons as their own, and can give them in defence of their actions to other rational agents. It is a matter of controversy, however, what this demand should amount to. Many philosophers offer theories of moral reasoning that expect agents to be highly articulate in arguing for their actions by specifying and justifying their reasons. Those inspired by Aristotle, however, often deplore the 'intellectualism' characteristic of so much analytic moral philosophy, maintaining that it fails to recognise that sound moral judgement depends on the exercise of a skill—practical wisdom—that resists codification into rules or principles that might be adduced to warrant particular judgements.[30] Rather, statements such as 'It was the kind thing to do' or 'I thought it might embarrass her' can, understood in context, exhaustively specify an agent's reason for action. Assessing such claims as reasons is a matter of thinking one's way into the circumstances of judgement to see why the situation necessitated a response of this kind. It is not a matter of weighing arguments pro and anti, but of reflecting upon different ways of seeing the situation at hand in order to discern those that carry conviction.[31]

Of course not *all* learning is learning through initiation. Once a person has facility with the concepts in some domain, she can acquire new knowledge by inference and testimony, and she can imagine, invent and discover. But the idea of learning through initiation illuminates the infant's initial entry into the space of reasons and the cultivation of virtue, as well as many situations of schooling in which learners are introduced to knowledge domains where they possess only rudimentary conceptual resources to enable them to find their way. The conception also yields insight into the relation of teacher and learner. At the early stages of such learning, what the teacher offers by example or instruction the learner must simply appropriate. They are engaged in what is essentially a joint activity, where the teacher addresses a student who is unable independently to engage with the subject-matter. The nature of this joint activity will depend on the character of the subject-matter. If the subject is theoretical, their interaction may begin as a kind of one-sided conversation. But if it is practical—if a skill is being taught—then they may literally be involved in collaborative activity, in which the teacher lends the student her skill in an exercise of collective intentionality. In any case, the learning process is one in which the student gradually attains independence until she is in command of the subject-matter. As this occurs, so a different kind of teaching and learning becomes possible, one based on two-way conversation and mutual enquiry. This new conversation, however, must be understood in light of what we have learned of the commingling of the rational and the non-rational. We cannot see it as a purely rational exchange of ideas. Teachers know very well that they need to establish a mood conducive to learning and, if I may speak metaphorically, that there must be a certain music to pedagogical experience. Inspiration, wonder and awe—powerful motives for learning—dwell on the border of the rational and the non-rational: they are open to rational assessment, but they do not present in the form of judgement or move us by argument. Their work is different, and their influence does not diminish as a person's rational autonomy increases. On the contrary, it is a mark of excellence in a teacher if she can help keep such feelings alive in her students.[32]

This vision of teaching and learning can also help illuminate the relation of passive and active elements in learning. It is tempting to operate with a distinction between pedagogical methods that treat learning as a process of passive absorption and those that focus on the learner's active role in acquiring concepts, skills and knowledge. At its most basic, the distinction contrasts instruction as the 'transmission' of knowledge from teacher to pupil with a 'child-centred' vision of students learning by actively constructing the knowledge domain. Our conception enables us to introduce more subtlety into the discussion. We have cast learning through initiation as a transition from passive appropriation to autonomous rational command. But even within that schema, we can acknowledge ways in which the learner is, or can be, active from the beginning. Even in the case of the infant's entrance into the space of reasons, where she lacks the resources actively to set out to learn, initiation is possible only by engaging with the child as agent, channelling her activity into patterns of common practice. And where learners already have significant conceptual resources they can bring them actively to bear as they approach new domains where they lack facility. They may have to begin by conforming to the norms of the knowledge domain as something given, but they can intend to do this, in a self-conscious effort to learn, and do it intelligently in a way that facilitates their emerging understanding. Moreover, observation, contemplation and listening—which might all be associated with learning as passive reception—are all things we *do*; indeed, they are things we must learn to do well. Conversely, even where learners are extremely active in their engagement with their subject-matter, their relation to the object of knowledge may yet include a significant element of passivity. For even where the learner is encouraged to take an active role in the learning process, constructing her subject-matter rather than simply acquiring it ready-made as received wisdom, much of her appropriation of that subject-matter may nonetheless proceed by a kind of osmosis, by 'growing into' the subject, by flashes of insight or understanding gratefully received, rather than by explicit deliberation and reasoning (see Claxton, 1997). Much learning is directed to acquiring the ability to apprehend the subject-matter for what it is. Learners may be active enquirers, but what their enquiries aim to disclose to them is the nature of an object that is not an object of their activity. Finally, if we are to think of the relation of teacher and student on the model of conversation, then once again we will find both passive and active dimensions essentially at work throughout the learning process, sometimes in an unruly dialectic, sometimes in considered balance, but always together. This, it seems to me, is something that any plausible pedagogical theory must have firmly in its sights.

CONCLUSION

The primary purpose of this chapter has been to correct a potential misconception arising from the view that rational animals are 'at home in the space of reasons'. This is the idea that our status as inhabitants of the space of reasons is best exemplified by the exercise of pure, unencumbered spontaneity, and that it is in this that our authentic personhood ultimately resides. Navigating the space of reasons is a matter of freely, self-consciously and deliberately tracing rational relations. As an antidote to this view, I first sought to bring out how many transactions in the space of reasons cannot be construed on the model of deliberate inference or other modes of self-conscious ratiocination. This is true of perceptual judgement, and of those forms of responsiveness to reasons that lend themselves to construal on the model of perception. But more dramatically, it is true of many insights that simply come to us, either unbidden, or at some remove from conscious deliberation. I then turned to the interplay of the rational and non-rational in our lives. The distinction between rational and scientific modes of intelligibility, so crucial to McDowell's thought, invites us to think that we can factor episodes and states neatly into those that are within the space of reasons and those that are not. This is fine if the contrast is between events such as thinking that the cat is on the mat, on the one hand, and accidentally spilling wine on the cat, on the other. But much that goes on in our lives resists such pigeon-holing. Mood is a phenomenon that exists on and around the border of the rational and the non-rational, and music another. No account of what it is to be at home in the space of reasons can fail to appreciate this. Of course, it might be countered that the idea of unencumbered spontaneity is merely an ideal. But even as an ideal it embodies a distorted conception of our nature, a mislocation of authentic personhood. The non-rational does not always figure as encumbrance, inhibiting our ability to respond to reasons. On the contrary, it can serve to enable that responsiveness.

After defending this position, I began to explore some of its implications for issues of education. The prominence I have given to the concept of autonomy might suggest that my position is located squarely in the tradition of liberal philosophy of education. As anticipated back in chapter 1, there are continuities between the view defended in this book and the idea of liberal education expounded by the London School of Paul Hirst, R. S. Peters and Robert Dearden. Their view of autonomy was, as Paul Standish puts it, 'internally related to a rich conception of the development of mind through initiation into public modes of thought and engagement in worthwhile activities. This involved "getting on the inside" of subjects of study in a gradual initiation into "the conversation of mankind"; this, it was sometimes said, was the creation of mind itself' (Standish, 2003a, p. 172). In this respect at least, their view is very like mine.

My position is rather different, however, from the kind of liberal philosophy of education propounded by those who succeeded Hirst, Peters and Dearden. In the work of these later thinkers autonomy tends to be equated with the ability to *choose*, specifically to choose how to live in way that best satisfies preferences that one has formed without coercion. On this view, education is charged with equipping individuals with the resources to form considered preferences and make unpressured choices about how best to satisfy them, while fostering the qualities of character necessary to assume the burdens of such choices (see, e.g., White, 1990, p. 23). My view gives the notions of choice and preference-satisfaction far less prominence. On my account, the fundamental notion of autonomy is the idea of the power to make up one's mind what to think and do in light of what there is reason to think and do. The power to determine one's thought and action by reasons is not primarily a power of choice. Only sometimes does the outcome of theoretical or practical deliberation permit a choice about what to think or do. Of course, there are many ways of living a good life, many ways of flourishing, and life puts before each person the question of how to live well. But ways of life are not laid before us like samples of cloth to be chosen for a garment. We are thrown into life and must find our way. The more we can make up our minds about what to think and do in light of good reasons, the greater our self-conscious control over ourselves, and the greater our chance of living a life informed by a compelling conception of what is genuinely worthwhile. However, the process in which we attain the power of autonomy—*Bildung*—is one in which we are formed as agents with values, preferences, concerns and commitments; that is, we emerge as rational beings already possessed of views about the good, however partial, confused or incoherent they may be. Our task is to bring those views to consciousness and subject them to critical thought. The more we are autonomous, the more we are able to reflect upon what we value, so that we can embrace a conception of the good we can endorse and live by. To idealise this as the unencumbered choice of free individuals is to distort the situation in which we find ourselves. Standish offers a far more accurate depiction when he writes:

> We are founded in the ways that we find ourselves, in the culture with its givens, with the acknowledgement and observance that it requires of us. It is in relation to these given practices that we find our voice. In the culture we are schooled in we find the words that make possible our aversion from conformity, not least in the rich traditions of subjects of study. And this aversion ... is internally related to the possibility of our living better, of our orientation toward perfection. It is a moral imperative that comes from neither authority nor law but that speaks to our own best, attained yet unattained, selves. Finding our voice in this way is our most authentic engagement with the world. (Standish, 2003b, p. 230)

Standish's words, inspired by Cavell's reading of Emerson, are in harmony with a conception of autonomy, properly understood. For to attain the power to determine one's thoughts and actions in light of what there is reason to think and do is to find one's voice—to speak for oneself in one's own name. Thus in educating for autonomy, we educate to enable not choice, but judgement. The ingredients of good judgement are knowledge, powers of theoretical and practical reasoning and the many qualities of character essential for their judicious exercise. What Standish reminds us is that when we see these powers not as simply already given, but set them rather in the process of their formation, problems of the cultivation of autonomy and of the search for authenticity are sides of the same coin.

Because I see the idea of autonomy as internally related to the idea of knowledge, and have no sceptical concerns about knowledge of value, I have little regard for the view that educational systems and institutions should be neutral with respect to conceptions of the good. The rhetoric of neutralist liberalism sits uneasily with the reality of schooling.[33] Educational institutions embody and promote values in so many ways, sometimes strongly and explicitly. So do teachers, who often inspire students precisely because they project a powerful conception of what *matters*. *Bildung* is the formation of character, so it had better be informed by plausible conceptions of the good. I do believe, however, that schools should promote open-minded pluralism about values, and tolerance of diverse conceptions of the good, but not out of relativism or agnosticism about the good. The reasons are three. First, value pluralism is true, we are fallible, and there is much room for reasonable dispute about where the good lies. Such dispute must be sensitive to the particular circumstances of people's lives, for only some worthwhile lives are real options for a person, and it is easy for the decisions one makes to further delimit one's options than to open up new ones.[34] So it is vital that educational contexts stretch students' imaginations about what is possible for them. Second, schools are societies of individuals, who bring with them a variety of contrasting conceptions of how to live, and have to get along with one another. Third, and most importantly, only if a person deliberates in such a way as to arrive at judgements that she can endorse are those judgements truly her own. People must decide how to live because that decision cannot be made for them without affronting their autonomy and slighting their nature as rational animals. An education must aspire to equip students to determine what to think and how to act in light of reasons for so doing, but if it determines this on their behalf it diminishes them. The question of how to live is posed for each of us in the first person and we must answer in the first person, and do so authentically with responses we genuinely endorse. The precondition of this is a culture of critical reflection on truth and goodness in an atmosphere of tolerance, where intellectual risks can be taken free of prejudice and fear. This is what schools must aspire to create.

NOTES

1 Many representatives of the Russian socio-historical tradition considered questions of the nature of education to be philosophically central, so central indeed that they did not recognise a specific subdiscipline of philosophy of education (see, e.g., Mikhailov, 2001, pp. 401–552; Ilyenkov, 2002a).
2 My use of the idea of a power is inspired by Rödl's treatment of the notion (see Rödl, 2007, especially ch. 5).
3 It would be a bad mistake to attribute to McDowell the kind of rationalism targeted by Michael Oakeshott in his famous essay 'Rationalism in Politics' (1962/1991). Oakeshott himself makes clear that the rationalism he attacks should not be taken to be definitive of the terms 'reason', 'rational', 'rationality' and so on (see ibid., pp. 22–23, n. 24, and especially 1950/1991).
4 As one might expect, given the fact that McDowell's view of moral judgement cited above emerges in the course of a discussion of Aristotle's notion of *phronesis* (McDowell, 1979/1998a).

We should note that in a later exchange Dreyfus concedes that his 2005 critique of McDowell was flawed by a number of misunderstandings. He acknowledges both that McDowell is not committed to the view that 'mind at its best is detached from immersion in activity', and that McDowell holds that 'conceptuality is situation-specific' (Dreyfus, 2007, pp. 371–72). Nonetheless, Dreyfus continues to complain about McDowell's view that 'embodied coping' is permeated by the conceptual (see Dreyfus, 2007a, 2007b; McDowell, 2007b/2009b, 2007c/2009b).
5 One should be wary of the kind of contrast between rule-following and the exercise of educated sensitivity that Dreyfus's objection seems to presuppose. As we observed earlier (chapter 5, note 12), McDowell invokes Wittgenstein to argue that the ability to follow a rule rests ultimately upon a form of understanding—the ability to 'see' what the rule asks of one—that cannot itself be codified on pain of regress. So it is not that someone's acting is either the result of adherence to articulable rules or a manifestation of an embodied sensibility, for the latter is a presupposition of the former.

Reason and Its Limits: Music, Mood and Education   145

6 Both Rouse and Dreyfus draw inspiration, in different ways, from Todes's *Body and World* (2001).
7 As noted in chapter 5, note 3, McDowell originally cast the distinction as one between rational explanation and explanation by appeal to scientific law, but he has recently modified the contrast by recognising that not all scientific explanation need be strictly nomological in the sense originally implied (see McDowell, 1994, pp. 70–1; 2000a, pp. 6–7; 2006b, pp. 235–6). Much that goes on in the lives of non-human animals cannot be represented as the inexorable outcome of scientific law, though it can be rendered intelligible by biology. So McDowell now draws the contrast as one between space-of-reasons intelligibility, on the one hand, and a rather catholic view of 'natural-scientific intelligibility', on the other.
8 The objection is undoubtedly encouraged by speaking of some episodes as 'in' the space of reasons and others as 'outside' it and 'in' the realm of law, rather than talking only of states and episodes being open to different styles of explanation. But since McDowell himself deploys the problematic idiom, I think it is fair to use it in setting up the objection (e.g., McDowell, 2000a, p. 7).
9 Perhaps this is partly what underlies Dreyfus's objections.
10 To speak of 'passivity within spontaneity' might seem oxymoronic, but if spontaneity is 'the mind's power of producing representations from itself' (Kant, 1781/1933, A 51/B 75) there should be no obstacle to recognising passive elements in the manifestation of that power.
11 Brandom would no doubt disavow the fantasy that the space of reasons is a province in which reason enjoys total control. It is interesting, however, that McDowell chides him for failing to appreciate the options that are opened up in epistemology once the fantasy is rejected (see McDowell, 2002a/2009b).
12 Guy Claxton's *Hare Brain, Tortoise Mind* (1997) contains interesting reflections on the passive dimensions of creativity; see, e.g., the many relevant quotations from scientists and scholars on pp. 56–60.
13 We should briefly consider how these remarks relate to the discussion of freedom and rational necessity in chapter 4. There I gave two cases, strikingly similar to those under consideration here, to illustrate how freedom can be exhibited in subordination to rational necessity. The first was that of a concert pianist brilliantly playing a piece just so; the second that of a scholar making an exhilarating response in debate. In such cases, I suggested, it is appropriate to describe their respective performances as manifestations of freedom, even though both might say that they had no choice in the matter of how to play or what to say. We so describe them in part because we see the pianist and scholar as in command of their material. How does this relate to the similar examples I give here to burst the bubble of unencumbered reason? In the present examples, where more improvisation and spontaneity are at stake, it seems more appropriate to describe the agents, not so much as commanding their subject-matter, but as commanded by it. They have, as it were, given themselves over to the currents of reason. In contrast to the earlier cases, where pianist and scholar may be said to know exactly what they are doing, the present examples are cases where competence is consistent with the agents' not quite knowing how things will turn out. In these cases, we can think of the agents as attuned to rational necessity, and their freedom expressed in the fact that they are the kinds of beings that can tune themselves into the appropriate 'wavelength'. Of course, they are *agents*, not mere vehicles, even if they sometimes feel as if they are spectators of their own actions. There is an element of control in the manner of their attunement and in their judgements about how things are turning out— which must involve continuous reflective endorsement if they are to acknowledge their doings as their own—and in their anticipations of where they might be going. Their control may also take the form of legitimate confidence that, wherever things lead, they will not lose a grip on what they are playing or saying. So despite the differences, I see the two pairs of examples as situated on a spectrum. Not all forms of responsiveness to reasons exhibit the command we attribute to agents in those cases that best exemplify the expression of freedom in subordination

146   *The Formation of Reason*

to rational necessity, but even where reason is at its most passive it still enjoys essential elements of control. In *all* cases control is not unconditional but subject to a variety of contingencies. There are many ways the world must cooperate if our judgements are to be in tune with the facts and our activity successful.

14 McDowell denies that the same notion of mental content can be deployed for intentional states and sub-personal mechanisms. Only persons can have states that are contentful in the sense of bearing on the world. So it makes no sense to think of a person delegating problems to her subconscious. The most we can say is that the sub-personal mechanisms that enable thinking continue working during sleep and causally contribute to the production of something that we can later locate in the space of reasons and treat as a potential solution to our problem (see McDowell, 1994/1998a). In this, McDowell differs dramatically from Claxton, who is at ease with the idea that we can allow our unconscious to think on our behalf.

15 To emphasise the point, consider the manner in which rational considerations influence moods. Sometimes the effect is immediate and total. Suppose I am sad because I regret having lost something of great sentimental value. If I suddenly find it, my sadness is gone right away. In contrast, some moods lift only gradually, and may do so under the influence of entirely non-rational factors, or of a complex mix of rational and non-rational elements. Consider the way in which 'time heals'. It is tempting to say that the influence of the passage of time is entirely non-rational. After all, there is often no less reason to regret someone's death 20 years after the fact than there is on the day of his funeral. It is, we might surmise, just a fact of human nature that our loss becomes less vivid and all-consuming. But this would be too simple a picture. Grief is a complex emotional state held in light of the recognition of loss. We acknowledge the natural fact that distress diminishes over time by taking it up into the domain of reason and establishing an intuitive normative standard governing how it is appropriate to grieve and for how long. Hence, the healing influence of time is mediated by rational considerations about when it is appropriate to 'let go', considerations that are open to critical scrutiny. The issue turns from one about how people typically do feel into one about how it is *fitting* to feel if we are properly to acknowledge the loss of those we love. No sense can be made of this if we work with a sharp opposition between rational and non-rational influences.

16 The notion of shape can be deployed to illuminate the phenomenon of what we might call 'objective moods'. We speak of places or events as having moods, such as the mood of a room, or of a gathering, or of a piece of music. To say that a room is 'cheerful' is not just to make a causal claim about how it affects the mood of those who enter it. There is also a normative dimension. The room has qualities that warrant a certain kind of positive response.

17 It might be denied that McDowell is so committed on the grounds that the perceptual content on which he focuses is 'world-disclosing', the sort of thing that can justify empirical beliefs. This sort of content, he argues, must be conceptual in character. He does allow, however, that non-conceptual content might play a role elsewhere in our theory. Might he not therefore concede that musical experience is non-conceptual in character because musical experience is not world-disclosing? I do not think, however, that this strategy is open to him. Musical experience is world-disclosing in the sense that it opens the subject to organised configurations of sound in her environment, configurations that the subject can integrate into her world-view. Indeed, I think McDowell would say that all content available to consciousness is conceptual in character—it is all available to be integrated into the subject's conception of the world, even as mere hallucination. When McDowell allows non-conceptual content into his philosophy, he portrays it as operating at a sub-personal level (see note 14 above). He grants that cognitive scientists can legitimately operate with something called 'content' when they theorise about the mechanisms of mind. But he is adamant that this is a conception of content different from bone fide conceptual content (he sometimes speaks of '"as if" content attribution') (see McDowell, 1994/1998a, pp. 351–2).

18 McDowell's arguments for conceptualism have been the subject of much critical attention. Michael Luntley (2003) has argued that the conceptualist cannot give a plausible account of

musical experience, which he argues is better treated as non-conceptual in character. Luntley's argument rests on the claim that if content is conceptual, the subject must be able to deploy it in the rational organisation of her behaviour. I think he takes too demanding a view of what the latter criterion commits us to. Nonetheless, the discussion is insightful, and well versed in the relevant literature on conceptualism in general and musical experience in particular.

19 Many examples could be given, but some particularly good ones can be found in the songs of Elvis Costello (e.g., *I Don't Want to go to Chelsea*; *Watching the Detectives*). Although his lyrics are carefully constructed, it is often difficult to say what the songs are *about*. Yet the mood they create is deliberate and determinate.

20 In using the expression 'making up one's mind', I should again acknowledge the influence of Richard Moran, who deploys the notion in articulating his conception of the deliberative stance, on which I have drawn earlier in this work (Moran, 2001).

21 I think it is important to respect the distinction between theoretical and practical reasoning, the former resulting in the formation of belief, the latter in action. However, it will be important to the discussion of learning that follows that we do not work with an artificially sharp distinction between them. It is critical to recognise that belief is essentially manifest in action, and that an action is essentially the expression of a thought. Moreover, theoretical reasoning is itself a practice, and learning science, or mathematics or history involves learning to *do* lots of things. Simple truths, though easily neglected.

22 Of course the power of autonomy can be misused or its exercise thwarted by circumstance. An autonomous being retains that power even in cases where its exercise goes awry, just as a juggler retains the power to juggle even if unfavourable circumstances make it impossible for her to keep the balls in the air (the example is Rödl's from his expert discussion of the power of reflective knowledge in his 2007, ch. 5). And where things go awry we can ask whether and to what degree the agent is culpable. Should she have known that conditions were unfavourable? Error can be blameless—we are, after all, fallible creatures who do not enjoy full control over their epistemic circumstances—or it can bespeak lack of attention or diligence on our part.

23 Of course, a more conceptually adept learner than the infant may approach the learning task intentionally from the outset, deliberately setting out to reproduce the activities in question as a first step to acquiring knowledge of the domain.

24 Some 'social pragmatist' or 'communitarian' readings of Wittgenstein's rule-following considerations falter on this point. Competence with a concept amounts to more than conformity with the linguistic community. I can use a concept in conformity with others, and know that I do, yet not understand the concept. Understanding requires me to appreciate the grounds on which the concept is correctly deployed, which should not be conflated with facts about how others use it.

25 The trajectory is consistent with the model of concept development sketched in chapter 1.

26 Myles Burnyeat invokes the notion of second nature in his outstanding commentary on Aristotle's view, to which I am much indebted (Burnyeat, 1980, p. 74). Interestingly, Irwin and Fine offer a different translation of the relevant passage from the *Nicomachean Ethics* (1147a21–22), speaking not of second nature, but of knowledge 'growing into' the learner (Aristotle, 1995, p. 415).

27 As students of McDowell will know, I am here deploying texts that McDowell himself cites. He refers approvingly to Burnyeat's paper (McDowell, 1994, p. 84), and quotes the same passage from Cavell with admiration (McDowell, 1979/1998a, p. 60; 1981/1998a, pp. 206–7).

28 If we are to do justice to these thoughts, we must be careful not to be misled by certain connotations of the term *Bildung*. Though McDowell's immediate source is Gadamer, the term inevitably invokes Hegel's conception of learning in which the subject overcomes the otherness of the object. Rational understanding thus involves the relation of 'being with oneself in another'; and this, for Hegel, constitutes a form of freedom. Although we can agree with Hegel that

through *Bildung* 'the freedom of spirit is vindicated over the mere positivity of what is given in nature', as Allen Wood aptly puts it (Wood, 1998, p. 302), we should not even flirt with Hegel's comprehensive vision of the cancelling of otherness (which McDowell occasionally appears to do (1994, p. 44; 2000b, p. 97), notwithstanding the reassurances he gives (e.g., 1994, p. 183)). That only invites us to see the *Bildungsprozess* as aspiring to subjugate the non-rational. If we are to have a this-worldly conception of rationality we must appreciate that our ability to navigate the world is essentially mediated by sensibilities, moods, emotions, sensitivities, modes of feeling, and so on, in which the rational and non-rational commingle. Of course, we can work upon such states and dispositions, cultivating and refining them, learning to understand and control them. But the idea that the formation of reason involves liberation from their influence is to be resisted at all costs.

29 As McDowell puts it, responding to Dreyfus: 'The practical concepts realized in action are concepts of things to do. Realizing such a concept is doing the thing in question, not thinking about doing it' (McDowell, 2007c/2009b, p. 325). It is important that there are ways of acting that exemplify understanding even if that understanding cannot be put into words.

30 Here, of course, I have in mind thinkers like McDowell, Wiggins and Dancy, whose views about moral reasons I drew on earlier in this chapter in the discussion of mood. Burnyeat criticises 'intellectualism' in moral philosophy (1980, p. 70).

31 The point is not limited to cases of practical reasoning. Consider mathematics. If successful learning in mathematics entails the learner acquiring self-conscious understanding of the grounds of mathematical judgements, in what form should such understanding be expressed? Doing mathematics depends on an ability to 'see' mathematical relations, but the student need not be able to describe what she sees in any other idiom than the mathematical notation, deployment of which is a precondition of acquiring all but the most simple of mathematical concepts. This is educationally important. It is pedagogically fashionable to ask pupils learning mathematics to explain in words what they are doing (see, for example, the emphasis on oral and mental work in mathematics in the UK's National Numeracy Strategy). This is warranted if the purpose is to encourage learners to reflect upon mathematical activity, thereby stimulating the movement from habitualised responses to action-with-understanding. It would be wrong, however, to assume that the ability to produce a verbal reconstruction is a necessary condition of mathematical understanding. Mathematical competence is exemplified by the ability to think and do *mathematics*, not the ability to speak or write about mathematics.

32 One consequence of these remarks on teaching, consistent with the socio-historical position as a whole, is that we cannot hope to understand expertise in teaching if we employ social scientific strategies modelled on natural science. We need interpretative methods, fit to elucidate the idea of conversation between reasoners. (This is partly what Bruner seeks to capture with the idea of 'meaning-making', prominent in Bruner, 1990. I resist this notion because it invites constructionist excesses, but applaud the intention.)

33 My views about the shortcomings of neutralist liberalism owe much to Christine Sypnowich; see, e.g., Sypnowich, 2003.

34 I have in mind the idea of 'real options' developed by Bernard Williams in his famous article 'The Truth in Relativism' (1974–5).

7
Education Makes Us What We Are

At the outset of this book I posed two questions. First: to what degree do human beings owe their distinctive psychological powers to history, society, and culture? Second: if our relatedness to others is a precondition of our mindedness, to what extent can this be demonstrated or illuminated by philosophical reflection? In answer, I have expounded a socio-historical conception of mind, according to which our characteristically human psychological capacities reside in our responsiveness to reasons. This responsiveness is not simply a gift of nature, but emerges as a child acquires conceptual capacities through initiation into traditions of thinking and reasoning. Enculturation thus effects a gradual transformation, elevating the child into a rational agent in self-conscious control of her thoughts and actions.

Though they make only cameo appearances here, my approach is much inspired by the Russian thinkers on whom I have written in the past. But the most conspicuous influence on the present work is John McDowell. Let me briefly summarise again the position he outlines in *Mind and World*. To be a thinker, McDowell contends, 'is to be at home in the space of reasons'. Human beings are not born with this standing. Indeed, it is 'not even clearly intelligible' that they could be. Rather, 'they are born mere animals, and they are transformed into thinkers and intentional agents in the course of coming to maturity' (McDowell, 1994, p. 125). As we mature, we acquire a 'second nature' through enculturation, or *Bildung*. Our second nature includes conceptual capacities that enable us to move within the space of reasons, so that we think and act in light of a conception of the world, rather than simply respond, as non-human animals must, to biological imperatives. This ability to determine our thoughts and actions by reasons, rather than merely react to the affordances of a local environment, is constitutive of our freedom.

McDowell contends that the space of reasons is autonomous or *sui generis*: that is, it cannot be rendered intelligible by natural-scientific means, but must

The Formation of Reason, First Edition. David Bakhurst.
© 2011 David Bakhurst. Published 2011 by Blackwell Publishing Ltd.

be understood in its own terms. For all that, he argues, there is nothing contrary to nature about second nature, or about the minds it makes possible. *Bildung*, McDowell stresses, is part of the normal maturation of human beings. It will seem mysterious only if we identify the natural exclusively with what falls within the scope of scientific explanation. But we can resist that identification and work with a broader conception of nature that encompasses the life activity of rational animals. And if we do, we can say, contrary to my initial formulation, that mind *is* a gift of nature, but it is second, rather than 'first', nature that is the provider.¹

Much of this book can be read as a sympathetic commentary on McDowell's thought, though one that, I hope, has an orientation somewhat different from most treatments of his work in the contemporary literature. The outcome is a position that gives us reason to bring education to the centre of philosophical attention. In this concluding chapter, after various points of clarification, I consider directions that further discussion of the socio-historical conception might take, concluding with some final thoughts on education.

A RESIDUAL INDIVIDUALISM

A distinctive feature of the view I have defended is that the social is portrayed as enabling the life of the mind, but not as constituting it.² We acquire rational powers through *Bildung*, but neither the exercise of those powers, nor what we achieve through their exercise, is determined by, or otherwise hostage to, the relations we bear to others. As McDowell puts it:

> [A] rational animal could not have acquired the conceptual capacities in the possession of which its rationality consists except by being initiated into a social practice. But as I see things, the capacities transform their possessor into an individual who can achieve standings in the space of entitlements [i.e. the space of reasons] by her own efforts. (McDowell, 2002a/2009b, p. 287)

Whether she achieves such standings is not constitutively dependent on the presence, opinions, attitudes or actions of other people.³ Throughout this book, I have consistently rejected views that cast the social in a stronger, constitutive role; that is, those that portray mind, or mental content, or meaning, or normativity as in some way socially constructed or constituted. In this, McDowell and I are at one. An attraction of such views is that they appear to yield answers to grand philosophical questions, such as *How does normativity get into the world?*; *How is meaning possible?*; *In what do truth, objectivity, and rationality consist?* But the answers they offer distort the nature of our mindedness and its social preconditions. Better to challenge the rationale for the questions themselves.

Some will feel that resistance to the constitutive view bespeaks a tacit commitment to individualism. McDowell discerns Brandom making this accusation, and responds:

> Which is closer to individualism: a position according to which initiation into a social practice yields individuals of a special kind, able to achieve standings in the space of reasons by, for instance, opening their eyes; or a position according to which we supposedly accommodate the very idea of such standings by contemplating subjects individually incapable of achieving them, who somehow nevertheless keep one another under surveillance? At any rate, one can find the second picture unhelpful without denying that sociality is important in understanding our capacities for objective purport. (McDowell, 2002a/2009b, p. 287)

The rhetorical question McDowell poses might surprise the reader. We are invited to conclude that Brandom's view—on which my entitlement to claim knowledge that *p* depends upon whether *others* are prepared to commit to *p*—is actually more (or at least no less) individualistic than McDowell's. But on what grounds? I suggest the following answer. Anti-individualism is sometimes motivated by a yearning to restore a missing sense of community, to counter the bleak picture of individuals as independent, self-contained atoms that informs so much Western thinking about society and the conditions of economic life. McDowell asks which picture best recognises the profundity of our indebtedness to others: one that claims that through enculturation there emerge beings capable of genuine independence of mind, or one that holds that a person's cognitive purchase is constitutively dependent on the judgements and attitudes of others? Surely it is the first view, because it can paint a compelling picture of our dependence upon real relations to real people—those who brought us up, nurtured and educated us—as well as more amorphous relations to our culture, sustained as it is by the countless actions of countless real people, and the ever-present background that is our common form of life. If we read the second view as making our standing as rational beings dependent on the actual attitudes and judgements of others, the result is an Orwellian vision (note the reference to 'surveillance'), where the status of our thoughts (and, on some theories, their very *content*) is somehow conferred upon them by the thoughts and attitudes of others. To counter the excesses of individualism, we are better off casting the social as enabling of mind, rather than constitutive of it.

It would be disingenuous, however, to deny that the socio-historical approach contains elements that can appropriately be described as individualism. After all, its focal point is the individual person—the autonomous subject of a life, self-conscious, responsible, creative. The space of reasons is the realm of freedom, and that freedom is manifest only by the individuals who inhabit it. But this is individualism without the myth of individuals as ready-formed and self-contained prior to society, and, as McDowell would put it, deprived of the fantasy that there is a domain over which reason's control is total. Nevertheless, as we have seen, the notion of an individual's control over her life and mind, albeit partial and subject to contingency, is central to our conception of responsible agency and to the idea of the first-person perspective. And concomitantly, for all our dependency on culture, whatever we inherit or internalise becomes for us a possible object of criticism, for it is only through reflective endorsement that we make our beliefs and values our own. One might call the socio-historical conception, understood in this way, 'individualism without atomism'.

VYGOTSKY'S LEGACY

My hope is that this book will be a stimulus to further enquiry in socio-historical style, especially in regard to issues of education. It is controversial, however, what form future studies should take. In virtue of his Wittgensteinian aversion to constructive philosophising, McDowell does not invoke the notions of *Bildung* and second nature with a view to their being the focus of a research programme, and much of what he says about them is deflationary and minimalistic. Consider, for example, his comment that second nature 'is no more than the idea of a way of being ... that has been acquired by something on the lines of training', an idea we are to invoke only for reassurance that 'for all the *sui generis* character of responsiveness to reasons, there is nothing spooky about it' (McDowell, 2000b, pp. 98–9). There is no suggestion that the concepts of second nature and *Bildung* stand in need of theoretical development. On the contrary, 'the bare invocation' of these ideas is said to suffice (p. 99).

Here McDowell and I appear to disagree. I think we need a compelling account of how rationality is engendered by initiation into social being. This need not be motivated by the desire—which McDowell forswears—systematically to unify first and second nature. The point is that the reassurance McDowell wants will be forthcoming only if our story about the acquisition of rationality is persuasive. But many will be sceptical that we can achieve this by laying so much weight on such notions as 'training'.[4] It will no doubt be asked how a creature that is less than a rational agent, that lacks conceptual powers and is hence not a subject of experience or of world-directed thought, can be 'trained' to acquire the conceptual capacities that will put it in touch with reality? Those who hold that engaging in certain social practices is constitutive of mindedness might get away with the claim that the acquisition of second nature essentially amounts to training in the relevant practices, but once we disavow the constitutive thesis, it looks obvious that the notion of training is too thin. Children are trained to use the toilet or to sleep through the night. But training is the wrong notion even to do full justice to the habituation invoked in chapter 6 to characterise the first steps of 'learning through initiation', let alone the rich social dimensions of language learning or the development of moral, aesthetic or musical sensibilities. At best, it is relevant to *some* aspects of development in these cases, but only some. Children are influenced by adults and peers in many and diverse ways, and any account of the formation of reason must capture this.

The temptation to think exclusively in terms of training derives from operating with too austere a picture of the pre-rational child. We need a sophisticated appreciation of the child's initial state and a nuanced conception of the influences upon her as she becomes an inhabitant of the space of reasons. At this point, we may turn for inspiration to Vygotsky, a thinker with whom the term 'socio-historical' has long been associated, and whose work contains a blueprint of the kind of framework for which we are looking.[5]

Vygotsky portrays the mature human mind as a system of 'higher mental functions'. These include linguistic thought and reasoning, intelligent speech, voluntary memory and attention, rational perception, deliberate volition, reasonable desire, considered emotion. These capacities are 'interfunctionally related'; that is, the nature and development of each is determined in part by the relations it bears to the others. For example, increasing facility with linguistic thought makes possible more articulate speech, more accurate factual memory, better developed practical reasoning, and so on; more effective control of desire and emotional reaction makes for better reasoning, both practical and theoretical, and for more sophisticated self-understanding, and so on. The system of higher mental functions is unified in two ways. First, they share a common currency—*meaning*: that is, they traffic in contentful states that can be given propositional form, so that what is remembered can be thought of or spoken about, what is wanted can be willed, what is feared can be reasoned about, and so on. Second, the higher mental functions are unified by their role in sustaining the integrity of a person's mental life.

It is an enduring theme of Vygotsky's writings that the higher mental functions are social in origin. Their development cannot be portrayed as the outcome of biological maturation, but essentially involves the child's appropriation of culture. This, and the fact that meaning is the medium of the higher mental functions, entails that the higher mental functions resist explanation by appeal to natural-scientific law.[6]

Vygotsky contrasts the higher mental functions with those 'elementary mental functions' which define the psychology of the pre-rational child. These include non-verbal thought (simple problem-solving activity), involuntary or associative memory, primitive speech, basic forms of attention, sensory awareness, volition, desire and emotion. These capacities develop as part of the biological maturation of the organism, and their nature and functioning is tractable in natural-scientific terms. Vygotsky represents the elementary mental functions as fundamentally independent capacities. Their deliverances are related causally—the child's perceptual sensitivity to a certain smell may cause in her a memory of her last meal, causing in turn a desire for more food of that kind, and so on—but the structure of the elementary functions is essentially modular: each has its own biological path of development. They are unified, and yet the principle of their unity is not the maintenance of a first-person perspective on a unified world, but their subservience to biological imperatives, the fulfilment of needs for food, protection, comfort, and so on.

In his masterwork *Myshlenie i rech'* (*Thought and Speech*) (1934/1986), Vygotsky describes the key moment in the transition from elementary to higher mental functions. This is the point at which the developmental trajectories of thought and speech converge. Prior to this, non-verbal thought and pre-intellectual speech are essentially independent of each other. When the child begins to use articulate sound or gesture in problem-solving activity, the seeds of language are sown on the soil of reason: intellectual speech and verbal thought become possible, and that possibility is made actual as the child acquires language. This collision of elementary thought and speech issues largely from the child's natural development, but it is facilitated by social factors, not least of all by the fact that the child lives in an environment in which meaning constantly mediates the activity of those around her. Moreover, the child is encouraged to catch on to meaning precisely because

154   *The Formation of Reason*

adults read it into her movements.[7] As the child's proficiency with language increases, so she becomes an inhabitant of the space of reasons. Now she is open to myriad social influences on concept development, and she begins to internalise styles and methods of intellectual activity.[8] Vygotsky is clear that the emergence of the higher mental functions represents a fundamental transformation in the child's mental life. The elementary functions should not be seen as embryonic versions of those that succeed them. The whole structure of the mind is transformed by the unity of thought and language.

Vygotsky's account is broadly consistent with the vision of human development defended in this book. What is especially notable is that he in no way represents the mind of the pre-rational child as a *tabula rasa*, or portrays the child's behaviour as mere mechanism. The elementary mental functions may be 'purely animal' in nature, but they represent a sophisticated, organised system in the service of a distinctive form of animal life, one open to the formation of reason.

An attraction of the Vygotskian framework is that it enables a sensible approach to questions of innateness. Very often, social theories of mind adopt a radical nurturism, denying that any interesting qualities of the human mind are innate. Ilyenkov, for example, frequently comes across as arguing that all aspects of distinctively human psychological functioning are '100% social' (see, e.g., Ilyenkov, 2002b, p. 75). Such extreme environmentalism is not entailed by Vygotsky's psychology. Although he argues that the elementary functions are fundamentally transformed with the emergence of the higher, nothing prevents Vygotsky from holding that aspects of elementary mental functioning have an enduring influence.[9] Moreover, for all that the higher mental functions are social in character, there is no reason why a particular person's aptitude at mathematics or music, or their proneness to anxiety, or their cheerful disposition, should not be explained, at least in part, by appeal to their first-natural endowment. It is foolish to think that, say, 'intelligence' denotes a measurable quality of human beings that is simply an innate capacity. But it is equally misguided to insist that how well someone does at tests designed to measure intelligence is entirely the outcome of environmental factors. The Vygotskian framework avoids both kinds of silliness.

RECONCILING VYGOTSKY AND McDOWELL

There are differences of style and substance between Vygotsky and McDowell that need to be worked out. For example, since McDowell maintains that experience is available only to a creature capable of conceptual thought, and that the child acquires conceptual capacities only with the acquisition of language, it follows that the child is not a subject of experience until some time in its second year or beyond. Vygotsky, however, holds that it is not until adolescence that the child becomes capable of genuine conceptual thought (see Vygotsky, 1998, p. 42). Since it would be mad to deny that the pre-adolescent is a subject of experience, we might conclude that Vygotsky and McDowell are on different wavelengths.

It is relatively easy, however, to reconcile the two thinkers. Their apparent disagreement derives from their different foci. McDowell is preoccupied with the contrast between the rational and the pre-rational, between being an inhabitant of the space of reasons and not—or not yet—being one. Vygotsky, in contrast, is focused on the development of forms of thinking and reasoning, from infancy to adulthood. Both emphases have their side-effects. McDowell's can give the impression that entrance into the space of reasons involves an abrupt transformation—the image of cognitive baptism that I tried to correct in chapter 1. Vygotsky can write as if only the final stage of development manifests the genuine article under investigation.[10] Accordingly, he reserves the term 'conceptual thinking' for operating with scientific concepts at what in chapter 1 I called the fourth stage of conceptual development. The criteria for possessing such concepts are demanding, requiring that a person know not just *which* items falls within the extension of the concept, but *why* they do so. At the ideal, the concept-holder understands the principle that unites the items in the extension of the concept. Thus in the case of natural kind concepts, such as *gold*, or biological kind concepts, such as *tiger*, possession of the concept demands at least some knowledge of the relevant atomic or biological theory. This in turn requires knowledge of theoretical concepts and an appreciation of scientific methods and styles of analysis and explanation. Naturally, facility with such concepts develops principally in adolescence and as a result of formal instruction. However, it is not true that Vygotsky consistently represents scientific concepts as the only concepts. In *Thought and Language*, for example, he contrasts them with 'everyday' concepts that, though they stand in holistic relations, are not embedded in the kind of theoretical knowledge that gives content to scientific concepts. Everyday concepts are contrasted in turn with various kinds of 'complex', in which items are united by associative, rather than rational, principles. Though Vygotsky refers to thinking in complexes as 'pre-conceptual' (because of an invidious comparison with scientific reasoning), such thinking would count as conceptual by McDowell's lights. Indeed, it would not be contrary to the spirit of Vygotsky's thought to characterise the transition effected by the convergence of thought and speech as the child's entering the domain of the conceptual, even though her facility with concepts and modes of reasoning develops gradually and undergoes many changes before she meets the expectations of educated, mature thinkers.

Of course the need for clarification is not all on the Vygotskian's side. McDowell, for example, represents Sellars as holding that 'the intentionality, the objective purport, of perceptual experience in general' depends 'on having the world in view, in a sense that goes beyond glimpses of the here and now' (McDowell, 1998c, p. 435 [2009a, p. 7]). But when is it legitimate to say of a child that she 'has the world in view'? On the same page, McDowell proceeds to write as if having the world in view presupposes possession of a world-view. This looks a demanding criterion for membership of the space of reasons. Does a 3-year-old have a world-view? Does a 6-year old?

It would be a mistake to think that we are compelled to find precise answers to such questions. We can continue to say that the child is in the space of reasons if her activity warrants interpretation in the normative terms of rational explanation. There is obviously no moment of entry. This is in part because the child's emerging rationality admits of degrees and in part because adults project rational capacity onto the child, treating her as more able than she actually is. The influence of prolepsis is of great developmental significance, and it makes a mockery of attempts to consider the child's developing rational capacity by focusing exclusively on the child in isolation.

We must also be careful not to adopt too individualistic an account of what it is to *possess* a world-view. We are inclined to think of the world-view of some individual as a set of beliefs and values that she holds. We then suppose that to recognise a person's debt to society is to acknowledge how many of those beliefs and values she has inherited from her culture. It is critical, however, that in many cases she is indebted not just for the beliefs and values themselves, but for the grounds on which she holds them. Just as, wandering a foreign city, I can come to know where the cathedral is situated from the testimony of a reliable informant (e.g., in this case, a native of the city) even if I lack access to the grounds on which my informant bases what he tells me, so I can come to know facts about the nature of the world from a physics textbook even though it is beyond me to justify the beliefs that constitute my knowledge.[11] In the latter case, my cognitive purchase on the facts depends upon the cogency of the wider world-view from which my beliefs derive their authority, but in this case the world-view in question is not my possession in the sense considered above. It does not comprise a set of beliefs I can fully articulate or that I would assent to if asked. It is my possession in a more amorphous sense: by having an articulate understanding of some part of it, I thereby gain access to part of the rest, so that it may lend authority to those beliefs I do overtly hold.

A conceptual holist must say something similar about concepts. Each of us has many concepts we are rightly said to possess even though we are ignorant of (or of the details of) many of the inferential relations that give the concepts their content. We need enough competence with a concept to count as possessing it, but this can fall far short of a comprehensive appreciation of the inferential structures of which the concept is part. We have to borrow that knowledge from the world-view inherent in our culture. So, *contra* Vygotsky, it is not just that we have either everyday concepts, spontaneous and untheoretical, or scientific concepts, fully articulated theoretically. Both scientific and everyday concepts derive their content from the world-view in which they are embedded, and we may possess either only in virtue of our relation to that world-view. As is clear in the case of scientific concepts, the relevant parts of the wider world-view may not be transparent to us. What we need is enough facility with the concept, together with some appreciation of that from which the relevant authority derives and some understanding of the kind of expertise necessary to establish entitlement to the thoughts the concepts permit us to formulate.

Just as the scientific concepts and beliefs of a mature thinker depend upon the thinker's relation to a world-view that is only partially within her grasp, so the early stages of the child's conceptual development exhibit a similar dependence. By getting a toehold in language, the child gains access to a world-view that enables her to attain standings in the space of reasons that she could not achieve without that access, just so long as she has competence enough. This dependency serves to justify the adult's proleptic interpretation of the child, on which I commented above. Prolepsis is not wishful thinking that somehow magics into existence its own object. The child's individual development is propelled by the fact that she is lent entitlements that are more use to her if she can make them her own. The gap between what we can achieve unaided and what we can achieve only with assistance is an incentive to individual development[12] whether that assistance comes from the agency of others or our relation to the world-view that underwrites our concepts and beliefs. We could not rid ourselves of assistance of either kind.[13]

I have been suggesting that the contributions of McDowell and Vygotsky can be brought into fruitful dialogue to describe the formation of reason. And there are many other thinkers who might be invited to join the conversation, not least of all Ilyenkov and others among Vygotsky's Russian followers. Of course, the success of the socio-historical project will depend ultimately on whether it is consistent with genuinely explanatory empirical theories of mind and its development. But that is as it should be.[14]

PERSONALISM

At this point we should remind ourselves that, as we noted in chapter 1, notwithstanding McDowell's protestation that he does 'not mean to be objecting to anything in cognitive science' (McDowell, 1994, p. 121), a psychology that took the socio-historical approach to heart would operate on assumptions very different from those that inform much contemporary empirical research into the mind. The idea that a person's cognitive purchase on the world is enabled by her relation to a wider world-view that she cannot fully articulate with her own resources is a dimension of the world–mind relation that has come into view in contemporary psychology only relatively recently.[15] Moreover, implicit in the socio-historical perspective is a conception of mental states and processes that challenges entrenched ideas about the character of mind. If we take seriously McDowell's view that to be a thinker is to be an inhabitant of the space of reasons, and if (reading McDowell in Ilyenkovian style) we represent the space of reasons as coinciding with the world as we encounter it, we open up the possibility of identifying our mindedness with a certain way of living in the world, one that exhibits openness to reality in experience, identity with the world in thought, and engagement with the world in activity mediated by reasons. This is a conception that invites us to abandon the idea that our mental lives consist in states and episodes occurring in some self-contained 'inner' realm, of which our behaviour is merely the outward sign, and to think of mind as present in activity.

A natural complement to this position is a doctrine to which both McDowell and Ilyenkov subscribe, which we can call 'personalism' about the mental.[16] This is the view that mental states and properties can properly be attributed only to persons. It is people who think, imagine, wonder, remember, intend, and so on, not any of their parts. Although a person cannot be in any such state unless her brain is functioning appropriately, it is wrong to ascribe psychological properties to the brain or to its parts or systems. The location of mental phenomena is therefore nowhere inside the person, but simply where the person is (though of course we may be able to locate neural correlates of mental functioning, the areas of the brain in which sub-personal mechanisms subserve specific kinds of mental functioning, and so on).

This view of mind as immanent in the life activity of the person complements the various insights about the nature of the mental attributed to the socio-historical conception in earlier chapters.[17] It is not easy, however, to give it substance in a way that might recommend it to mainstream psychology. In a number of papers, McDowell speaks eloquently against the assumption 'that mental occurrences are, as such and in themselves, *internal* to the person in whose mental life they take place' (McDowell, 2000a, p. 14). He recognises, however, that the assumption is deeply rooted: 'there are many influences', he writes, 'that conspire to give this picture of the "inner" and the "outer" its hold on us' (1982b/1998b, p. 393). Paramount among them is 'the *objectifying* mode of conceiving reality' familiar in natural science, which, by representing the constituents of objective reality as bereft of meaning or significance, is unable to find mindedness in bodily movement and is thereby forced to locate mind in an inner realm 'behind' behaviour. The fact is, however, that so deeply entrenched is the assumption, not just in theoretical but in everyday discourse, that diagnosing the philosophical misconceptions that encourage it does not suffice, as McDowell hopes, to 'restore us to a conception of thinking as the exercise of powers possessed, not mysteriously by some part of a thinking being ... but unmysteriously by a thinking being itself, an animal that lives its life in cognitive and practical relations to the world' (1992/1998b, p. 289). There is not, or there is no longer, a natural position for our thinking about mind to come to rest when the distorting influence of philosophical confusions is overcome. Much work remains to be done before the conception of the mental that McDowell cautiously advances in these papers will seem as natural and as philosophically unassuming as he would have it seem. If this can be achieved, the socio-historical conception of the nature and development of mind will be the stronger, and the prospect of a new and innovative psychology will be the more real.

FINAL THOUGHTS ON EDUCATION

Let me conclude with some final reflections on education. In the last chapter, I defended the view that the end of education is autonomy, where an autonomous person enjoys the control over herself and her life befitting a rational agent because she has the power to make up her mind what to think and do. I now want further to develop the view by considering a metaphor of which McDowell makes use: the idea of 'being at home in the world'.[18] McDowell has a singular purpose invoking this image from Gadamar (and ultimately from Heiddeger and Hegel): to contrast the situation of human beings, whose conceptual powers equip them to stand in relation to the world as a totality (everything that is the case), with the situation of non-human animals, whose life activity is defined by the contours of a more or less local environment. But we can take up the metaphor and work with the evocative notion of *being at home*. Here we can find resources to enrich our conception of the ends of education, yielding ideas from which educators might draw direction or inspiration.

Of course, the metaphor does not speak for itself. We need to invest it with sense. And there are certainly ways of reading the phrase that do not convey a satisfying vision of what formal education should offer. 'At home' can suggest contentment, even complacency, invoking the mood of an inward-looking consciousness finding a haven from trouble by acquiescing in the narrow horizons of the familiar and secure. This is exactly *not* the image I want to capture. Nor do I want the idea of being at home to imply reconciliation with actuality. If the world is unjust, then one should not be at home in it in the sense of being complicit, resigned or quiescent. On the contrary, we must take seriously the coalescence of the world and the space of reasons, and recognise that to be at home in the space of reasons is to be alive, not just to what is, but to what ought to be. Sometimes, being at home in the world is being at odds with the actual.

We can arrive at a more rewarding reading by considering what we might mean by describing someone as 'not at home' in some situation. We might depict him as 'not knowing his way around', as not knowing what to think, unable to grasp how to behave, ill at ease, anxious and confused, or at odds with himself. Inverting and extending this example, we can say that to be at home in the world is to be in possession of knowledge or, perhaps better, understanding of the world that enables one to 'find one's way about' with poise and confidence.[19]

The position defended in this book, though thoroughly fallibilist, is not squeamish about the idea that we can attain genuine knowledge of the world and has no qualms about portraying education as directed to the cultivation of knowledge and understanding. Indeed, I have stressed what I see as an internal relation between knowledge and autonomy. To the question 'Knowledge of *what*?' we can reply: knowledge of the world, in its human and non-human aspects, fitting a person to contribute to what Oakeshott famously called 'the conversation' of humankind, enabling her autonomy and thereby the opportunity to lead a worthwhile life, to engage in productive work, to benefit from satisfying leisure and to enjoy happy relationships with others. This of course says nothing about exactly what to teach and when to teach it, about which disciplinary divisions to draw, what forms of understanding to cultivate, and when and how … Such curricula issues are beyond the purview of this book. They demand to be treated in detail, with due regard for their complexity and contentiousness.[20] I can say more, however, in clarification of my basic proposal.

First, as should be obvious from the tenor what has gone before, my emphasis on knowledge and understanding is not intended to privilege the theoretical at the expense of the practical. We need to understand knowledge in its relation to activity and action, and to this end it is best to eschew a sharp contrast between the theoretical and the practical (see above, chapter 6, note 21). My emphasis on knowledge in the service of 'finding our way about' is styled as an antidote to unduly contemplative representations of knowledge (though contemplation as an *activity* should not be disparaged). Art, craft, music, sport and other forms of practice are, in my view, essential parts of any serious curriculum, together with applied science and technology. To use a hackneyed distinction, a curriculum must aspire to a balance between, and to the harmonious interplay of, knowledge-how and knowledge-that.[21]

Second, moral knowledge is an essential ingredient of the practical knowledge possessed by people at home in the world. They understand the needs and aspirations of others, and appreciate what they can and should do to enhance their flourishing or alleviate their suffering. Being at home in the world incorporates the idea of living well, and to live well in the requisite sense requires recognition of, and adherence to, moral reasons.[22] Thus, if the idea of being at home in the world is to serve as an educational ideal, we must take moral education seriously as integral to this.

The appropriate form and content of moral education is a matter of lively controversy, as is the question of whether moral education should be the province of schools. Here I will simply explain how my opinion on such matters is influenced by my views in moral philosophy. I am committed to a form of ethical particularism, and the arguments in chapters 5 and 6 drew at various points on the views of its primary exponent, Jonathan Dancy, who, as I observed, is much influenced by McDowell.[23] Particularism, a descendant of virtue theory, holds that sound moral judgement issues from the exercise of a sensibility that cannot be codified into principles. So the project of moral education is not, or is not primarily, the teaching of moral rules.[24] Rather, particularism embraces the Aristotelian view of learning through initiation described above. Thus moral education must concern itself with the cultivation of the sensitivity necessary to discern the salient moral dimensions of particular cases, to appreciate how they influence the overall moral significance of the situation and how they are relevant to reasons for action. Such sensitivity is learnt by attention to the example of others (both those who are skilled at moral judgement and those who are not) and by acquaintance with and reflection upon moral situations, including those, commonplace or dramatic, in which one finds oneself. In this regard, one's skills as a moral agent are formed and honed rather like the skills of a musician or literary critic: by engaging in the appropriate kind of practice with the appropriate willingness to improve, and only later by critical self-reflection and argument. In light of this, I take the view that moral education is a poor candidate for a school subject in its own right, however it might be dressed up (e.g., 'values education'). Rather, we should look to other disciplines to provide settings for the cultivation of character and moral judgement: the study of literature, history, politics, society and culture, together with the opportunities afforded by participation in collaborative endeavours in music, games, drama and similar practices. Not that these subjects and activities should be moralised, so that they are dominated by a heavy-handed preoccupation with ethical questions. But it is important that we take advantage of the opportunities they provide for moral development. It is also vital that schools understand themselves as moral communities where all are expected to treat each other with dignity and respect, and to be attentive to each other's feelings.

Third, the knowledge a person must have to be at home in the world includes self-knowledge. When philosophers speak of self-knowledge they often have in mind a type of knowledge that it is impossible for someone to lack while remaining a person. This is the kind of knowledge of one's own states discussed in chapters 2 and 3 above: the form of self-awareness often called self-consciousness, which is expressed in the self-ascription of psychological states—*I am thinking of Vienna, I am in pain, I am hungry, I see a cat*, etc. This capacity for this kind of self-knowledge is obviously not taught, but emerges with the child's acquisition of conceptual capacities as she learns her native language.

There is, however, a second form of self-knowledge, presently given less attention in the philosophical literature. I have in mind a person's knowledge of her own character, of her own convictions and desires, and of how she appears in the eyes of others. This kind of self-knowledge is all too easy to lack. I can falsely believe that I am courageous or humble, that I respect my siblings, that I want a career in university administration, that others see me as poised and confident, and so on. Such failures of self-knowledge can be of tremendous significance in a person's life, affecting her self-esteem and influencing key decisions she might take about family and career, as well as about how to act in particular cases. I believe that the cultivation of self-knowledge of this kind is a worthy educational ideal.[25] The appropriate vehicle for this is, I believe, the study of the humanities, particularly literature, drama and creative writing, though the development of self-knowledge can be an indirect aim of many subjects, and can be facilitated by educational institutions encouraging a culture of reflection and self-understanding.

It is important that to extol self-knowledge is not to encourage narcissism. I am not suggesting that the primary reason to study, say, English literature is for what it can tell you about yourself. Learning about yourself in this sense is one among the possible fruits of literary study (though it is often more likely to be acquired the less one aims at it). What I have in mind, however, is self-knowledge of a rather different kind. This is, as Rödl puts it, knowledge of oneself as *one of a kind*. The expression 'one of a kind' is commonly taken to denote uniqueness. When we say of someone that he is one of a kind, we usually mean that he is the *only* one of his kind. I have in mind a more literal reading. Self-knowledge involves understanding oneself as one of a kind; namely as a human being, so that light cast on the nature of the human condition by the study of literature, history, politics, biology, and so on should increase our understanding of the kinds of beings we are and thereby enhance our self-understanding. To understand your particularity, you have to understand yourself as one of a kind, as a human being.[26]

I have been suggesting that we can supplement the socio-historical approach's commitment to autonomy as the end of *Bildung* by developing the idea of 'being at home in the world' so that, suitably understood, it should serve as an ideal that might regulate the educational process. I have argued that being at home in the world presupposes knowledge, theoretical and practical, including moral knowledge and self-knowledge, and that the cultivation of such knowledge is an ideal that should inform and inspire formal education. Such an ideal is congruent with the claim that the proper end of education is autonomy: that is, to put us, so far as possible, in control of our lives and ourselves by empowering us to determine what to think and do. What I have said is but a sketch of some part of what it means to be at home in the world, and a fuller account would yield further insights germane to our understanding of what education can and should be. I have said something about what cannot be taught head-on, but little or nothing about the form and content of what should be taught, and when and how. Moreover, much of what I have said about moral knowledge and self-knowledge pertains to secondary school students and beyond, while the issue of whether and how these forms of knowledge should be cultivated in primary school is another matter. I acknowledge such questions merely to leave them open here.

This book itself aspires to self-knowledge by providing an account, speculative in I hope the best sense, of the kinds of beings that we are and how we come to be such. If the position I have endorsed carries conviction, then education, broadly conceived, should no longer be neglected by philosophical enquiries into the character of the human condition, as so often it is in contemporary philosophy. We should keep in mind a commonplace truth too often overlooked: education makes us what we are.

NOTES

1 Or perhaps it is better to say that we can think of mind as a gift of nature just so long as our conception of nature embraces second nature.
2 An enabling/constitutive distinction is deployed in McDowell, 1994/1998a, p. 352, where he argues that sub-personal brain processes enable mental states and episodes but do not constitute them. McDowell does not explain the distinction, and it is not easy to elucidate in part because the idea of 'constitution' is notoriously obscure. In saying that the social enables the mental, I mean to claim that social facts, processes, practices and relations are among the conditions of possibility of the mental. They are factors that make mind possible—where the 'making-possible' relation can take different forms and be of various degrees of strength. In denying that the mental is socially constituted, I mean to reject the idea that a person's being in some particular mental state, or undergoing some particular mental process, is to be analysed in terms of the occurrence of social facts, processes, practices or relations, or that the normative standing of mental states and processes is determined by such social facts, processes, practices or relations.
3 As McDowell goes on to note, 'by her own efforts' does not mean 'by her own unaided resources', as if her standing in the space of reasons does not depend upon co-operation from the world. It just does not depend on the beliefs or attitudes of others, except of course in cases where the presence, opinions, attitudes or actions of other people are the objects of her thoughts and actions.
4 The idea of training is lent gravitas by its Wittgensteinian pedigree. The most impressive discussion of Wittgenstein's notion is in Williams, 1999 (though see Brandom, 2008, for a highly original attempt to develop the notion). In my view, the better we understand the process of the child's initiation into culture, the less adequate the concept of training looks. Admittedly, in later writing McDowell takes a broader view, speaking of 'education, habituation, or training' (2008, p. 220), but he tells us nothing about how these notions are to be distinguished and understood.
5 Although Vygotsky's working life was little more than a decade long—he died from tuberculosis in 1934 at the age of 38—he was a prolific writer (the six-volume edition of collected works is by no means complete). My sketch of Vygotsky's framework is distilled from a number of his writings, particularly Vygotsky, 1997 and 1934/1986. Since his views were complex and constantly developing, a brief discussion like this risks distortion and simplification. I give more detailed readings in Bakhurst, 1990; 1991, ch. 3; and 2007b.
6 Note, however, that Vygotsky does not deny that scientific psychology is possible. Just as McDowell would broaden our conception of nature, so Vygotsky would widen our conception

Education Makes Us What We Are   163

of science to encompass methods for the systematic study of human rationality that fall short of establishing explanatory laws.

7   Vygotsky gives a spectacular example of how by interpreting a child's grasping movements as *pointing* to a desired object, those around the child create the possibility of the child gradually coming to deploy the movement as a gesture (see Vygotsky, 1997, pp. 143–4). Here we see the significance of the 'proleptic' or anticipatory mode of relating to children we noted in chapter 1, note 19, and of which more below.

8   Vygotsky's notion of internalisation is complex and multifaceted (see my discussion in Bakhurst, 1991, pp. 76–83). I believe it is best understood in the context of the kind of Aristotelian view of learning discussed in chapter 6. (Interestingly, Burnyeat uses the term 'internalisation' in his reconstruction of Aristotle's view (Burnyeat, 1980, pp. 72, 76)). Rather than indicating a transition between an activity going on in the external world and one occurring in a private mental space, the concept marks the child's gaining command over some concept or activity, so that it can be integrated into her capacity to think and act intentionally.

9   Vygotsky would have agreed with McDowell's remark that 'in some respects, the lives of mature human beings simply match the lives of mere animals; it would be absurd to suppose that *Bildung* effects a transfiguration, so to speak, of everything that happens in a human life' (McDowell, 1994, p. 183).

10 Because Vygotsky sees development as a series of qualitative transformations, he is inclined to stress that what we see in the earlier stages in a developmental process is not of the same kind as in later stages.

11 The cathedral example is McDowell's (1993/1998b).

12 As Vygotsky recognised with his concept of the zone of proximal development (1934/1986, pp. 186–90), which deserves to be an important complement to any view of learning through initiation.

13 These reflections are designed to bring out important social dimensions of knowledge and belief. It would be a mistake, however, to infer that they represent a retreat from the claim that our rational powers are enabled, but not constituted, by social factors. Consider testimony: when I come to know that it is snowing in Woodley because my sister tells me so in a telephone conversation, I come to share her warrant for belief. Her telling me enables me to know, but it does not in itself suffice for knowledge. Whether I know or not depends on the quality of her warrant for belief, but there is nothing distinctively social about that. In the case of our dependence on a world-view, it is the case that I can think, say, that oxygen has six valence electrons only because of my relation to a tradition of enquiry, but the content of that thought is not determined by that tradition, but by the truth-conditions of the claim 'Oxygen has six valence electrons'. Once again the role of the socio-historical is to enable rather than constitute our thinking.

14 I do not pretend that invoking Vygotsky lends empirical support to my position. Vygotsky took empirical enquiry very seriously and was a brilliant experimenter (though his experimental methods were cavalier by today's standards). But what endures most in his legacy is his philosophical vision of mind and its place in nature, and this is scarcely less speculative than McDowell's. Vygotsky offers a framework in which to do psychology in socio-historical style, not an empirical confirmation of any of its theses.

15 There is perhaps some common ground worth exploring with work on 'distributed', 'situated', and 'embodied' cognition (The literature is enormous: Robbins and Aydede, 2009, is a good point of entry. Classics include Lave and Wenger, 1991; Hutchins, 1995; Clark, 1997).

16 See Arsen'ev et al., 1966; Ilyenkov, 1974, p. 183, 1984, p. 29, 2009b, p. 22 (the relevant passage does not appear in the 1979/1991 version of this text); McDowell, 1992/1998b, 2000a. Western advocates of personalism are often inspired by Wittgenstein (e.g., Bennett and Hacker, 2003). I give a fuller treatment of the issues in Bakhurst, 2008.

17 Though it might be wise to revisit the formulation of those insights. It is tempting to speak of mind as 'on the surface', but that metaphor trades on a distinction between the inner and the

outer that personalism would prefer to be rid of. It is also fashionable to speak of minds as 'embodied' (and I have succumbed to the fashion a number of times in this book), but such talk is problematic. Bennett and Hacker contend that such talk contains remnants of Cartesianism: 'It is mistaken to suppose that human beings are "embodied" at all—that conception belongs to the Platonic, Augustinian, and Cartesian tradition that should be repudiated. It would be far better to say, with Aristotle, that human beings are *ensouled* creatures (*empsuchos*)—animals endowed with such capacities that confer upon them, in the form of life that is natural to them, the status of persons' (Bennett and Hacker, 2007, p. 160).
18 See, e.g., McDowell, 1994, pp. 117–19; there is a thoughtful discussion of the notion in de Gaynesford, 2004, pp. 179–82.
19 I should add the qualification 'where poise and confidence are appropriate to the situation in which one finds oneself'. Sometimes they are not.
20 A good place to start would be to revisit Kieran Egan's provocative *The Educated Mind* (1997), which rejects the three supposedly dominant contemporary ideas of education (education for socialisation, for intellectual cultivation, and for personal growth) in favour a vision of education as a journey that recapitulates the course of human culture, through five 'kinds of understanding' (somatic, mythic, romantic, philosophical and ironic) understood as Vygotskian 'cognitive tools'. There is much in Egan's position with which I disagree, but his is a stimulating position with which to engage on these questions. See also Michael Young's recent *Bringing Knowledge Back In* (2007).
21 Oakeshott approvingly quotes William Cory, an Eton schoolmaster: '[Y]ou go to a great school not so much for knowledge as for arts and habits; for the habit of attention, for the art of expression, for the art of assuming at a moment's notice, a new intellectual position, for the art of entering quickly into another person's thoughts, for the habit of submitting to censure and refutation, for the art of indicating assent or dissent in graduated terms, for the habit of regarding minute points of accuracy, for the art of working out what is possible in a given time, for taste, discrimination, for mental courage and mental soberness. And above all you go to a great school for self-knowledge' (Oakeshott, 1962/1991, pp. 491–2, n. 1). The problem with this otherwise fine passage (apart from its preoccupation with 'great' schools) is that it rests on a false contrast between knowledge, on the one hand, and 'arts and habits', on the other. Not only does the exercise of the latter presuppose knowledge, the kinds of arts and habits Cory has in mind *are* forms of practical knowledge. Moreover, the passage concludes (as my argument will) with an appeal to the importance of self-knowledge as an educational end. Cory's proper target is not knowledge, as such, but what we might call 'information'. Gradgrind is the enemy, not I.
22 The relevant notion of living well, or well-being, presupposes a conception of moral good. I do not mean living well by some criterion that might be rendered intelligible in non-moral terms (such as what Bernard Williams wittily called the 'ethological standard of the bright eye and the gleaming coat' (Williams, 1985, p. 46)).
23 In Bakhurst, 2000 and 2007a, I explore aspects of particularism, and these texts contain references to much relevant literature. I discuss particularism in relation to moral education in Bakhurst, 2005d, and address the once (but now much less) controversial issue of whether there really is moral *knowledge* in Bakhurst, 1999.
24 It should be noted that many particularists, myself among them, find a residual role for moral principles and accord their recognition a role in moral education. Moreover, nothing in particularism suggests that, where social practices are rule-governed, participants should take a cavalier attitude to the rules that bind them. Particularism need have no argument with proceduralism and the rule of law.
25 It should be clear from what has gone before that I am not implying that within each of us resides something, 'the self' or (worse) 'the true self', that we must seek to know. By 'self-knowledge' I mean no more (or no less) than a person's knowledge of him- of herself.

26 Rödl suggests that even the most austere 'I-thought' presupposes reference to oneself as one of a kind (Rödl, 2007, p. 194), or, as Michael Thompson would put it, a member of a certain life-form (Thompson, 2008)). What I think when I think 'I am in pain' is a thought of a being of a certain kind, namely, a human being. These are deep philosophical waters, but from them a channel flows back to the issues surrounding the nature of persons discussed in chapter 3.

References

Allen, B. (1993) *Truth in Philosophy* (Cambridge, MA, Harvard University Press).
Anscombe, G. E. M. (1957) *Intention* (Oxford, Blackwell). 2nd edn, rev. (Cambridge, MA, Harvard University Press, 2000).
Arsen'ev, A. S., Ilyenkov, E. V. and Davydov, V. V. (1966) Mashina i chelovek, kibernetika i filosofiya [Machine and human being, cybernetics and philosophy], in: *Leninskaya teoriya otrazheniya i sovremennaya nauka [Lenin's Theory of Reflection and Contemporary Science]* (Moscow, Politizdat), pp. 265–85.
Aristotle (1993) *Metaphysics: Books gamma, delta, and epsilon*, 2nd edn, trans. C. Kirwan, with notes (Oxford, Clarendon Press).
Aristotle (1995) *Selections*, trans. T. Irwin and G. Fine, with introduction, notes and glossary (Indianapolis, Hackett).
Astington, J. (1993) *The Child's Discovery of the Mind* (Cambridge, MA, Harvard University Press).
Baker, G. P. and Hacker, P. M. S. (1984) *Scepticism, Rules and Language* (Oxford, Blackwell).
Baker, G. P. and Hacker, P. M. S. (1990) Malcolm on Language and Rules, *Philosophy* 65, pp. 167–179.
Bakhtin, M. M. (1952–3/1986) The Problem of Speech Genres, in his: *Speech Genres and Other Late Essays*, trans. V. McGee, ed. C. Emerson and M. Holquist (Austin, University of Texas Press, 1986), pp. 60–102.
Bakhurst, D. (1990) Social Memory in Soviet Thought, in: D. Middleton and D. Edwards (eds), *Collective Remembering* (London, Sage), pp. 203–226.
Bakhurst, D. (1991) *Consciousness and Revolution in Soviet Philosophy. From the Bolsheviks to Evald Ilyenkov* (Cambridge, Cambridge University Press).
Bakhurst, D. (1995a) Social Being and the Human Essence: An Unresolved Issue in Soviet Philosophy, *Studies in East European Thought* 47, pp. 3–60.
Bakhurst, D. (1995b) Wittgenstein and Social Being, in: Bakhurst and Sypnowich, 1995, pp. 30–46.
Bakhurst, D. (1995c) Lessons from Ilyenkov, *Communication Review* 1.2, pp. 155–78.
Bakhurst, D. (1997) Meaning, Normativity, and the Life of the Mind, *Language and Communication* 17.1, pp. 33–51.
Bakhurst, D. (1999) Pragmatism and Moral Knowledge, in: C. Misak (ed.), *Pragmatism, Canadian Journal of Philosophy*, suppl. vol. 24, pp. 227–252.
Bakhurst, D. (2000) Ethical Particularism in Context, in: B. Hooker and M. Little (eds), *Moral Particularism* (Oxford, Oxford University Press) pp. 157–177.

The Formation of Reason, First Edition. David Bakhurst.
© 2011 David Bakhurst. Published 2011 by Blackwell Publishing Ltd.

Bakhurst, D. (2001a) Ilyenkov on Aesthetics: Realism, Imagination, and the End of Art, *Mind, Culture, and Activity* 8.2, pp. 187–199.

Bakhurst, D. (2001b) Wittgenstein and 'I', in: H.-J. Glock (ed.), *Wittgenstein: A Critical Reader* (Oxford, Blackwell), pp. 224–245.

Bakhurst, D. (2001c) Memory, Identity, and the Future of Cultural Psychology, in: Bakhurst and Shanker, 2001, pp. 184–198.

Bakhurst, D. (2002) Skromnoe velikolepie Vladislava Lektorskogo [The Quiet Brilliance of Vladislav Lektorsky], in: *Sub'ekt, poznanie, deyatel'nost'. K 70-letiyu V. A. Lektorskogo [Subject, Cognition, Activity: In honour of Vladislav Lektorsky]* (Moscow, Kanon), pp. 79–106.

Bakhurst, D. (2005a) Strong Culturalism, in: D. Johnson and C. Erneling (eds), *The Mind as a Scientific Object: Between Brain and Culture* (New York: Oxford University Press), pp. 413–431.

Bakhurst, D. (2005b) Ilyenkov on Education, *Studies in East European Thought* 57.3, pp. 261–275.

Bakhurst, D. (2005c) Wiggins on Persons and Human Nature, *Philosophy and Phenomenological Research* LXXI.2, pp. 462–469.

Bakhurst, D. (2005d) Particularism and Moral Education, *Philosophical Explorations* 8.3, pp. 265–279.

Bakhurst, D. (2007a) Pragmatism and Ethical Particularism, in: C. Misak (ed.), *New Pragmatists* (Oxford, Oxford University Press), pp. 122–141.

Bakhurst, D. (2007b) Vygotsky's Demons, in: M. Cole, H. Daniels, and J. Wertsch (eds), *The Cambridge Companion to Vygotsky* (Cambridge, Cambridge University Press), pp. 50–76.

Bakhurst, D. (2008) Minds, Brains and Education, *Journal of the Philosophy of Education* 42.3–4, pp. 415–432. Repr. in: Cigman and Davis, 2009, pp. 56–74.

Bakhurst, D. and Padden C. (1990) The Meshcheryakov Experiment: Soviet Work on the Education of Blind-Deaf Children, *Learning and Instruction* 1.3, pp. 201–215.

Bakhurst, D. and Dancy, J. (1988) The Cartesian Straightjacket, *Times Higher Education Supplement*, 22 April, p. 18.

Bakhurst, D. and Sypnowich C. (eds) (1995) *The Social Self* (London, Sage).

Bakhurst, D. and Shanker S. (eds) (2001) *Jerome Bruner: Language, Culture, Self* (London, Sage).

Beiser, F. (2003) Romanticism, in: Curren, 2003, pp. 130–141.

Bennett, M. and Hacker, P. M. S. (2003) *Philosophical Foundations of Neuroscience* (Oxford, Blackwell).

Bennett, M. and Hacker P. M. S. (2007) The Conceptual Presuppositions of Cognitive Neuroscience: A Reply to Critics, in: Bennett et al., 2007, pp. 127–162.

Bennett, M., Dennett, D., Hacker, P. M. S. and Searle J. (2007) *Neuroscience and Philosophy: Brain, Mind, and Language* (New York, Columbia University Press).

Berkeley, G. (1710/1998) *A Treatise Concerning the Principles of Human Knowledge*, ed. J. Dancy (Oxford, Oxford University Press, 1998).

Bernstein, R. (2002) McDowell's Domesticated Hegelianism, in: Smith, 2002, pp. 9–24.

Blake, N. Smeyers, P., Smith, R. and Standish, P. (eds) (2003) *The Blackwell Guide to Philosophy of Education* (Oxford, Blackwell).

Bonnett, M. and Cuypers, S. (2003) Autonomy and Authenticity in Education, in: Blake et al., 2003, pp. 326–340.

Brandom, R. (1994) *Making it Explicit* (Cambridge, MA, Harvard University Press).

Brandom, R. (1995a) Knowledge and the Social Articulation of the Space of Reasons, *Philosophy and Phenomenological Research* LV.4, pp. 895–908.

Brandom, R. (1995b) Perception and Rational Constraint, *Philosophical Issues* 7, pp. 241–259.

Brandom, R. (2000) *Articulating Reasons: An Introduction to Inferentialism* (Cambridge, MA, Harvard University Press).

Brandom, R. (2002) *Tales of the Mighty Dead. Historical Essays in the Metaphysics of Intentionality* (Cambridge, MA, Harvard University Press).
Brandom, R. (2008) *Beyond Saying and Doing* (Cambridge, MA, Harvard University Press).
Brandom, R. (2009) *Reason in Philosophy: Animating Ideas* (Cambridge, MA, Harvard University Press).
Bruner, J. (1990) *Acts of Meaning* (Cambridge, MA, Harvard University Press).
Bruner, J. (2001) In Response, in: Bakhurst and Shanker, 2001, pp. 199–215.
Bruner, J. (2002) *Making Stories: Law, Literature, Life* (Cambridge, MA, Harvard University Press).
Buber, M. (1923/1959) *I and Thou*, 2nd edn, trans. R. Smith (New York, Charles Scribner's Sons, 1959).
Bubner, R. (2002) *Bildung* and Second Nature, in: Smith, 2002, pp. 209–216.
Burge, T. (1979/2007) Individualism and the Mental, in his: *Foundations of Mind: Philosophical Essays Volume 2* (Oxford, Clarendon Press, 2007), pp. 100–150.
Burnyeat, M. (1980) Aristotle on Learning to be Good, in: A. Rorty (ed.), *Essays on Aristotle's Ethics* (Berkeley, University of California Press), pp. 69–92.
Carey, S. (1985) *Conceptual Change in Childhood* (Cambridge, MA, MIT Press).
Cavell, S. (1969) *Must We Mean What We Say?* (New York, Charles Scribner's Sons).
Churchland, P. (1988) *Matter and Consciousness*, rev. edn (Cambridge, MA, MIT Press).
Cigman, R. and Davis, A. (eds) (2009) *New Philosophies of Learning* (Oxford, Wiley-Blackwell).
Clark, A. (1997) *Being There. Putting Brain, Body, and World Together Again* (Cambridge, MA, MIT Press).
Claxton, G. (1997) *Hare Brain, Tortoise Mind: Why Intelligence Increases When You Think Less* (London, Fourth Estate).
Cohen, G. A. (1996) Reason, Humanity and the Moral Law, in: Korsgaard, 1996, pp. 167–188.
Connolly, C. (writing as Palinurus) (1944/2002) *The Unquiet Grave*, in his: *Selected Works of Cyril Connolly, Vol. 2: The Two Natures* (London, Picador, 2002), pp. 134–259.
Curren, R. (2003) *A Companion to the Philosophy of Education* (Oxford, Blackwell).
Dancy, J. (1985) *Introduction to Contemporary Epistemology* (Oxford, Blackwell).
Dancy, J. (1993) *Moral Reasons* (Oxford, Blackwell).
Dancy, J. (2000) *Practical Reality* (Oxford, Oxford University Press).
Dancy, J. (2004) *Ethics Without Principles* (Oxford, Oxford University Press).
Dancy, J. (2006) Acting in the Light of Appearances, in: Macdonald and Macdonald, 2006, pp. 121–134.
Danziger, K. (1997) *Naming the Mind: How Psychology Found its Language* (London, Sage).
Darwell, S. (2006) *The Second-Person Standpoint* (Cambridge, MA, Harvard University Press).
Davidson, D. (1963/1980) Actions, Reasons, and Causes, in: Davidson, 1980, pp. 3–19.
Davidson, D. (1970/1980) Mental Events, in: Davidson, 1980, pp. 207–225.
Davidson, D. (1971/1980) Agency, in: Davidson, 1980, pp. 43–61.
Davidson, D. (1974/1984) On the Very Idea of a Conceptual Scheme, in: Davidson, 1984, pp. 183–198.
Davidson, D. (1980) *Essays on Actions and Events*. (Oxford: Oxford University Press; 2nd edn 2001).
Davidson, D. (1983/2001) A Coherence Theory of Truth and Knowledge, in: Davidson, 2001, pp. 137–153.
Davidson, D. (1984) *Inquiries into Truth and Interpretation* (Oxford, Oxford University Press; 2nd edn 2001).
Davidson, D. (1984/2001) First-Person Authority, in: Davidson 2001, pp. 3–14.
Davidson, D. (1986/2005) A Nice Derangement of Epitaphs, in: Davidson, 2005, pp. 89–107.
Davidson, D. (1991/2001) Three Varieties of Knowledge, in: Davidson, 2001, pp. 205–220.
Davidson, D. (1992/2001) The Second Person, in: Davidson, 2001, pp. 107–121.
Davidson, D. (1992/2005) The Third Man, in: Davidson, 2005, pp. 159–165.
Davidson, D. (1994/2005) The Social Aspect of Language, in: Davidson, 2005, pp. 109–125.

Davidson, D. (1997/2001) The Emergence of Thought, in: Davidson, 2001, pp. 123–134.
Davidson, D. (2000/2005) Truth Rehabilitated, in: Davidson, 2005, pp. 3–17.
Davidson, D. (2001) *Subjective, Intersubjective, Objective* (Oxford: Oxford University Press).
Davidson, D. (2005) *Truth, Language, and History* (Oxford, Oxford University Press).
Davis, A. (1999) *The Limits of Educational Assessment* (Oxford, Blackwell).
Davis, A. (2005) Social Externalism and the Ontology of Competence, *Philosophical Explorations* 8.3, pp. 297–308.
Davis, A. (2008) Ian Hacking, Learner Categories and Human Taxonomies, *Journal of Philosophy of Education* 42.3–4, pp. 441–445. Repr. in: Cigman and Davis, 2009, pp. 81–97.
Dearden, R. (1972) Autonomy and Education, in: Dearden et al., 1972, pp. 448–465.
Dearden, R, Hirst, P. and Peters, R. (eds) (1972) *Education and the Development of Reason* (London, Routledge and Kegan Paul).
de Gaynesford, M. (2004) *John McDowell* (Cambridge, Polity).
Dennett, D. (2007) Philosophy as Naive Anthropology, in: Bennett et al., 2007, pp. 73–95.
Derry, J. (2008a) Abstract Rationality in Education: From Vygotsky to Brandom, *Studies in Philosophy and Education* 27.1, pp. 49–62.
Derry, J. (2008b) Technology-Enhanced Learning: A Question of Knowledge, *Journal of the Philosophy of Education* 42.3–4, pp. 505–519. Repr. in: Cigman and Davis, 2009, pp. 142–155.
deVries, W. (2005) *Wilfrid Sellars* (Montreal and Kingston, McGill-Queen's Press).
Dickens, C. (1854/1901) *Hard Times and Christmas Books* (London, Thomas Nelson and Sons, 1901).
Dreyfus, H. (2005) Overcoming the Myth of the Mental: How Philosophers Can Profit from the Phenomenology of Everyday Expertise, *Proceedings of the American Philosophical Association* 79.2, pp. 47–65.
Dreyfus, H. (2007a) The Return of the Myth of the Mental, *Inquiry* 50.4, pp. 352–365.
Dreyfus, H. (2007b) Response to McDowell, *Inquiry* 50.4, pp. 371–377.
Edwards, D., Ashmore, M. and Potter J. (1995) Death and Furniture: The Rhetoric, Politics and Theology of Bottom Line Arguments against Relativism, *History of the Human Sciences* 8.2, pp. 25–49.
Egan, K. (1997) *The Educated Mind: How Cognitive Tools Shape our Understanding* (Chicago, IL, Chicago University Press).
Elder, C. L. (2004) *Real Natures and Familiar Objects* (Cambridge, MA, MIT Press).
Elder, C. L. (2011) Carving Up a Reality in which There Are No Joints, in: S. D. Hales (ed.), *A Companion to Relativism* (Oxford: Wiley-Blackwell), pp. 604–620.
Fink, H. (2008) Three Sorts of Naturalism, in: Lindgaard, 2008, pp. 52–71.
Fodor, J. (1998) *Concepts: Where Cognitive Science Went Wrong* (Oxford, Clarendon Press).
Foster, I. (1998) Across the S–S Divide, in: Parker, 1998, pp. 107–117.
Franks, P. (2005) *All or Nothing. Systematicity, Transcendental Arguments, and Skepticism in German Idealism* (Cambridge, MA, Harvard University Press).
Gadamer, H.-G. (1975) *Truth and Method*, 2nd edn, trans. W. Glen-Doepel, rev. J. Weinsheimer and D. Marshall (New York: Continuum).
Gaskin, R. (2006) *Experience and the World's Own Language: A Critique of John McDowell's Empiricism* (Oxford, Clarendon Press).
Gergen, K. (1985) The Social Constructionist Movement in Modern Psychology, *American Psychologist* 40.3, pp. 266–273.
Gergen, K. (1999) *Invitation to Social Constructionism* (London, Sage).
Gergen, K. (2001) *Social Constructionism in Context* (London, Sage).
Geuss, R. (1996) Morality and Identity, in: Korsgaard, 1996, pp. 189–199.
Geuss, R. (1999) *Morality, Culture, and History: Essays on German Philosophy* (Cambridge, Cambridge University Press).
Goldie, P. (2000) *The Emotions: A Philosophical Exploration* (Oxford, Oxford University Press).

170   References

Gopnik, A. and Meltzoff, A. (1996) *Words, Thoughts, and Theories* (Cambridge, MA, MIT Press).
Gopnik, A., Meltzoff, A. and Kuhl, P. (1999) *The Scientist in the Crib: What Early Learning Tells Us About the Mind* (New York, Harper Collins).
Gubeljic, M., Link, S., Müller, P. and Osburg, G. (2000) Nature and Second Nature in McDowell's *Mind and World*, in: Willaschenk, 2000, pp. 41–49.
Hacking, I. (1986/2002) Making Up People, in his: *Historical Ontology* (Cambridge, MA, Harvard University Press, 2002), pp. 99–114.
Hacking, I. (1991) The Making and Molding of Child Abuse, *Critical Inquiry* 17, pp. 253–278.
Hacking, I. (1995) Why Multiple Personality Tells Us Nothing About the Self/Mind/Person/Subject/Soul/Consciousness, in: Bakhurst and Sypnowich, 1995, pp. 159–179.
Hacking, I. (1999) *The Social Construction of What?* (Cambridge, MA, Harvard University Press).
Hacking, I. (2006) What is Tom Saying to Maureen?, *London Review of Books* 28.9, 11 May, pp. 3–7.
Halbig, C. (2008) Varieties of Nature in Hegel and McDowell, in: Lindgaard, 2008, pp. 72–91.
Hamlyn, D. (1978) *Experience and the Growth of Understanding* (London, Routledge and Kegan Paul).
Hand, S. (ed.) (1989) *The Levinas Reader* (Oxford, Blackwell).
Haslanger, S. (1995) Ontology and Social Construction, *Philosophical Topics* 23.2, pp. 95–125.
Haslanger, S. (2003) Social Construction: The 'Debunking' Project, in: F. Schmitt (ed.), *Socializing Metaphysics: The Nature of Social Reality* (New York, Rowman & Littlefield), pp. 301–325.
Haslanger, S. (2005) What Are We Talking About? The Semantics and Politics of Social Kinds, *Hypatia* 20.4, pp. 10–26.
Haugeland, J. (1995/1998) Mind Embodied and Embedded, in his: *Having Thought. Essays in the Metaphysics of Mind* (Cambridge, MA, Harvard University Press, 1998), pp. 207–237.
Hegel, G. W. F. (1807/1977) *The Phenomenology of Spirit*, trans. A. Miller, foreword and analysis by J. Findlay (Oxford, Oxford University Press, 1977).
Hegel, G.W.F. (1821/1967) *The Philosophy of Right*, trans. T. Knox (Oxford, Clarendon Press, 1967).
Heidegger, M. (1976) *Piety of Thinking: Essays of Martin Heidegger*, trans. J. Hart and J. Maraldo (Bloomington, IN, Indiana University Press).
Hornsby, J. (1987) *Simple-Mindedness: In Defence of Naive Naturalism in the Philosophy of Mind* (Cambridge, MA, Harvard University Press).
Hutchins, E. (1995) *Cognition in the Wild* (Cambridge, MA, MIT Press).
Hume, D. (1748/1975) *An Enquiry Concerning Human Understanding*, in his: *Enquiries Concerning Human Understanding and Concerning the Principles of Morals*, repr. from the 1777 edn, with an Introduction and Analytical Index by L. A. Selby-Bigge, 3rd edn, ed. P. H. Nidditch (Oxford, Oxford University Press, 1975).
Ilyenkov, E. V. (1956/1997) *Dialektika abstraktnogo i konkretnogo v nauchno-teoreticheskom myshlenii* [*The Dialectics of the Abstract and the Concrete in Scientific-Theoretical Thinking*] (Moscow, ROSSPEN, 1997). Uncensored version of Ilyenkov, 1960.
Ilyenkov, E. V. (1960) *Dialektika abstraktnogo i konkretnogo v 'Kapitale' Marksa* (Moscow, Academiya nauk). Trans. S. Surovatkin, as *The Dialectics of the Abstract and the Concrete in Marx's* Capital (Moscow, Progress, 1982).
Ilyenkov, E. V. (1962) Ideal'noe [The Ideal], in: *Filosofskaya entsiklopediya* [*Philosophical Encyclopedia*], vol. 2., pp. 219–227. Repr., amended, in: Ilyenkov, 1974, pp. 183–210.
Ilyenkov, E. V. (1964) Vopros o tozhdestve myshleniya i bytiya v domarksistskoi filosofii [The Question of the Relation of Thinking and Being in Pre-Marxist Philosophy], in: *Dialektika – teoriya poznaniya* [*Dialectics – The Theory of Knowledge*] (Moscow, Nauka), pp. 21–54. Trans. as Ilyenkov, 1997.
Ilyenkov, E. V. (1970) Psikhika cheloveka pod "lupoi vremeni" [The Human Mind Under the 'Magnifying Glass of Time'], *Priroda [Nature]*, no. 1, pp. 87–91.
Ilyenkov, E. V. (1974) *Dialekticheskogo logika. Ocherki istorii i teorii.* [*Dialectical Logic. Essays in its History and Theory*] (Moscow, Politizdat), 2nd edn, rev. and enlarged (Moscow, Politizdat, 1984). First edn trans. as Ilyenkov, 1977b; repr. in: Ilyenkov, 2009a, pp. 1–214.

References

Ilyenkov, E. V. (1977a) The Concept of the Ideal, in: *Philosophy in the USSR. Problems of Dialectical Materialism*, trans. R. Daglish (Moscow, Progress), pp. 71–99. Repr. in: Ilyenkov, 2009a, pp. 253–284.

Ilyenkov, E. V. (1977b) *Dialectical Logic. Essays in its History and Theory*, trans. H. Campbell-Creighton (Moscow, Progress).

Ilyenkov, E. V. (1977c) Soobrazhenie po voprosu ob otnoshenii myshleniya i yazyka [Reflections on the Relation of Thought and Language], *Voprosy filosofii [Questions of Philosophy]*, no. 6, pp. 92–96. Repr. in: Ilyenkov, 1991, pp. 270–274.

Ilyenkov, E. V. (1979/1991) Dialektika ideal'nogo [The Dialectic of the Ideal], in: Ilyenkov, 1991, pp. 229–270. Originally published as 'Problema ideal'nogo' [The Problem of the Ideal], *Voprosy filosofii [Questions of Philosophy]*, 1979, no. 6, pp. 145–158, and no. 7, pp. 128–140. Repr. in: Ilyenkov, 1984, pp. 8–77, and (further amended and supplemented) as Ilyenkov, 2009b. An earlier, and shorter, version published in English translation as Ilyenkov, 1977a.

Ilyenkov, E. V. (1984) *Iskusstvo i kommunisticheskii ideal [Art and the Communist Ideal]* (Moscow, Iskusstvo).

Ilyenkov, E. V. (1991) *Filosofiya i kul'tura [Philosophy and Culture]* (Moscow, Politizdat).

Ilyenkov, E. V. (1997) The Question of the Identity of Thought and Being in Pre-Marxist Philosophy, *Russian Studies in Philosophy* 36.1, pp. 5–33.

Ilyenkov, E. V. (2002a) *Shkola dolzhna uchit' myslit' [School Must Teach How to Think]*. (Moscow-Voronezh, MODEK). Trans. in its entirety in *Journal of Russian and East European Philosophy* 45.4, 2007.

Ilyenkov, E. V. (2002b) Biologicheskoe i social'noe v cheloveke [The Biological and the Social in the Person], in: Ilyenkov, 2002a, pp. 72–77.

Ilyenkov, E. V. (2002c) K razgovoru o Meshcheryakove [A Contribution to the Conversation about Meshcheryakov], in: Ilyenkov, 2002a, pp. 95–106.

Ilyenkov, E. V. (2009a) *The Ideal in Human Activity* (Pacifica, CA, Marxist Internet Archive).

Ilyenkov, E. V. (2009b) Dialektika ideal'nogo [The Dialectic of the Ideal], *Logos* 65.1, pp. 6–62.

Johnson, D. M. (2003) *How History Made the Mind: The Cultural Origins of Objective Thinking* (Chicago and La Salle, Open Court).

Kant, I. (1781/1933) *Critique of Pure Reason*, trans. N. Kemp Smith (London, Macmillan, 1933).

Kant, I. (1785/1948) *Groundwork of the Metaphysics of Morals*, trans. as H. Paton, (ed.) *The Moral Law* (London, Hutchinson, 1948).

Kant, I. (1786/1949) What is Orientation in Thinking?, in his: *Critique of Practical Reason and Other Writings in Moral Philosophy*, ed. L. W. Beck (Chicago, IL, University of Chicago Press, 1949), pp. 293–305.

Kant, I. (1803/2003) *On Education*, trans. A. Churton (Mineola, NY, Dover).

Keil, F. (1989) *Concepts, Kinds, and Cognitive Development* (Cambridge, MA, MIT Press).

Korsgaard, C. (1996) *The Sources of Normativity*. The 1992 Tanner Lectures, ed. O. O'Neill, with replies by G. A. Cohen, R. Geuss, T. Nagel and B. Williams (Cambridge, Cambridge University Press).

Korsgaard, C. (2003/2008) Realism and Constructivism in Twentieth-Century Moral Philosophy, in: Korsgaard, 2008, pp. 302–326.

Korsgaard, C. (2008) *The Constitution of Agency: Essays on Practical Reasoning and Moral Psychology* (Oxford, Oxford University Press).

Korsgaard, C. (2009) *Self-Constitution: Agency, Identity, and Integrity* (Oxford, Oxford University Press).

Lave, J. and Wenger, E. (1991) *Situated Learning: Legitimate Peripheral Participation* (Cambridge, Cambridge University Press).

Levinas, E. (1958/1989) Martin Buber and the Theory of Knowledge, in: Hand, 1989, pp. 59–74.

Levinas, E. (1984/1989) Ethics as First Philosophy, in: Hand, 1989, pp. 75–87.

Levitin, K. (1982) *One is Not Born a Personality*, trans. Y. Filoppov (Moscow, Progress).

Lingaard, J. (2008) *John McDowell: Experience, Norm, and Nature* (Oxford, Blackwell).

References

Locke, J. (1689/1975) *An Essay Concerning Human Understanding*, ed. P. H. Nidditch (Oxford, Oxford University Press, 1975).
Lovibond, S. (2006) Practical Reason and its Animal Precursors, *European Journal of Philosophy* 14.2, pp. 262–273. Repr. in: Lingaard, 2008, pp. 112–123.
Lovibond, S. and Williams, S. (eds) (1996) *Essays for David Wiggins: Identity, Truth and Value* (Oxford, Blackwell).
Løvlie, L. (2003) The Promise of *Bildung*, in: Løvlie et al., 2003, pp. 151–170.
Løvlie, L., Mortensen, K. and Nordenbo, S. (eds) (2003) *Educating Humanity:* Bildung *in Postmodernity* (Oxford, Blackwell).
Løvlie, L. and Standish, P. (2003) Introduction: *Bildung* and the Idea of a Liberal Education, in: Løvlie et al., 2003, pp. 1–24.
Luntley, M. (2003) Nonconceptual Content and the Sound of Music, *Mind & Language* 18.4, pp. 402–426.
Macdonald, G. (2006) The Two Natures: Another Dogma?, in: Macdonald and Macdonald, 2006, pp. 222–235.
Macdonald, C. and Macdonald G. (eds) (2006) *McDowell and his Critics* (Oxford, Blackwell).
MacIntyre, A. (1981) *After Virtue* (London, Duckworth).
MacIntyre, A. (1999) *Dependent Rational Animals: Why Human Beings Need the Virtues* (Chicago and La Salle, IL, Open Court).
Macmurray, J. (1961) *Persons in Relation* (London, Faber and Faber).
Maidanskii, A. (2009) Editorial Introduction, *Logos* 69.1, pp. 3–5.
Malcolm, N. (1986) *Nothing is Hidden* (Oxford, Blackwell).
Mann, W. (2003) The Past as Future? Hellenism, the *Gymnasium* and *Altertumswissenschaft*, in: Curren, 2003, pp. 143–160.
Marx, K. (1844/1977) *Economic and Philosophical Manuscripts of 1844*, 5th edn (Moscow, Progress).
McDowell, J. (1978/1998a) Are Moral Requirements Hypothetical Imperatives?, in: McDowell, 1998a, pp. 77–94.
McDowell, J. (1979/1998a) Virtue and Reason, in: McDowell, 1998a, pp. 50–73.
McDowell, J. (1981/1998a) Non-Cognitivism and Rule-Following, in: McDowell, 1998a, pp. 198–218.
McDowell, J. (1981/1998b) Anti-Realism and the Epistemology of Understanding, in: McDowell, 1998b, pp. 314–343.
McDowell, J. (1982a/1998b) Truth-Value Gaps, in: McDowell, 1998b, pp. 199–213.
McDowell, J. (1982b/1998b) Criteria, Defeasibility, and Knowledge, in: McDowell, 1998b, pp. 369–394.
McDowell, J. (1984/1998a) Wittgenstein on Following a Rule, in: McDowell, 1998a, pp. 221–262.
McDowell, J. (1984/1998b) *De Re* Senses, in: McDowell, 1998b, pp. 214–227.
McDowell, J. (1985/1998a) Functionalism and Anomalous Monism, in: McDowell, 1998a, pp. 325–340.
McDowell, J. (1987/1998b) In Defence of Modesty, in: McDowell, 1998b, pp. 87–107.
McDowell, J. (1991/1998b) Intentionality *De Re*, in: McDowell, 1998b, pp. 260–274.
McDowell, J. (1992/1998b) Putnam on Mind and Meaning, in: McDowell, 1998b, pp. 275–291.
McDowell, J. (1993/1998b) Knowledge by Hearsay, in: McDowell, 1998b, pp. 414–443.
McDowell, J. (1994) *Mind and World*, 2nd edn, with a new introduction by the author, 1996 (Cambridge, MA, Harvard University Press).
McDowell, J. (1994/1998a) The Content of Perceptual Experience, in: McDowell, 1998a, pp. 341–358.
McDowell, J. (1995) Reply to Gibson, Byrne, and Brandom, *Philosophical Issues* 7, pp. 283–300.
McDowell, J. (1995/1998a) Might There Be External Reasons?, in: McDowell, 1998a, pp. 95–111.
McDowell, J. (1995/1998b) Knowledge and the Internal, in: McDowell, 1998b, pp. 395–413.
McDowell, J. (1996/1998a) Two Sorts of Naturalism, in: McDowell, 1998a, pp. 167–197.

McDowell, J. (1997) Brandom on Representation and Inference, *Philosophy and Phenomenological Research* LVII.1, pp. 157–162.
McDowell, J. (1997/1998a) Reductionism and the First Person, in: McDowell, 1998a, pp. 359–382.
McDowell, J. (1998a) *Mind, Value, and Reality* (Cambridge, MA, Harvard University Press).
McDowell, J. (1998b) *Meaning, Knowledge, and Reality* (Cambridge, MA, Harvard University Press).
McDowell, J. (1998c) Having the World in View: Sellars, Kant, and Intentionality, *The Journal of Philosophy* XCVV.9, pp. 431–491. (Repr. as essays 1–3 in: McDowell, 2009a, pp. 3–65).
McDowell, J. (1999/2009b) Naturalism in the Philosophy of Mind, in: McDowell, 2009b, pp. 257–275.
McDowell, J. (2000a) Experiencing the World, in: Willaschenk, 2000, pp. 3–18.
McDowell, J. (2000b) Responses, in: Willaschenk, 2000, pp. 91–114.
McDowell, J. (2000/2009b) Towards Rehabilitating Objectivity, in: McDowell, 2009b, pp. 204–224.
McDowell, J. (2002) Responses, in: Smith, 2002, pp. 269–305.
McDowell, J. (2002a/2009b) Knowledge and the Internal Revisited, in: McDowell, 2009b, pp. 279–287.
McDowell, J. (2002b/2009b) Gadamer and Davidson on Understanding and Relativism, in: McDowell, 2009b, pp. 134–151.
McDowell, J. (2002c/2009b) How Not to Read *Philosophical Investigations*: Brandom's Wittgenstein, in: McDowell, 2009b, pp. 96–111.
McDowell, J. (2006a) Response to Jonathan Dancy, in: Macdonald and Macdonald, 2006, pp. 134–41.
McDowell, J. (2006b), Response to Graham Macdonald, in: Macdonald and Macdonald, 2006, pp. 235–239.
McDowell, J. (2006/2009a) Conceptual Capacities in Perception, in: McDowell, 2009a, pp. 127–144.
McDowell, J. (2007a/2009a) Avoiding the Myth of the Given, in: McDowell, 2009a, pp. 256–272.
McDowell, J. (2007b/2009a) On Pippin's Postscript, in: McDowell, 2009a, pp. 185–203.
McDowell, J. (2007a/2009b) Gadamer and Davidson on Understanding and Relativism, in: McDowell, 2009b, pp. 134–151.
McDowell, J. (2007b/2009b) What Myth?, in: McDowell, 2009b, pp. 308–323.
McDowell, J. (2007c/2009b) Response to Dreyfus, in: McDowell, 2009b, pp. 324–328.
McDowell, J. (2008) Responses, in: Lingaard, 2008, pp. 200–267.
McDowell, J. (2008/2009a) Towards a Reading of Hegel on Action in the 'Reason' Chapter of the *Phenomenology*, in: McDowell, 2009a, pp. 166–184.
McDowell, J. (2009a) *Having the World in View: Essays on Kant, Hegel, and Sellars* (Cambridge, MA, Harvard University Press).
McDowell, J. (2009b) *The Engaged Intellect: Philosophical Essays* (Cambridge, MA, Harvard University Press).
McGeer, V (2001) Psycho-practice, psycho-theory and the Contrastive Case of Autism, *Journal of Consciousness Studies*, 8.5–7, pp. 109–132.
Mikhailov, F. T. (1964) *Zagadka chelovecheskogo ya [The Riddle of the Self]* (2nd edn, rev. and expanded, 1976) (Moscow, Politizdat). 3rd edn (Moscow, Ritm, 2010).
Mikhailov, F. T. (1980) *The Riddle of the Self*, 1976 Russian edn trans. R. Daglish (Moscow, Progress).
Mikhailov, F. T. (1995) The Soviet Self: A Personal Reminiscence, in: Bakhurst and Sypnowich, 1995, pp. 67–83.
Mikhailov, F. T. (2001) *Izbrannoe [Selected Works]* (Moscow, INDRIK).

Mikhailov, F. T. (2003) *Samoopredelenie kul'tury: filosofskii poisk [The Self-Determination of Culture: A Philosophical Quest]* (Moscow, INDRIK).
Moore, A. (1996) On There Being Nothing Else to Think, or Want, or Do, in: Lovibond and Williams, 1996, pp. 165–184.
Moran, R. (1994) Interpretation Theory and the First Person, *Philosophical Quarterly* 44.175, pp. 154–73.
Moran, R. (2001) *Authority and Estrangement: An Essay on Self-Knowledge* (Princeton, NJ, Princeton University Press).
Munzel, G. (2003) Kant, Hegel, and the Rise of Pedagogical Science, in: Curren, 2003, pp. 113–129.
Neuhouser, F. (2000) *Foundations of Hegel's Social Theory: Actualizing Freedom* (Cambridge, MA, Harvard University Press).
Niiniluoto, I. (2000) Opening Words, in: Oitennen, V. (ed.) *Evald Ilyenkov's Philosophy Revisited* (Helsinki, Kikimora Publications), pp. 7–8.
Nordenbo, S. (2003) *Bildung* and the Thinking of *Bildung*, in: Løvlie et al., 2003, pp. 25–36.
Oakeshott, M. (1950/1991) Rational Conduct, in: Oakeshott, 1991, pp. 99–131.
Oakeshott, M. (1962/1991) Rationalism in Politics, in: Oakeshott, 1991, pp. 5–42.
Oakeshott, M. (1991) *Rationalism in Politics and Other Essays*, new and expanded edn. (Indianapolis, Liberty Fund).
Owens, D. (2000) *Reason Without Freedom: The Problem of Epistemic Normativity* (London, Routledge).
Parfit, D. (1971) Personal Identity, *Philosophical Review* 80.1, pp. 3–27.
Parker, I. (ed.) (1998) *Social Constructionism, Discourse and Realism* (London, Sage).
Patterson, D. (1988) *Literature and Spirit: Essays on Bakhtin and his Contemporaries* (Lexington, KY, University Press of Kentucky).
Perner, J. (1991) *Understanding the Representational Mind* (Cambridge, MA, MIT Press).
Pippin, R. (2000) What is the Question for which Hegel's Theory of Recognition is the Answer?, *European Journal of Philosophy* 8.2, pp. 155–172.
Phillips, D. C. (1995/2007) The Good, the Bad, and the Ugly: The Many Faces of Constructivism, in: R. Curren (ed.), *Philosophy of Education: An Anthology* (Oxford, Blackwell, 2007), pp. 398–409, originally published in *Educational Researcher* 24.7 (1995), pp. 5–12.
Phillips, D. C. (2003) Theories of Teaching and Learning, in: Curren, 2003, pp. 232–245.
Plummer, K. (ed.) (1981) *The Making of the Modern Homosexual* (London: Hutchinson).
Popper, K. (1972) *Objective Knowledge: An Evolutionary Approach* (Oxford, Oxford University Press).
Popper, K. (1978) Three Worlds, The Tanner Lecture on Human Values, delivered at the University of Michigan, 7 April 1978. http://www.tannerlectures.utah.edu/lectures/documents/popper80.pdf.
Putnam, H. (1988) *Representation and Reality* (Cambridge, MA, MIT Press).
Readings, B. (1996) *The University in Ruins* (Cambridge, MA, Harvard University Press).
Robbins, P. and Aydede, M. (eds) (2009), *The Cambridge Handbook of Situation Cognition* (Cambridge, Cambridge University Press).
Rödl, S. (2007) *Self-Consciousness* (Cambridge, MA, Harvard University Press).
Rorty, R. (1979) *Philosophy and the Mirror of Nature* (Oxford, Blackwell).
Rorty, R. (1989) *Contingency, Irony, and Solidarity* (Cambridge, Cambridge University Press).
Rorty, R. (1984/1991) Solidarity or Objectivity? in his: *Objectivity, Relativism, and Truth* (Cambridge, Cambridge University Press, 1991), pp. 21–34.
Rosen, G. (1997) Who Makes the Rules Anyway?, *Philosophy and Phenomenological Research* LVII.1, pp. 163–171.
Rouse, J. (2005) Mind, Body, and World: Todes and McDowell on Bodies and Language, *Inquiry* 48.1, pp. 38–61.
Ryle, G. (1949) *The Concept of Mind* (Harmondsworth, Penguin).

Schacht, R. (1972) Hegel on Freedom, in: A. MacIntyre (ed.), *Hegel: A Collection of Critical Essays* (Notre Dame, IN and London, University of Notre Dame Press), pp. 289–328.
Sellars, W. (1956/1963) Empiricism and the Philosophy of Mind, in his: *Science, Perception, and Reality* (London: Routledge and Kegan Paul, 1963), pp. 127–196.
Sismondo, S. (1996) *Science Without Myth: On Constructions, Reality, and Social Knowledge* (Albany, NY, SUNY Press).
Smeyers, P., Smith, R. and Standish, P. (2007) *The Therapy of Education* (Basingstoke, Palgrave Macmillan).
Smith, N. (ed.) (2002) *Reading McDowell: Essays on* Mind and World (London, Routledge).
Standish, P. (2003a) Out of the Fold: A Plurality of Parts, in: White, 2003, pp. 169–173.
Standish, P. (2003b) The Ends of Education, in: Curren, 2003, pp. 221–231.
Strawson, P. F. (1959) *Individuals. An Essay in Descriptive Metaphysics* (London, Methuen).
Strawson, P. F. (1962/1974) Freedom and Resentment, in his: *Freedom and Resentment and Other Essays* (London, Methuen, 1974), pp. 1–25.
Strawson, P. F. (1966) *The Bounds of Sense* (London, Methuen).
Sypnowich, C. (2003) Equality: From Marxism to Liberalism (and Back Again), *Political Studies Review* 1, pp. 333–343.
Taylor, C. (1975) *Hegel* (Cambridge, Cambridge University Press).
Thompson, M. (2008) *Life and Action: Elementary Structures of Practice and Practical Thought* (Cambridge, MA, Harvard University Press, 1976).
Thornton, T. (2004) *John McDowell* (Montreal and Kingston, McGill-Queen's University Press).
Todes, S. (2001) *Body and World* (Cambridge, MA, MIT Press).
Triplett, T. and deVries, W. (2007) Does Observational Knowledge Require Metaknowledge? A Dialogue on Sellars, *International Journal of Philosophical Studies* 15.1, pp. 23–51.
Voloshinov, V. N. (1927/1976) *Freudism*, trans. I. Titunik, ed. I. Titunik and N. Bruss (Bloomington and Indianapolis, Indiana University Press, 1976).
Voloshinov, V. N. (1929/1973) *Marxism and the Philosophy of Language*, trans. L. Matejka and I. Titunik (Cambridge, MA, Harvard University Press, 1973).
von Glasersfeld, E. (1984) An Introduction to Radical Constructivism, in: P. Watzlawick (ed), *The Invented Reality: How Do We Know What We Believe We Know? Contributions to Constructivism* (New York, W.W. Norton), pp. 17–40.
von Glasersfeld, E. (1995) *Radical Constructivism* (London, The Falmer Press).
Vygotsky, L. S. (1934/1986) *Thought and Language*, rev. edn, ed. A. Kozulin (Cambridge, MA, MIT Press, 1986).
Vygotsky, L. S. (1997) *The Collected Works of L. S. Vygotsky, Volume 4: The History of the Development of the Higher Mental Functions* (New York, Plenum Press), trans. M. Hall, from L. S. Vygotsky, *Sobranie sochinenii, tom 3: Problemy razvitiya psikhiki* (Moscow, Pedagogika, 1983).
Vygotsky, L. S. (1998) *The Collected Works of L. S. Vygotsky, Volume 5: Child Psychology* (New York, Plenum Press), trans. M. Hall, from L. S. Vygotsky, *Sobranie sochinenii, tom 4: Detskaya psikhologii* (Moscow, Pedagogika, 1984).
White, J. (1982) *The Aims of Education Restated* (London, Routledge).
White, J. (1990) *Education and the Good Life* (London, Kogan Page).
White, J. (2003) Five Critical Stances Towards Liberal Philosophy of Education in Britain, with responses from W. Carr, R. Smith, P. Standish, and T. McLaughlin, *Journal of Philosophy of Education* 37.1, pp. 147–184.
Wiggins, D. (1967) *Identity and Spatio-temporal Continuity* (Oxford, Blackwell).
Wiggins, D. (1975–6/1991) Deliberation and Practical Reason, in: Wiggins, 1991, pp. 213–237.
Wiggins, D. (1980) *Sameness and Substance* (Oxford, Blackwell).
Wiggins, D. (1987) The Person as Object of Science, as Subject of Experience, and as Locus of Value, in: A. Peacocke and G. Gillett (eds), *Persons and Personality* (Oxford, Blackwell), pp. 56–74.

Wiggins, D. (1991) *Needs, Values, Truth*, 2nd edn (1st edn, 1987) (Oxford, Blackwell).
Wiggins, D. (1996) Replies, in: Lovibond and Williams, 1996, pp. 219–284.
Wiggins, D. (2001) *Sameness and Substance Renewed* (Cambridge, Cambridge University Press).
Wiggins, D. (2005) Replies, *Philosophy and Phenomenological Research* LXXI.2, pp. 470–476.
Wiggins, D. (2006) *Ethics: Twelve Lectures on the Philosophy of Morality* (Cambridge, MA, Harvard University Press).
Willaschenk, M. (ed.) (2000) *John McDowell: Reason and Nature. Lecture and Colloquium in Münster 1999* (Münster, Hamburg, London, LIT Verlag).
Williams, B. (1970a/1973) Are Persons Bodies?, in: Williams, 1973, pp. 64–81.
Williams, B. (1970b/1973) Deciding to Believe, in: Williams, 1973, pp. 136–151.
Williams, B. (1970c/1973) The Self and the Future, in: Williams, 1973, pp. 46–63.
Williams, B. (1973) *Problems of the Self* (Cambridge, Cambridge University Press).
Williams, B. (1974–5) The Truth in Relativism, *Proceedings of the Aristotelian Society*, LXXV, pp. 215–228. Repr. in his: *Moral Luck* (Cambridge, Cambridge University Press, 1981), pp. 132–143.
Williams, B. (1985) *Ethics and the Limits of Philosophy* (Cambridge, MA, Harvard University Press).
Williams, M. (1999) *Wittgenstein, Mind, and Meaning. Toward a Social Conception of Mind* (London, Routledge).
Wittgenstein, L. (1953) *Philosophical Investigations*, trans. G. E. M. Anscombe (Oxford, Blackwell).
Wittgenstein, L. (1958) *The Blue and Brown Books*, 2nd edn, 1960, (Oxford, Blackwell).
Wittgenstein, L. (1969) *On Certainty*, ed. G. E. M. Anscombe and G. H. von Wright, trans. D. Paul and G. E. M. Anscombe (Oxford, Blackwell).
Wittgenstein, L. (1978) *Remarks on the Foundations of Mathematics*, rev. edn (original edn, 1956), ed. G. H. von Wright and R. Rhees, trans. G. E. M. Anscombe (Oxford, Blackwell).
Wittgenstein, L. (2005) *The Big Typescript*, trans. and ed. C. G. Luckhardt and M. A. E. Aue (Oxford, Blackwell).
Wood, A. (1998) Hegel on Education, in: A. Rorty (ed.), *Philosophers on Education: New Historical Perspectives* (London, Routledge), pp. 300–317.
Wright, C. (1987) On Making Up One's Mind: Wittgenstein on Intention, in: P. Weingartner and G. Schurz (eds), *Logic, Philosophy of Science and Epistemology. Proceedings of the XIth International Wittgenstein Symposium* (Vienna, Holder-Pickler-Tempsky), pp. 391–404.
Young, M. (2007) *Bringing Knowledge Back In: From Social Constructivism to Social Realism in the Sociology of Education* (London, Routledge).

Index

action, 70n, 74, 97n, 145n, 150, 151
    and autonomy 142–3
    bodily movement and 58, 65
    explanation of 90–2, 97n, 100–1, 132
    freedom manifest in 93
    identity and 88
    intelligence manifest in 38
    intentional 6, 49n, 56, 120n
    knowledge and 159
    manifest in practical judgement 16, 17
    mind present in 64, 66
    mood and 31–2
    moral 81
    partial responsibility for 128
    permeated by conceptual rationality 125–6
    practical concepts realised in 148n
    practical reasoning and 147
    rational 86
    rational agents and 42, 45, 69, 149
    reasons and 19n, 34, 48n, 87, 112, 114, 122n, 124, 125, 133, 137, 139, 140, 149, 160
    reflective control and 81
    reflective endorsement of 83, 85
    self-knowledge of 58
    space of reasons and 101–3, 111, 119–20nn, 129
    understanding exhibited in 118n
    understanding as a form of 130
    verbal articulation of 139
    virtue and 138

activity 15, 67, 84, 112, 113, 120n, 121, 122n, 128, 139, 141, 154, 155, 157, 163n
    brain 109
    conceptual 20n
    contemplation as 159
    creativity and 130
    embodied 61
    form of life as background to 139
    ideality and 110–11
    in accord with virtue 92
    intelligent 117n
    instituting norms 118n
    joint 15, 39, 121n, 140
    knowledge and 159
    meaning as product of 35
    mind in 61, 64, 126, 144n, 157, 158
    mundane 58, 64
    objectification of 112
    pedagogical 116
    practical 22
    principle of 21
    problem-solving 153
    rational 73n
    rationality present in 63
    space of reasons and 96n, 129
    spontaneous 72n
    see also life activity
Aydede, Murat 163n
Allen, Barry 31
altruism 53, 54
analytic philosophy 3, 23n, 49n
Anscombe, G. E. M. 15

The Formation of Reason, First Edition. David Bakhurst.
© 2011 David Bakhurst. Published 2011 by Blackwell Publishing Ltd.

178 Index

anthropocentrism 28–9, 84, 87, 112
Aristotle 9, 10, 16, 71n, 88, 92, 97n, 125, 139, 144n, 160, 163n, 164n
  Metaphysics 33
  Nicomachean Ethics 138, 147n
Arsen'ev, A. S. 163n
Ashmore, Malcolm 29
assertion 33, 37, 101, 119n, 136, 139
  and entitlement 105
  inferential articulation of 106
  sincere 40, 50n
Astington, Janet 23n
Augustine, St 71n
automata 71–2nn
autonomy 74, 86, 123, 144, 147n
  education and 75, 93, 124, 125, 136–7, 143, 158, 161
  fundamental notion of 142
  knowledge and 159
  law of 91–2
  in liberal philosophy of education 142
  rational 9, 61, 93n, 140
  supreme expression of 84

Baker, Gordon 5, 18n
Bakhtin, Mikhail 36, 42, 48n
Bakhurst, David 18n, 19n, 20n, 22n, 23n, 45n, 46n, 48n, 66, 70n, 97n, 119n, 120n, 121n, 162n, 163n, 164n
behaviourism 38
Beiser, Frederick 20n
Bennett, Maxwell 163–4nn
Berkeley, George 30, 46n
Bernstein, Richard 68
Bibler, V. S. 18n
Bildung 7, 15–16, 20n, 22n, 23n, 24, 47n, 51n, 62, 66, 68, 72n, 82, 83, 94n, 99, 101, 118n, 120n, 122n, 123, 124, 127, 128, 137, 138, 139, 143, 147–8nn, 150, 152, 161, 163n
  freedom and 74, 93
  idea of 8–10
  philosophy of education and 69
  rational capacities acquired through 113
  second nature acquired through 149
  significance of 92
Bildungsprozess 9, 18, 39, 45, 63–4, 69, 111, 148n
  conceptual development and 10–14
  social influences upon 17

Blake, Nigel 20n
Bonnett, Michael 93n
Brandom, Robert 9, 11, 13, 42, 99, 112, 115, 118–19nn, 122n, 129, 145n, 150–1, 162n
  inferentialism 105–9, 120n
Bruner, Jerome 13, 25, 26, 33–4, 35, 44, 45n, 46n, 47n, 48n, 148n
Buber, Martin 72n
Bubner, Rüdiger 20n
Burge, Tyler 48n, 50n
Burnyeat, Myles 138, 139, 147n, 148n, 163n

Carey, Susan 23n
Cartesianism 6, 17–18, 26–7, 28, 35, 37–9, 40, 49n, 54, 65, 70n, 164n
categories 11
  see also psychological categories
causal factors 2, 4, 79, 91
Cavell, Stanley 73n, 138–9, 143, 147n
child development 14
Churchland, Paul 34
Churton, Annette 20n
Clark, Andy 163n
Claxton, Guy 94n, 141, 145n, 146n
cognitive science 17, 18, 146n, 157
Cohen, G. A. 85–6
coherentism 89
communication 4, 71n
  understanding 33
concepts 11, 16, 20n, 75
  and beliefs 22n
  everyday and scientific 14, 156
  understanding of substance 12–14
  Vygotsky and McDowell on 156
  see also conceptual capacities
conceptual capacities 7, 16, 24, 61, 72n, 76, 94n, 102, 104, 114, 117n, 124, 125, 136, 137, 138, 149, 150, 152, 154, 161
Connolly, Cyril 70n
consciousness 20n, 36, 51n, 52, 54, 56, 66, 70n, 71n, 111, 143, 146n
  continuity of 59
  inward-looking 159
  logic of 37
  reflective structure of 86
  social 109–10
  third-personal approach and 49n
  unity of 65
  see also self-consciousness
content *see* mental content
Cory, William 164n

creativity 130
critical thought 143
cultural psychology 2, 25
culture 2, 3, 110, 111
   child's initiation into 121n
   intellectual 7–8
   oral 18n
   see also Bildung; enculturation
Curren, Randell 20n
Cuypers, Stefaan 93n

Dancy, Jonathan 38, 70n, 97n, 114, 122n, 133, 148n, 160
Danziger, Kurt 43
Darwall, Stephen 72n
Davidson, Donald 3, 4–6, 7, 18n, 19n, 31, 40, 44, 47n, 48n, 49n, 61, 70n, 71n, 89, 96n, 100, 102, 116n
Davis, Andrew 50n, 71n, 94n
Davydov, V. V. 18n, 121n
Dearden, Robert 9, 20n, 93n, 97n, 142
Dennett, Daniel 48n
Derrida, Jacques 26
developmental psychology 6, 17, 38
deVries, Willem 21n, 39, 116n
dialectic 130
Dickens, Charles 15
discursive psychology 2
division of linguistic labour 22n
Dreyfus, Hubert 15, 125–6, 144n, 145n, 148n
dualism 59, 124, 127, 128
   scheme-content 31, 117n
   two-worlds 121n

education 14, 20n, 45n, 123, 136–41, 164n
   autonomy and 75, 93, 124, 125, 136–7, 143, 158, 161
   of blind-deaf children 121n
   and social engineering 74
   theory and practice of 43, 78
   see also Bildung; philosophy of education
Edwards, Derek 29, 32
Egan, Kieran 164n
Elder, Crawford 47
Elkonin, D. B. 121n
Emerson, Ralph Waldo 143
empiricism 46n, 93n
enculturation 14, 47n, 62, 64, 74, 82, 94n, 95n, 111, 151
   musical 135
   rational capacities acquired through 114

   second nature acquired through 149
   significance of 92
epistemology 4, 53, 54, 66, 80, 84, 88, 89, 145n
   intellectual freedom and 78–9
   ontology and 47n
   testimony and 94n
   virtue-centred approach to 92
experience 7, 8, 12, 27, 31, 46n, 52, 61, 72n, 75, 104, 114, 117n, 121n 122n, 125, 129
   a priori conditions of 112
   conceptually unified 135
   conscious 36, 64
   content of 90, 101, 134
   musical 134, 135, 146n, 147n
   necessary preconditions of 84
   openness to reality in 157
   pedagogical 140
   perceptual 20n, 21n, 89, 125, 129, 134, 155
   propositional content of 19n
   reality confronted in 111
   sensory 119n
   subjective 36
   subjects of 53, 55, 56, 57, 66, 69n, 152, 154
   visual 35, 134, 135
experience-memory 60
explanation 13, 100, 106, 107, 113, 115, 139
   of action 90–2, 97n, 100–1, 132
   causal 101
   nomological 101, 116
   non-rational modes of 117
   rational 101, 117, 128, 145, 155
   scientific 96, 127, 128, 145, 150, 153, 155
   space-of-reasons 132
external reality 52, 111
   bridging the gap between mind and 107
externalism
   epistemic 79, 95n, 117n
   social, 48n 50n

fact and opinion 30, 31
fallibilism 32, 37, 78, 80, 118n, 143, 147n, 159
false beliefs 41, 49n, 50n, 161
   trivial and momentous 33
feminist theory 2, 24
Fichte, Johann Gottlieb 20n, 72n
Fine, Gail 147n
Fink, Hans 68

first-person perspective 19n, 37–8, 41, 42, 44, 53, 63, 70n, 72n, 79, 100, 123, 151
  pronoun 6, 55
  psychological ascription 37, 39–40, 50n, 56–8
Fodor, Jerry 11
folk psychology 25, 33–4, 38, 48n
Foster, Ian 27
Franks, Paul 20n, 72n, 112
freedom 127
freedom 69, 74, 96n
  coincidence of rational necessitation and 83
  compromised 90
  education and 75
  rational agency conception of 90–1, 137
  see also intellectual freedom
Frege, Gottlob 11, 20n, 102
Freud, Sigmund 26

Gadamer Hans-Georg 8, 20n, 28, 84, 96n, 147n
Gaskin, Richard 48n, 68, 93n
Gaynesford, Maximilian de 19n, 119n, 164n
gender 25, 45n
Gergen, Kenneth 26–8, 29, 32, 37, 40, 45n, 51n, 70n
Geuss, Raymond 20n, 97n
Glasersfeld, Ernst von 46n
Goodman, Nelson 46n
Gopnik, Alison 23n, 49n
Gubeljic, Mischa 68, 71n

Hacker, P. M. S. 5, 18n, 163–4nn
Hacking, Ian 24, 26, 42–3, 44, 45n, 50–1nn
Halbig, Christoph 68, 71n, 73n
Hamlyn, David 49n, 95n
Haslanger, Sally 25, 45n
Haugeland, John 113
Hegel, Georg Wilhelm Friedrich 1, 8, 20n, 28, 70n, 71n, 84, 95n, 96n, 104, 113, 147–8nn, 158
Heidegger, Martin 28, 48n
Helmholtz, Hermann von 8
Herder, Johann Gottfried von 8
Hirst, Paul 9, 142
Hornsby, Jennifer 116n
human nature 74, 146n
  Wiggins on persons and 59–64, 72n
Humboldt, Wilhelm von 8, 20n
Hume, David 93n
Hutchins, Edwin 163n

idealism 29, 91, 103, 104, 113
  see also transcendental idealism
ideality 110, 120–1nn
ideological signs 37
idiolects 6, 19n, 48n, 61
Ilyenkov, E. V. 18n, 22n, 74, 99, 109–14, 115, 118n, 120n, 121–2nn, 126, 133, 144n, 154, 157, 163n
individualism 26, 150–1, 156
individuation 59
inference 11, 39, 58, 86, 103, 107, 108, 119–20nn, 122n, 125, 129,135, 140, 141
inferentialism 105–9, 120n
intellectual freedom 75–6, 77, 83, 89, 93, 94n
  defence of 78–82
intelligibility 27, 39, 56, 57, 60, 69, 70n, 73n, 96n, 100, 107, 115, 117n, 122n, 128, 129
  natural-scientific 68, 116n, 127, 142, 145n, 149
  rational 118n, 142
  space-of-reasons 103, 104, 116n, 127, 145n
intentional states 38, 102, 106, 146n
internalisation 121n, 163n
intersubjectivity 5, 39
  development of 62,72n
Irwin, Terence 147n

Johnson, David Martel 18n
judgement 13, 40, 44, 74, 90, 93, 94n, 101, 102, 104, 124, 145n, 146n, 151
  aesthetic 114
  agreement in 47n
  correctness in 65
  epistemic 114
  good 143
  inference and 129
  informed 137
  mathematical 148n
  McDowell on 7, 21n, 75–6, 116n, 126–7, 144n
  moral 114, 125, 139–40, 144n, 160
  musical 135–6
  objective 133
  perceptual 20n, 21n, 141
  practical 16, 81, 100
  rational agency and 69
  rational constraints on 129
  reflective 77
  responsible 80

theoretical 84, 100
justification 13, 94, 95n, 99, 100–1, 103, 120, 129, 132, 136, 138, 139, 146, 156, 157
   coherentist view of 89

Kant, Immanuel 11, 31, 65, 66, 75–6, 81, 82, 83, 84, 85, 86, 87, 96n, 97n, 129, 145n
   Groundwork on the Metaphysics and Morals 127
   On Education 20n
Keil, Frank 22–3nn
knowledge
   abstract 15
   acquisition of 75, 140
   autonomy and 159
   background 14
   infallible 37, 48n
   linguistic 13
   local 15
   moral 160
   practical 15, 16, 139, 160, 164n
   propositional 92
   of self and others 4–5
   theoretical 15, 22n, 135, 155
   verbal 15
   see also epistemology; self-knowledge
Korsgaard, Christine 46n, 47n, 77, 81, 84–8, 89, 96–7nn, 98n, 101

language 6, 28, 33, 51n, 59, 110, 116, 135, 136, 138
   acquisition of 7–8, 10, 121n, 153, 154, 161
   children play and revel in 13
   child's proficiency with 154
   conformity to norms of 92
   creative thought and 92
   diversity of practices 118n
   getting a toehold in 156
   initiation into 82, 124
   intimate connection between thought and 4
   learning 39, 152
   object 92
   passive understanding of 21n
   seeds sown on the soil of reason 153
   shared 4, 19n
   social character of 3–6
   sophisticated and reflexive skills 15
   as speaking us 48n
   standards of correctness 3, 5
   Tarksian theory for natural 19n, 107
   unity of thought and 154

   see also language games; linguistic thought; natural languages; philosophy of language; private language
language games 27, 105
Lave, Jean 163n
learning disabilities 43, 50n
Leibniz's law 54–5
Lektorsky, V. A. 18n
Leontiev, A. N. 121n
Levinas, Emmanuel 28, 72n
Levitin, Karl 121n
life activity 61, 62, 66, 110, 111, 120n, 150, 158
linguistic
   abilities 11
   awareness 12
   expression 16, 106, 107
   knowledge 13
   representations 26
   thought 134, 135, 152, 153
   understanding 19n
   usage 13
Locke, John 3, 59, 93n
London School *see* Dearden; Hirst; Peters
Lovibond, Sabina 20n, 95n
Luntley, Michael 146–7nn
Løvlie, Lars 8, 20n, 51n

Macdonald, Graham 68
MacIntyre, Alasdair 92, 95n
Macmurray, John 71n, 72n
making up people 42–3
Malcolm, Norman 4, 5
Mann, Wolfgang 20n
Marx, Karl 28, 70n
Marxism 1, 109, 112, 113
materialism 109
   dialectical 1
   eliminative 34, 48n
   historical 1
mathematics 46n, 148n
McDowell, John 7–8
   on action 64–5
   on being at home in the world 9, 67, 158
   on causation 96–7nn, 116n
   on concepts 11
   on experience 7, 19n, 20n, 35, 125, 126, 134
   on freedom and rational necessitation 81–2, 83, 87
   individualism in philosophy of 150–1

182 Index

McDowell, John (*cont'd*)
  on intellectual freedom 75–6, 78–82, 94n
  on judgement 7, 21n, 75–6, 116n, 126–7, 144n
  on language 7, 39
  on the location of mind 17–18, 157–8
  on mental content 146n
  moral philosophy of 88, 102, 114, 125, 138
  on non-human animals 24n, 95n
  on normativity 89, 91
  on other minds 39
  on philosophy 101–2
  on platonism 87, 96n
  on rational agency conception of freedom 90–1, 97n, 137
  on relation between thought and reality 53, 117–18nn, 144n
  on scheme-content dualism 31, 117n
  on self 65–6
  views criticised as rationalistic 15, 124–5
  and Vygotsky 152, 154–7
  see also Bildung; conceptual capacities; experience; mindedness; persons; rationality; responsiveness to reasons; second nature; space of reasons
McGeer, Victoria 20n
meaning 3, 37, 48n, 112, 121n
  borrowed 50n
  mental content and 35–7, 50n, 95n
  mind being moved by 18
Meltzoff, Andrew 23n, 49n
Mendelssohn, Moses 8
mental content 17, 114, 117n, 146n, 150
  causation and 4
  empiricist theory of 46n
  meaning and 35–7, 50n, 95n
mental representations 11, 17, 26
mental states 17, 19n, 44, 48n, 49n, 59, 102–3, 121n
  ascription of 55–6, 100, 157
  causes of 4
  first-person authority about 58
  normative standing of 162n
  relations between 117
  social construction of 33–42
Meshcheryakov, A. I. 121n
metaphysics 20n, 47n, 52, 53, 62, 65, 66, 68, 71n, 73n, 88, 89, 97n, 107, 109, 111, 114
Mikhailov, F. T. 2, 18n, 72n, 74, 144n
mind 7, 9, 37
  culture and 3

  epistemological gap between world and 66
  independence of 74
  infant acquires 10
  place in nature 163n
  preconditions of 2, 4
  socio-historical character/vision of 2, 8, 123, 149
  spontaneity of 131
  theory of 38
mindedness 7, 10, 17, 38, 56, 59, 61, 64, 66, 157, 158
  actions as bodily movements infused with 58
  of child 24, 62
  of community 20
  engagement with reality permeated by 126
  preconditions of 1, 149, 150
  present in bodily engagement with world 16
  and rational agency 3
  and responsiveness to reasons 109
  social practices constitutive of 115, 152
moods 129, 131–4, 136, 137, 139, 140, 142, 148n, 159
  deliberate and determinate 147n
  influence of rational considerations on 146n
Moore, Adrian 96n
moral
  development 138, 139
  education 160, 164n
  knowledge 160, 161–2, 164n
  sensibilities 152
  see also particularism
moral philosophy 72n, 84, 97n, 114, 125, 160
  analytic 139–40
  constructivism in 46n
  intellectualism in 148n
  problem of self and other in 53
Moran, Richard 40–1, 42, 44, 50n, 58, 70n, 79, 95n, 123, 147n
Munzel, G. Felicitas 20n
music 95n, 129, 134–6, 146n, 147n
  interpretative context 96n

natural languages 19n
nature–nurture debate 2–3
Neuhouser, Frederick 96n
Niiniluoto, Ilkka 121n
nominalism 31, 46n
  dynamic 43
Nordenbo, Sven Erik 8

normativity 102, 106, 108, 118–19nn, 122n, 150
  sources of 82–98, 101, 112

Oakeshott, Michael 20n, 144n, 159, 164n
objectification of activity 112
objective reality 32, 32, 110, 158
  disenchantment of 8
objectivity 108, 112, 119n, 120n, 150
  and solidarity 31, 87
obrashchenie 72n
ontological pluralism 121n, 122n
Owens, David 77–83, 86, 92, 93n, 94n, 95n, 98n

Padden, Carol 121n
Parfit, Derek 70n
particularism 97n, 122n, 160, 164n
Patterson, David 48n
Peirce, C. S. 68
perception 11, 15, 37, 77, 83, 85, 89, 91, 92, 97n, 116n, 117n, 126, 129, 130, 141
  accurate 134
  causal and situational elements of 61
  challenged and vindicated inferentially 119–20nn
  deliverances of 7, 86
  influence of mood upon 133
  objects in 108, 119n
  rational 153
  sense 94n, 125
  warped or obscured 91
Perner, Josef 23n
persons 18, 20n, 66, 67, 70n, 72n, 73n, 78, 82, 100, 104, 116, 123, 129, 146n, 165n
  attributes of 17, 157
  control of mental lives 78
  double-aspect or two-standpoints view of 128
  McDowell on 78
  rational agents as 42, 124
  rational requirements that govern 92
  status of 164n
  Strawson on 49n, 55–8, 64
  Wiggins on 59–60, 61, 62, 63
  Wittgenstein on 6
Peters, R. S. 9, 142
phenomenalism 106, 108, 109, 119n
Phillips, D. C. 28, 45n, 46n
philosophy of education 75, 93, 123, 124, 142, 144n

philosophy of language 20n, 23n, 102, 106
philosophy of mathematics 46n
philosophy of mind 51n
  analytic 49n
  challenge to representationalist tradition of 106
  folk psychology in 34
  third-personal turn in 38, 39
phronesis 16, 125–6, 138, 144n
Piaget, Jean 21n
Pippin, Robert 84
Plummer, Kenneth 42
political matters 9, 25, 26, 32–3, 43, 53, 54, 67
  extreme ideology 91
political philosophy 53
  communitarian 2
  constructivism in 46n
Popper, Karl 121n, 122n
poststructuralism 2
Potter, Jonathan 29
pragmatism 15
predicates 11, 13, 40, 55–8, 64
pre-linguistic ability 9, 12
private language 3, 18n
psychological categories 2, 25
  social construction of 42–5
  see also folk psychology
Pufendorf, Samuel von 118n
Putnam, Hilary 22n, 50n

Quine, W. V. O. 26, 46n

race 45n
radical constructivism 46n
rational agency 8, 41–2, 44–5, 51n, 58, 63, 69, 75, 79, 93, 104, 149, 152, 158
  acquisition of second nature and 123
  autonomous, critical 9
  freedom and 90, 91, 137
  identity and 86
  irrational behaviour 70n
  moods and 139
  preconditions of 2, 4
rationality 10, 17, 47n, 60, 65, 68, 71n, 76, 96n, 124, 125, 126, 128, 129, 150, 163n
  animality and 64, 127
  constitutive ideal of 100
  elucidating the nature of 99
  emerging 63, 64, 155–6

rationality (cont'd)
  engendered by initiation into social
    being 152
  failure of 101
  freedom and 69
  ideas of 86
  mundane failures of 44–5
  natural being permeated with 82
  rule-following and 4
  this-worldly conception of 148n
  understanding of 118n
Readings, Bill 20n
reality 20n, 24, 25, 30, 33, 36, 45, 65, 101,
    108, 126, 152
  aboriginal 31
  disenchanted conception of 112
  empirical 125
  experience as openness to 7, 157
  features of 72–3nn
  imagination and 51n
  independence of 103
  independent 29
  intelligibility of 68
  minds open to 104
  moral requirements as aspects of 114
  normative character of 88, 113, 115
  oneness with 92
  rational requirements as genuine
    constituents of 87
  scientistic conception of 97n
  sensible 49n
  social construction of 26–8, 31
  space of reasons as tract of 96n
  thought and 32, 66, 89, 90, 111, 117n,
    118n, 119n, 122n
  see also external reality; objective
    reality
reasoning 36, 41, 55, 76, 96n, 125, 128, 129,
    137, 141, 149
  ethical 102
  linguistic 152
  logical norms of 110
  moral 139
  practical 81, 85–6, 97n, 120n, 124, 136,
    143, 147n, 148n, 153
  scientific 95n, 155
  theoretical 86–7, 124, 136, 143, 147n
reasons 19n, 114
  and causes 101, 116n
  see also action; responsiveness to reasons;
    space of reasons

reflective endorsement 76, 81–2, 82–3, 145n,
    151
relativism 27, 32, 96n, 143
responsiveness to reasons 60, 64, 68, 80, 81,
    90, 92, 95n, 99, 104, 105, 113, 125, 127,
    145–6nn, 149, 152
  enabling 134, 136
  forms of 16, 126, 141
  freedom and 69
  impaired 91
  mindedness and 109
  reflective endorsement and 82–3
  virtues and vices and 78
Robbins, Philip 163n
Rödl, Sebastian 49n, 70n, 72n, 91, 96n, 97n,
    98n, 144n, 147n, 161, 165n
Rorty, Richard 40–1, 46n, 47n, 54, 87, 89,
    107
Rouse, Joseph 126, 145n
rule-following considerations 3–4, 18n, 118n,
    125, 126, 144n, 147n
Russian philosophy 1, 18n, 70n
Ryle, Gilbert 38, 40

Schacht, Richard 95n, 96n
Schiller, Friedrich von 8
scientism 7, 8, 89, 97n, 112
  McDowell's hostility to 114
second nature 7, 10, 66, 67, 68, 71n, 72–3nn,
    82, 87, 95n, 96n, 101, 112, 127, 147n,
    162
  acquired through enculturation 149
  nothing contrary to nature about 150
  rational agent status acquired only through
    acquisition of 123
  refinement of 69
  responsiveness to reasons and 113
  robust view of 89
  significance of 61–5
  systematically unifying first and 152
  and virtue 138
second-person perspective 63, 64, 72n
self and other 4–5, 28, 52–73
self-consciousness 43, 53, 127, 161
  reflective endorsement and 82
self-determination 74, 84, 90, 92, 93, 131
  possibility of 2
  rational 95n
self-knowledge 5, 49–50nn, 160–1, 162
  education in 92
  importance as an educational end 164n

perceptual model of 38, 41
self-understanding 42, 44, 70n, 153, 161
Sellars, Wilfrid 7, 11, 21n, 39, 49n, 99–101, 116n, 117n, 118n, 155
sentience and sapience 9
Sismondo, Sergio 45n
Smeyers, Paul 73n
social constructionism 4, 18, 22n, 24–51, 52, 53, 70n, 86
  distinguished from constructivism 45nn
  global 26, 28–31
  in psychology 2
social externalism 48n, 50n
social interaction 2, 74
  mental content depends upon 4
Soviet philosophy 18n
space of reasons 9, 10–11, 13, 17, 18, 21n, 61–2, 63, 67, 75, 83, 93, 96n, 97n, 124–5, 126, 127, 133, 145n, 146n, 152, 154, 157
  being at home in 7, 8, 103, 104, 116, 141, 142, 149, 159
  depression and 132
  exploring 99–122
  entering 137, 138, 139, 140, 141, 155
  initiation into 7
  intellectualisation of 120n
  mood as within 132
  movement within 129, 149
  navigating 128, 134, 136, 141
  securing smooth passage through 91
  standings in 79, 129, 151, 156, 162n
  transactions in 129–30
  understood in its own terms 149–50
  see also activity; explanation; intelligibility; reality
Spinoza, Baruch 96n
Stalinist myths 74
Standish, Paul 8, 20n, 22n, 142, 143
stimuli 100
  differential responses to 119n
  reaction to 4, 71n
Strawson, P. F. 49n, 55–8, 64, 65, 69n, 70n, 132
subjectivity 37, 44, 54, 84
  mutual 63
  self-standing 104
sub-personal systems 17, 130, 146n, 158, 162n
Sypnowich, Christine 18n, 148n

Tarski, Alfred 6, 19n, 47n, 48n, 102
Taylor, Charles 84
third-person perspective 38, 49n

psychological ascription from 37, 39–40, 41, 56, 57, 58, 63, 64, 100
Thompson, Michael 165n
Thornton, Tim 19n, 49n
thought-experiments 2, 59
thought 7, 8, 9, 11, 13, 19n, 20n, 26, 36, 52, 54, 84, 91, 93, 130
  ability to form 14
  action essentially the expression of 147n
  bearing on the world 126
  command of 44
  concepts as constituents of 16, 75
  conceptual 82, 125, 154
  contents of 50n, 102, 104, 105, 151, 163n
  control of 69, 79, 123, 137, 149
  creative 92
  everyday 47n
  first-person 53
  framing 17, 104
  historically evolving cultural traditions of 48n
  influence of speech genres 42
  initiation into public modes of 142
  language and 6, 154
  mentalistic vocabulary for describing 6
  non-rational influences 82, 129
  non-verbal 153
  objects and 22n, 31, 53, 56, 108, 112, 121n, 147n, 162n
  occurrent 49n
  perceiving others' 39, 49n
  power to determine 143
  present in speech 38–9
  as pure activity 128
  rational and non-rational influences on 97n
  reality and 32, 66, 89, 90, 111, 117n, 118n, 119n, 122n
  reasons and 81, 83, 111, 114, 137, 142, 149
  responsibility for 42, 45, 75, 127, 137
  second-person 72n
  self-determination and 74
  separation in 61
  speech and 153, 155
  talk and 107, 108, 119n
  world-directed 152
  see also linguistic thought
Todes, Samuel 126
transcendental idealism 31, 47n

Index

triangulation 4–5, 6
Triplett, Timm 21n
truth 33
  and agreement 31
  intersubjective 5
  objective 4, 107
  relativistic conception of 27
  theories of 19n, 29, 48n

unjustified beliefs 41
utterances 12n 19n, 26, 31, 33, 36, 50n, 83, 102–3, 106, 139
  creative 37

value judgements 36
vocabularies
  mentalistic 6
  specialised 43
Voloshinov, V. N. 36–7, 48n
Vygotsky, L. S. 14, 18n, 66, 74, 111, 121n, 152–7, 162–3nn, 164n

Wenger, Etienne 163n
White, John 93n, 142
Wiggins, David 11, 55, 59–64, 70n, 71n, 72n, 96n, 116n, 133, 148n
Williams, Bernard 59, 70n, 93n, 148n, 164n
Williams, Meredith 162n
Wittgenstein, Ludwig 2, 5–6, 7, 19n, 26, 27, 40, 48n, 73n, 86n, 102, 105, 114, 121n, 122n, 138–9, 152, 162n, 163n
  rule-following considerations 3–4, 18n, 118n, 125, 126, 144n, 147n
  works: *Big Typescript* 18n; *Blue and Brown Books* 18n; *Foundations of Mathematics* 18n; *On Certainty* 94n; *Philosophical Investigations* 3, 18n, 37–8, 39, 47n, 71–2nn, 118n; *Tractatus* 20n, 104, 117n
Wright, Crispin 40, 41

Young, Michael 164n

Lightning Source UK Ltd.
Milton Keynes UK
UKOW031016240613

212727UK00010B/442/P